RELIGIONS IN DIALOGUE

East and West Meet

Edited by

Zacharias P. Thundy
Kuncheria Pathil
Frank Podgorski

UNIVERSITY
PRESS OF
AMERICA

LANHAM • NEW YORK • LONDON

OFFERIMUS

ERUDITIONIS HOC FLORILEGIUM

J. B. CHETHIMATTAM

AETATIS SUAE LX

"Gladly wolde he lerne and gladly teche" (Chaucer)

iii

Acknowledgements

The editor is grateful to the following for their invaluable help in bringing out this Festschrift. My fellow editors, Kuncheria Pathil and Frank Podgorski, were extremely helpful from the beginning of this editorial undertaking. Northern Michigan University and its Provost Robert B. Glenn provided me with research grants and secretarial help. Linda Cleary and Kimberly Ericson helped type the manuscript with speed and acuracy. My wife Gina offered me unflagging support and day-to-day encouragement. The CMI Order gave me friendship and support. Above all, my thanks to the contributors to this volume.

TABLE OF CONTENTS

WEST IS WEST: DIALOGUE IN THE WEST

EAST AND WEST MEET: BEYOND IDEOLOGIES?

EPILOGUE

x

INTRODUCTION

John Britto Chethimattam is a man of many sides and countless accomplishments. I have known him since I was twelve; he was teaching theology at the time at Sacred Heart Seminary, Chethippuzha, Kerala, India, where I was an altar boy. That was a long time ago. But our acquaintance grew into friendship as years rolled by, and in 1963 we found ourselves living and teaching in the same college, Dharmaram College, Bangalore, India. He was then the Dean of Studies at the college where I was an instructor in the Faculty of Philosophy. Again, that too was many moons ago. Yet, in retrospect, I remember him as the most courteous gentleman. Our personal friendship and professional camaraderie continued to grow as well as my personal esteem and professional admiration for Chethimattam.

I respect and admire Chethimattam primarily for what he is: the gentleman scholar. Geoffrey Chaucer describes such a man for us in the person of the Clerk from Oxford in the General Prologue to his Canterbury Tales. To render the Middle English Chaucer into Modern English with appropriate emendations and with a touch of sensible humor:

There was also an Indian guru who was long gone to lectures on logic [philosophy and theology]. His horse [car] was as old and lean as a rake, and he was not fat at all; he looked thin, but serious all the time [with his usual sense of humor and candor, notwithstanding]. His little outer cloak was thread-bare; he was not secular enough to aspire for political office and so never secured any benefices for himself. He would rather have had at his bed's head twenty volumes of Aristotle's Philosophy [as well as the Sacred Books of the East] than have rich robes or a fiddle or gay psaltery. Though he was a philosopher [a distinguished professor], he had but little gold in his money-box [bank]. But all that he had earned he spent on books and learning and he would pray for the souls of those who gave him the keep that he earned by teaching and writing. Above all, of study he took most heed and care. Seldom he spoke more words than was needful. The little that he said was formal and modest, in speech short and quick and full of high sentence. All that he said tended toward moral virtue. Indeed, he loved to learn and teach [And gladly wolde he lerne and gladly teche].

Chethimattam was born at Thottakkad, Kerala, India, on October 26, 1922. In 1919 he graduated with the highest honors from St. Ephrem's English High School, Mannanam. Upon graduation he entered the Order of the Carmelites (TOCD alias CMI, a religious order of the Syro-Malabar Church of India with Chaldean associations). After having completed two years of rigorous training in classical languages and one year of novicehood, he pronounced his religious vows and then continued his seminary studies in philosophy and theology at st. Joseph's Seminary, Mangalore, India, which was run by the Jesuits at that time. He was ordained a priest of the Roman Catholic Church on April 7, 1951. He taught theology after his priestly ordination, at Sacred Heart Monastery Seminary--where I first met him--from 1951 to 1952. Next he went to Rome and attended the Gregorian University where he took his Licentiate in Theology in 1953 (with the highest honors), Licentiate in Philosophy in 1955 (with honors), and Doctorate in Divinity in 1957. He returned to India the same year and have since then taught courses in Theology, Philosophy, and Comparative Religion at Dharmaram College, though not uninterruptedly. He became a graduate student once again, in 1965, first at Fordham University (1965-66) and later at Harvard University (1966-67). In the fall of 1967 he became an Instructor in the Department of Philosophy at Fordham University while completing his Ph.D. dissertation. Upon completion and defense of the doctoral dissertation, he was promoted to Assistant Professor at Fordham in 1968, to Associate Professor in 1970, and to Full Professor in 1979. Meanwhile, in 1972, Chethimattam returned to India to become Rector of Dharmaram College, which position he held with amazing grace till 1975 when he decided to give up administration and to resume teaching at Fordham. However, he never gave up his devotion and love for India: every summer he commutes to India to teach a full term at Dharmaram College without pay. In April 1984, he agreed to administer the Province of St. Joseph (East) as its provincial without relinquishing his academic responsibilities.

In this brief essay, I should not fail to refer to Chethimattam's editorial activities. He is the Book-Review Editor and Section Editor for "Ecumenism and Encounter of Religions" of the monthly Jeevadhara, a journal of Christian interpretation; Associate Editor of The Journal of Dharma; and a member of the Editorial Board of Indian Theological Studies, Religious Tradition, Kairali, and Indian Currents. The article on Chethimattam by Professor Kadankavil, which appears as Prologue in this volume dwells at length on the scholarly accomplishments of Chethimattam. It does not, however, say how effective a mentor he has been to thousands of his students. He has always been an encouraging, resourceful guide to young scholars and his colleagues. To all of them a scholar he is, but devoid of scholarly self-seriousness. I would use the following Skeltonics as Chethimattam's own:

> Let us leave such sad learning
> To spring daffodils turning
> And praty birds smale
> Warbeling in the vale
> - ug, ug,
> jug, jug
> Good day and good luck
> -But Chuck, I say Chuck.

Chethimattam has been in the vanguard of inter-religious dialogues during the last two decades in India, Europe, and America. He has tried constantly and successfully to bring followers of Eastern and Western religions together. In this cultural mission he shares the imagination, inspiration, and abandon of Walt Whitman:

> Coming westward from Hindustan,
> from the vales of Kashmere,
> From Asia - from the North - from
> the God, the sage, and the hero;
> From the South - from the flowery
> peninsulas, and the Spice Islands;
> Now I face the old home again -
> looking over to it, joyous, as
> after long travel, growth and sleep;
> But where is what I started for,
> so long ago?
> And why is it yet unfound?

> Passage to more than India!

> Passage immediate passage! The blood burns in my veins!
> Away! O soul! Hoist instantly the anchor!
> Cut the hawsers - haul out - shake out every sail!
> Sail forth - sail for the deep waters only,
> Reckless O soul, exploring, I with thee, and thou with me,
> For we are bound where mariner has not yet dared to go,
> And we will risk the ship, ourselves and all!

In deep appreciation for his contributions in the field ecumenical studies and comparative religion, his friends and colleagues dedicate with pleasure in his honor this volume of studies in religious dialogue which was planned when the days of his years were three score years - as a Shashtyabda-purtismaraka.

PROLOGUE

JOHN CHETHIMATTAM: CONSISTENCY AND TRUTH

Thomas Kadankavil

1. In the making: To some, commitment to consistency is the only way to be honest to truth. When there is consistency with all that a man was in the past in such a way that no change is possible, then stagnation, fixation, or death of the spirit results. To be human is to become and to become is to transcend. The famous Neo-Freudian, Erik Erikson identifies some psychological needs such as trust, autonomy, initiative, identity, generativity, and integration as basic needs in the epigenesis of a personality. As man grows, the nature of his need also changes. In growth there is always a transcendence from the earlier position. The transcendent stage cannot be identical with the earlier one, but the question can be asked whether the latter position is consistent with the former. If so, there is natural growth. The question whether John Chethimattam has a consistent system of thought or vision can be answered with any precision only after having squarely dealt with the concept of consistency itself.

Consistency is sometimes conceived as being in agreement with what has been already thought of and expressed in words. Is it possible, or is it prudent, for a man to be slavishly consistent to his vision of reality of a past moment? The question cannot be answered in the affirmative. As in the case of the physical, there is development and maturing in man's intellectual faculty. "To have the courage of one's diversity (identity) is a sign of wholeness in individuals and civilizations. But wholeness, too, must have defined boundaries."[1] The whole endeavour of man in becoming, especially in his adolescence is to find an identity, to keep his diversity in which he could synthesize all his experience and find his wholeness. The wholeness of the present moment necessarily has its defined boundaries. But the fact is that ever newer and better world-views evolving in the individual and the society constantly shift the boundaries of one's identity. It is the sign of the dynamism of life. In my mind the ability to embrace all diversities, keeping at the same time one's own diversity in the wholeness of the moment, is the supreme expression of consistency.Whether we are to be consistent with the expressions of our experience in a past moment or with the truth we experience afresh is not an open question at all. The consistency has to be with truth, and one's own core identity must be always made consistent with that truth. Whether John Chethimattam has made any remarkable contribution in this constant struggle we face all the time is the issue raised in this article. No attempt is made to characterize and define the core vision of the author. It is left to the reader to form a unified picture of his vision through the many-sided thought presented here.

2.   A preacher with Conviction: (1948-1957)

As a preacher, teacher, theologian, Indologist, philosopher of religion, ecumenist, a person involved in inter-religious dialogue, editor, author, administrator, Chethimattam has come out powerfully as a man of conviction, courage, and, above all, commitment.   He is there fully where he is found.   His eloquence, his written style, his ability to abstract and synthesize are remarkable.   His writings span through a period of thirty-four years.   His first five works in Malayalam, the mother tongue of the author, brings out the pastor and the preacher in him. Chethimattam published his first book, The Life of St. John Berchmans at the age of 26, an age at which usually the adolescent is doing the finishing touch with his ego-ideal, the hero of his choice.   The next three books, in Malayalam, namely The Image of Love (1950), Life of Maximilian Kolbe (1951), A Model for Catholic Action (1951), express the same idea of being a model of love in action.   The fifth book in this series, The Existence of God (1957), which discusses the five ways proposed by Aquinas in the Middle Ages to prove the existence of God, marks the end of the preacher-propagandist (missionary) period in Chethimattam's life.

3.   Prolific Writer

Ten years after the first period, that is, in 1967, he came out with his first serious philosophical work, Consciousness and Reality.   Since then to date he has authored, co-authored, and edited five more works.   They reflect the manifold influences to which he was open and sympathetic.   An analysis, moreover, of the innumerable articles he has published both in Malayalam and English -- the present study, is restricted to the articles in English -- during the long period of thirty years will help us to locate his major works in the appropriate phase of the development of his thought.

The fifty-one articles appearing in the bibliography can be grouped under several headings representing various stages in the development of his thought.   In passing from one stage to another, whether the author keeps a self-identity which is consistent with the process of growth is an issue left to the reader to find a solution for himself.   Two major thrusts with three phases can be distinguished here.   The first is the deepening of the initial christian faith and its broadening in contact with Hinduism resulting in a series of comparative studies. This may be the take-off period. All his books so far published belong to this period.

A) The three phases that can be distinguished in this first major thrust are indicated below with the articles belonging to each phase.

i)   Christian Faith:

"The Vine and the Brances" (1), "Theology for the Laity" (5), "The Priestly Life" (8), "Faith and Life" (9), "Concept of Love in the Christian Tradition" (11), "Religious Vocation" (15), "Problems of Formation of Evangelization: A Theological Perspective" (30), "The Process of Decentralization in the Church" (39), "The Local Church is the Catholic Church" (36), "The Church as the Communion of Churches According to the Oriental Fathers" (40), "Towards Renewal in Religious life - Problems and Orientations" (47)

These articles mostly dealt with certain issues related to religious and priestly life which the author lives in the context of an Oriental local Catholic Church. Hence they hit on the familiar themes discussed in Church circles.

The article "Mystical Experience: The Meeting Point between the East and the West" (3), published in 1959, however, marks the starting point of a new phase. The author began to think at this juncture of finding out some common meeting ground for Western Christianity and Eastern religions especially Hinduism. Though for the time being a meeting point was found in mystical experience, the author did not stop there. He took himself to the study of Hindu religion in depth.

ii)   Indology:

The following articles are studies in Indology. "Indian Mind" (4), "Indian Approach to Metaphysics" (7), "Recent Christian Studies on Hinduism" (16), "Psychology and Personality: The Samkhya view of Personality" (17), "Secular Values in the Religion of Guru Nanak" (21), "Rasa, the Soul of Indian Art" (29), "Authority in the Hindu Scriptures" (33), "Intuition and Reason: An Indian Approach" (37), "Morality Beside and Beyond Religion: An Indian Approach to Morality" (43).

3

These articles written during the period of sixteen years of reflection deal with a wide variety of philosophical subjects. Their main concern was to see whether an "Indian approach" is possible to the fundamental issues of philosophy such as mind, (epistemology), metaphysics, personality, values, aesthetic experience, authority, intuition and reason and morality. Chethimattam's works published during this period also manifest a great concern for developing a philosophical methodology which would take into account the Western and the Eastern philosophical disciplines. The only exception is the book, Unique and Universal, An Introduction to Indian Theology. It represents his second major thrust about which we will speak later.

iii)   Comparative Studies:

Reflective study of Indian thought led Chethimattam naturally to comparative studies. Articles mentioned below were written during a period of twenty-three years: "Mary and Meaning of Matter" (2), "Mystical Experience, the Meeting Point Between East and West" (3), "Christian and Vedantic Experience" (6), "III Christian Colloquy on Hinduism" (10), "St. Theresa and Indian Spirituality" (12), "Ananyatva: Hindu and Christian Concept of Incarnation" (14), "An Epistemological Critique of the Knowledge of Christ" (19), "Indian Interiority and Christian Theology" (22), "Religious Experience: Christian and Hindu" (23), "Human Suffering and World Religions" (27), "Faith and Belief in World Religions" (28), "Symbolism and Cult in World Religions Today" (31), "The Christian Art of India Today" (44), "Oriental Pneumatology" (50), "Christian Theology and other Religions" (address 3), "The Problem of Population Explosion and traditional Religions" (26), "Image of Man in Religion and Philosophy" (29), "Meditation, a Discriminating Realization" (38), "Man and Feast" (39), "Religion and Law" (46).

Though the accent on Hinduism and Indian experience and spirituality is very conspicuous, the interest of the author in World Religions, in their symbolism, cult, art, faith, belief and pneumatology is unmistakable in the writings of this period.

B)   The second major thrust we find in Chethimattam's writings is towards dialogue and transformation. Whoever be the partner, either members of other Christian denominations (Ecumenism) or believers of other religions, the fruit of the inter-religious interactions has to be preserved for the coming generations of seekers. It is in this context, it seems to me, the author developed his idea of Indian theology. This may be called the launch-out or creative period.

Though it came out at a very late date, the article "Philosophical Hermeneutics" (49) highlights the guiding principles of his creative period. He conceives hermeneutics primarily as a search for meaning through the interpretation of texts, sacred as well as secular. The article briefly explains some of the main approaches to interpretation. According to Chethimattam, hermeneutics also has a certain open-ended character. It goes on expanding and developing the capacity for understanding. We find this principle operative as a conviction all through his creative period. The article on the "Scope and Conditions of a Hindu Christian Dialogue" (13) made the initial breakthrough into the field of interreligious relations. The three phases we can distinguish during this period are the following:

i) <u>Inter-Religious Dialogue</u>:

The important articles written along this line are: "Scope and Conditions of a Hindu-Christian Dialogue" (13), "Man's Dialogical Nature and the Dialogue of Religions" (32), "Theology and Evangelization: Theology for Dialogue and Theology of Dialogue" (41), "Ministries in the Church in the context of Inter-religious Dialogue" (42), "Atman and Vishnu: Hindu Insights for Inter-Faith Dialogue" (45), "Objectives of Interfaith Dialogue in the Technological Age" (address - 5).

ii) <u>Ecumenism</u>:

A dialogical openness to all christian denominations also was one of his concerns. "Ecumenism Today" (35) is certainly an unfailing witness to the abiding interest of the author in this area.

iii) <u>Indigenous Theology</u>:

In a synthetic mind the demarcation line between Philosophy and religion is very hard to trace out. In the search for a terminal point for thought or absolute truth, if the mind hits on a god, the resultant experience and conviction turns out to be religious. Rooted firmly in this philosophico-religious climate, Chethimattam channels his scholarship and energy to formulate a broader value system which would help one to incarnate one's insights in one's own culture. This he calls indigenous theology and in the Indian context "Indian theology", which has a wider appeal than the specifying term "Indian" signifies. <u>Unique and Universal</u> the work he edited, is a methodological <u>introduction</u> to the kind of work one has to undertake in this field. The important articles on this topic are: "The Spirit and Orientation of an Indian Theology" (25), "Missionary Dimension of an Indian

Theology" (51), "Methodology for an Indian Theology" (address-1).

4. The take-off Period

In the spirit of the saying of the Delphic oracles, "Know thyself," the first concern of the author was to collect information and to clarify, explain, elaborate, criticise and renew them through classes, lectures, seminars and occasional publications. This period lasted for almost ten years (1955-65). At the end of this period he really plunged into a serious study of Hinduism and comparative religion.

Hinduism, for Chethimattam, is a natural religion and culture embodying in its various forms spiritual and intellectual experience and insights of a higher order which, though not properly recognized at the moment, could be still used to generate that same "higher order of" integrating experience (anubhava) in our souls. A fully developed and fully discovered self is the goal of his search. For him "to become a unique, free, responsible human being and to create a better world by constructive social change are the central concerns of education."[3] And again he believes that "a distinctive note of the present age is that the different fields of human knowledge do not remain disparate and apart, but in a way converge in their common subject, man. The different images of man are superimposed on one another to present the integral personality of the conscious human self."[4]

In this process of discovering the integral personality of the human self, he found the great Indian philosopher Sankara coming with a view that tells man that "Thou art That". This position contains an answer to the only worthwhile metaphysical question, namely "What is reality, 'I', 'thou' and 'that'?" Chethimattam in his book "Consciousness and Reality" approaches this central problem of Metaphysics from an Indian standpoint. The book is in the Indian Tradition. But the fact is that "no single tradition can claim a monopoly of truth, and none can pretend to be Perennial Philosophy all by itself. Each tradition has its own particular mode of approach, its own specific problems to handle and peculiar solutions to propose."[5] It is in this spirit he wrote the story of Dialogue in Indian Tradition. But in Consciousness and Reality he has taken the metaphysics of Ramanuja as a point of departure for the discussion of the most basic metaphysical problems, for he is generally acknowledged as the most representative philosopher of the Hindu tradition.[6] Chethimattam says that Ramanuja "found that the Advaita Philosophy was doing great damage to the religious spirit of the people through its abstract concept of the

Absolute and purely theoretical approach to the problems of religious philosophy."[7]   A sensitive reader can easily detect where the real sympathy of the author himself lies. Religion has to be an object of experience rather than speculation.

Both Consciousness and Reality and Dialogue in Indian Tradition were written with the explicit goal of inter-religious dialogue in view. In the preface to the first book he clearly states his aim:

> For any fruitful dialogue, each one has to be conscious of his own identity as well as of the individuality of his partner. Hence, a right understanding of the metaphysical genius of India is indispensable for an East-West religious dialogue. I have attempted here to rethink the principal questions discussed in Western metaphysics from the Indian angle of vision.[8]

He writes again in the same vein stressing the need for convergence of views for a fruitful dialogue: "But only when the convergence of these various approaches to man and his life problems is taken into account, will a true dialogue emerge. To keep up the dialogue, the identity and uniqueness of each tradition too have to be kept intact."[9]

The tension between the need for convergence of all into an integral whole and the richness in keeping the diversity or uniqueness distinctly pervades all his writings. In one moment he easily transcends to the unifying point of the Absolute and at another moment he reaches down to earth stressing the concreteness and immediacy of experience in which alone religious and philosophic insights could become life-bound experience or anubhava.

The next phase we note in this major thrust is the stage of comparative study. The aim of comparative study is the deeper understanding of the sides compared. For such studies phenomena common to both sides are chosen. Meaning of matter, mystical experience, interiority and spirituality, religious experience, suffering, faith, symbolism, cult, art, laws and such other themes could easily be the object of comparative studies, and precisely these were the topics Chethimattam chose to write on. For example, the inter-relation between faith and belief in the evolution of religion is such an area.

The encounter of religions with national cultures is

most clearly shown in the translation of faith into
beliefs. Faith is the central reality of religion
and it is also a characteristic quality or potentiality
of human life. But it can be expressed and realized
in actual life only through its application . . . This
application produces particular beliefs. Thus faith
and belief are intimately connected, but they are
not identical.[10]

Each religion has a history in this translation of faith into
belief which is comparable to any other religious history. Cult
and symbols of worship take shape in all religions from certain
fundamental insights of man.[11] The history of the evolution of
symbolism and cult in world religions is certainly a very fruitful
area of research for creating an atmosphere of inter-religious
dialogue. Innumerable are the topics Chethimattam chose for his
comparative study, but I would like to conclude this section with a
citation from his article on the "Christian and Vedantic Experience"
of religion.

Vedānta presents a substantially correct philosophy of
religious experience, especially when examined against the
background of the intentions of its teachers. It is a religious
philosophy which takes the consciousness of man as the
starting point. Religion is not merely an abstract theory
about God, a system of concepts about divinity, but it is
essentially the quest and discovery of the Supreme. It
demands that we transcend the particular concepts derived
from our experience by which we construct a figure of the
Godhead in our speculations. The god of Aristotle, as such,
is no God of religion. Religion means not simply cognition
but recognition, not abstraction but realization, not simply
understanding, but intelligent submission to the Final End.[12]

5. Launching out

One of the key concepts of this period is that man himself is
dialogical in nature and therefore his religions also have to enter
into dialogue. In developing this idea, the author has come a long
way forward from his earlier position expressed in the article,
"Scope and Conditions of a Hindu Christian Dialogue".[13] "Dialogue
is not a concession or a luxury." Spontaneously growing dialogue
among religions brings out a long-neglected dimension of man: his
dialogal psychic structure, which contemporary philosophical
thinking and religious experience have brought into focus".[14]
Psychologically, the human self is dialogal; all authentic human
activity is dialogue. Poetry is dialogue with the world; love is

8

dialogue with others, and prayer is dialogue with God."[15]
Openness to other men in dialogue should be based on the
wholeness and integrity of the person. Person unifies in himself
two complementary tendencies: one directed towards the
concentration and mastery of self and the other to expansion and
gift of self to others . . . Self-possession and self-gift constitute
the rhythm of personal life."[16] Thus the author presents dialogue
as the basic dimension of what one is. "The purpose of dialogue
is that men should draw closer to each other. For this, religion,
philosophy and culture should be bonds and links enabling people
to share experience, ideas and ideals instead of being dividing
fences between classes and groups."[17]

The fact of dialogue calls for two types of theology, namely,
the theology of a dialogue and the theology for a dialogue. The
former "demands that each tradition and though pattern of faith
should initiate an inner dialogue with itself to examine how its
own inner logic has relevance to ever-changing actual situations
and new facets presented by basic religious problems."[18] The
theology for a dialogue "is rather the common search of people
sharing in the same cultural situation, of believers and
non-believers alike, to discover the meaning and implication of
God's word in that situation, to find out how the Logos . . .
transforms the whole situation from within".[19]

In this spirit of dialogue Chethimattam takes up the issue of
incarnation and tries to gain insight from Hindu tradition: "I shall
discuss two of these insights, experience of an ultimate ground of
all reality designated as Atman, and the vision of a sublime ideal
of humanity in the figure of Vishnu. These two constitute the
theological and anthropological poles of all religious experience in
which all religions can discover their basic unity as well as the
areas where each man can make his own unique contribution."[20]
The concrete conclusions Chethimattam arrives at as a result of a
dialogical interaction is summarized in the following statement.
"Thus in honest inter-faith encounter Christianity has to learn a
great deal from the Hindu experience to view the Christ-event
from a transcendental point of view, and Hinduism can learn from
Christianity to face the concrete problems of man today: poverty,
social inequality, and suffering from a realistic human
perspective."[21]

The dialogical relation of religions are not restricted to
non-Christian religions alone. It also includes Christian
denominations. In the article "Ecumenism Today" (35),
Chethimattam recognizes the great work being done in this area,
although he has not much to contribute to that specific field.

Another major concern in his launch-out period is the formulation of an Indian theology. Being a committed Indian Christian, he is called to live his Christian faith in the context of the Indian religious tradition. "Those who find it difficult to reconcile the experience of their inner selves with Jesus of Nazareth, Son of God, may not"[22] understand and appreciate what Chethimattam presents as Indian Theology. Theology for him "is reflection on faith, lived in a community and disclosure expressing that experience."[23] It is a dialogue between theos and logos."[24] "Theology is not a system, but rather an activity."[25] It is the interpretation of an ineffable faith. "Any interpretation of the ineffable should have the humility to recognize its inadequacy and the wisdom to leave all doors open for further understanding."[26] All structures are limiting, including theologizing, which is a process by which a structure is put on faith. Hence Chethimattam points out that "Structure itself is against the spirit of Indian Theology, which is a constant quest for the ultimate unknowable. Hence any structure ascribed to it should be that of an open-minded questioning."[27]

What is possible in this context is to "have an open structure of perpetual enquiry." But it cannot be an "empty openness." It is the transparency of the human self to the continuing presence of the Paramātman. Theology has to be grounded on this experience. This presence or sharing in divine life is supernatural grace. The life of grace can be conceived as a presence like that of light illuminating glass.[28] The Trinitarian mystery and the mystery of incarnation also get new interpretation in this new structure of Indian theology.

> The internal experience of the spirit acting in us as the aham (our real I), and the encounter with the world as Tvam (Thou, the true word) become unified in the supreme reality of the Father, the real Tat: in this unified vision one is not primarily concerned with the historical Christ, Jesus of Nazareth, who appeared at a particular point on the globe. What is important is his being the summary and sum-total of the external expression of the individual divinity, a climactic point for the exteriorisation of interior experience. For this Krsna or Buddha may play the role of Christ. History and precision will be called for only when attention is directed to the structure of external experience located in time and space.[29]

The fact is that human experience is not merely abstract and impersonal. It is located in time and space. Hence to a certain extent, history, precision, and structure are necessary to maintain

10

the experience. Some through their faith find it possible to reconcile the God-experience of their inner selves with Jesus of Nazareth. Even then an Indian Christian has to live his Christian faith in the context of his cultural tradition. It is in this context the new missionary-ideal of Chethimattam emerges: "Conversion is not a one-way traffic, demanded only of the non-Christians. The Christian has first to be converted to the way of experience of the Hindu and of the Buddhist, before he can ask his Hindu or Buddhist brother to share the message of salvation he bears for all men."[30]

What all men aim at in this life is fullness on consciousness and liberation in contrast to the present state of bondage. While discussing "Sankarāchārya's Theological Method," Chethimattam writes: "The problem is how one can proceed from the extreme of misery and ignorance to the fullness of knowledge and bliss. For Sankara this is the scope and meaning of "Brahma-inquiry", which is theology and philosophy at the same time."[31] The rootedness of Sankara's Brahma-inquiry in human temporality and relatedness is well formulated in the following citation. "Sankara's method... is to analyse bondage and ignorance and to show that what is positive in them is consciousness itself, which has to be liberated by the removal of the factors that hide and distort it."[32]

Total liberation of man and the attainment of limitless freedom is the end of all faiths, religion and philosophy, according to Chethimattam. Ecumenism, dialogue, Indian theology are only passing phases in the process of a comprehensive convergence.

6. Towards a Higher Synthesis

The question is not whether at a historical or transtemporal moment all becoming would converge in the omega-point or in a plenum. What is being discussed is the human spirit's striving for attaining its wholeness through integration. The question of convergence or integration has different connotation for empirical psychology and metaphysics. From a psychological point of view human personality matures and gets integrated attaining greater degrees of freedom as it advances in age, provided the need satisfactions are squarely met. Structure of this dynamics can be detected even in our intellectual operation. Chethimattam's writings make us aware of that spiritual and internal dynamism in us and invite us to respond to this call to integration and wholeness positively.

Chethimattam, however, is not a visionary. He knows that our universe is "an unsynthesized, pluralistic world of experience. Religious pluralism is a universally acknowledged phenomenon in

the world of today."[33]   Religions formulate their faith in God.
But "any theory or conceptual framework is only an inadequate
abstraction from this ineffable life-experience"[34] of God.   Though
inadequate, each religion has its own contribution to make.   "The
benefit of religious pluralism in this matter is the reflective
process by which experience in different linguistic and cultural
situations converge on the ineffable Reality indicated by them."[35]

The basic assumption here, as Paul Ricoeur tries to maintain
in his discussion on hermeneutics, is that no system or method of
interpretation is capable of attaining the totality of meaning it is
thinking about and aiming at.[36]   In the search for the ultimate
unifying point, Chethimattam also seems to take a position similar
to that of Ricoeur.   "He creates a third way of approach in the
form of a limit idea, by opposing the two sides of a polarity by a
philosophy of hope postponing a synthesis between then, thus
limiting philosophy itself."[37]   A philosophy of hope ever
postponing the ultimate synthesis is very much operative in the
writing of Chethimattam.   This is well evident in his endorsement
of the attitude of tolerance taken by Vatican II and S.
Radhakrishnan.

> Vatican II in its document on religious freedom moved
> a step forward emphasizing a policy of psychological
> tolerance, since even the most sublime truths have to be
> accepted and articulated by the free human consciousness.
> Systems and religions should not be viewed and judged in
> themselves, but one must allow each man to arrive freely
> at a grasp of truth by himself.   This puts common sense
> before logic and practical necessity before theoretical
> consistency.

> As S. Radhakrishnan puts it, tolerance of religious
> systems and traditions one cannot understand is the homage
> the finite human mind pays to the infinite reality of the
> Divine; it is an expression of the reflexive awareness of
> the limits and limitations of the human mind.[38]

This openness, tolerance, postponement of synthesis in terms
of a philosophy of hope does not mean that there is no core
identity in Chethimattam's thought which is being perfected at
every moment.   He is deeply committed to Christ and to the
sharing of this faith-experience:
> Christian missionary activity is event-centered
> communicating to all men what happened to them in Jesus
> Christ.   Jesus Christ is not just one expression of the
> presence and activity of the divine logos like several

12

others such as Buddha, Mahavira, Confucius or Mohammed, but unique as the focal point of human history at which the divine Logos integrated himself with all human history through the Incarnation and the redemptive Resurrection.[39]

But elsewhere he also admits that, in the unified vision of the Supreme Reality, "one is not primarily concerned with the historical Christ, Jesus of Nazareth, who appeared at a particular point on the globe."[40] For him the Christ-event is the climactic point for the exteriorization of the interior experience of the Supreme Reality. For this Krṣṇa or Buddha may play the role of Christ.[41] Here the author transcends the historical expression of Jesus of Nazareth himself.

What he aims at is freedom, freedom in its true sense, namely freedom from misery, ignorance, and bondage to freedom for what one can genuinely be. "man's temporal liberation is not merely a condition for his spiritual liberation but an integral part of it."[42] The religious task for those living in this secular city is in its streets and slums and not outside it. This means man is the starting point of all technology and religion, not an abstract God out there. The one thing worth liberating at all costs is the human person. Hence liberation in the fullest sense is the process for freeing man and for freedom from natural constraints, from social restrictions, from those barriers which man himself has erected by his personal and collective selfishness.[43] Indian religious tradition itself is called muktimārga, a way of liberation. For believing Christians "the Church is also the image of the freedom that all men are aspiring after."[44] The puzzling question is whether the Church as the enduring proclamation of the mystery of redemption is showing forth forcefully enough this ideal of liberation and freedom. It is, however, refreshing to note that we have among us writers like Chethimattam who are relentlessly fighting for the total liberation of man and his limitless freedom.

NOTES

[1] Erik H. Erikson, Identity: Youth and Crisis, (London: Faber, 1971), p. 90.

[2] The serial number of the article in the bibliography is given in bracket at the end of the titles for easy reference.

[3] "Philosophical Hermeneutics", Journal of Dharma, 5 (1981), 65.

[4] Images of Man, (Bangalore: Dharmaram Publications, 1974), p. 1.

[5] Dialogue in Indian Tradition, (Bangalore: Dharmaram Publications, 1969), p. iii.

[6] Consciousness and Reality, p. 7.

[7] Ibid., p. 19.

[8] Ibid., p. ix.

[9] Dialogues in Indian Tradition, p. iii.

[10] Jeevadhara, 3 (1973), 412.

[11] Jeevadhara, 5 (1975), 347-54.

[12] "Christian and Vedantic Experience", Indian Ecclesiastical Studies (1963), 2 (1963), 282.

[13] Journal of Dharma, (1975), 29.

[14] Ibid., p. 10.

[15] Ibid., p. 14.

[16] Ibid., p. 16.

[17] Ibid., p. 18.

[18] Jeevadhara, (1977), 393.

[19] Ibid., p. 395.

[20] Meeting of Religions, (1978), p. 136.

[21] Ibid., p. 155.

[22] Jeevadhara, (1971), 462.

[23] Ibid., p. 452.

[24] Unique and Universal, p. 11.

[25] Jeevadhara, (1971), 453.

[26] Ibid., p. 452.

[27] Ibid., p. 453.

[28] Ibid., p. 454-456.

[29] Ibid., p. 455-56.

[30] Ibid., p. 462.

[31] Unique and Universal, p. 90.

[32] Ibid., p. 90.

[33] Jeevadhara, 11 (1981), 325.

[34] Jeevadhara, 11 (1981), 325.

[35] Ibid., p. 326.

[36] "Philosophical Hermeneutics", Journal of Dharma, 5 (1980), 74.

[37] Ibid., p. 74.

[38] Jeevadhara, 11 (1981), 329-30.

[39] Jeevadhara, 7 (1977), 386-87.

[40] Jeevadhara, Vol. I (1971), p. 455.

[41] Jeevadhara, Vol. I (1971), p. 455.

[42] Jeevadhara, Vol. II (1972), p. 26.

[43] Ibid., p. 32.

[44] Ibid., p. 31.

Chethimattam: A Select Bibliography of His Publications

A. Books

In Malayalam

1. Visuddha Yohannan Berchmans (Life of St. John
   Berchmans) Thevara, India, 1948 pp. 180.

2. Snehasvarupan (The Image of Love), Mannanam, 1950,
   pp. 175.

3. Oru Vidushakan (Life of Maximilian Kolbe) Mannanam,
   1951, pp. 48.

4. Katholicapravarthanathinoru Matrka (A Model for
   Catholic Action) Mannanam, 1951, pp. 58.

5. Daivastittvam (The Existence of God), Mannanam, 1957,
   pp. 78.

In English

1. Consciousness and Reality, An Indian Approach to
   Metaphysics, Bangalore, 1967, London & New York, 1971.

2. Dialogue in Indian Tradition, Bangalore, 1969, pp. vii,
   162 re-edited as Patterns of Indian Thought, A Student
   Introduction, London: G. Chapman & Maryknoll: Orbis,
   1971, trans. into Polish: Nurty Myslii Indijewski,
   Warsaw: Pax, 1975.

3. A Philosophy in Song Poems (co-authored with
   Dr. A. de Nicholas) Bangalore, 1971.

4. Unique and Universal, An Introduction to Indian
   Theology, ed. Bangalore: Dharmaram Publications, 1972.

5. Images of Man (co-authored with Dr. T. M. Thomas,
   Bangalore, 1974.

6. Glimpses of Reality, A First Book of Metaphysics.
   E. Orange: Dharmanivas, 1980.

B. Articles: In English

1. "The Vine and the Branches," Unitas, Mangalore 1950

16

2. "Mary and the Meaning of Matter" India and the Fullness of Christ, Madras, 1957.

3. "Mystical Experience, the Meeting Point between East and West" Indian Philosophical Quarterly, 1959.

4. "The Indian Mind" Clergy Monthly, 1961.

5. "Theology for the Laity", Clergy Monthly, 1961.

6. "Christian and Vedāntic Experience" Indian Eccl. Studies 1 (1962) and 2 (1963).

7. "Indian Approach to Metaphysics" Indian Eccl. Studies 2 (1963) 236-54.

8. "The Priestly Life" Unitas, Mangalore, 1963.

9. "Faith and Life" a chapter in the book: The Art of Living ed. Prem Nath, Jullundur, 1963.

10. "III Christian Colloquy on Hinduism," Ind. Eccl. Studies, 3 (1964).

11. "Concept of Love in the Christian Tradition," Bulletin for the Study of Religion and Society, Bangalore, 13 (1964).

12. "St. Teresa and Indian Spirituality," Eucharist and Priest, Alwaye, 1964.

13. "Scope and Conditions of a Hindu Christian Dialogue," Concilium 3 (March 1965), Ind. Eccl. Studies 4 (1965); summarised in Catholic Digest Oct. 1965.

14. "Ananyatva, Hindu and Christian Concepts of Incarnation," The Guardian, Bangalore, March 1965, trans. into German in Stimmen auf Asien, Stuttgart, 1968.

15. "Religious Vocation" In Christo, 1965.

16. "Recent Christian Studies on Hinduism" Paper presented at the Indian Universities Colloquium on Comparative Religion, Bangalore, Sept. 1967, Examiner, Bombay, Oct. 1967.

17. "Psychology and Personality, The Samkhya View of Philosophy," Ind. Eccl. Studies, 7 (1968).

18. "The Church in Ceylon; Impressions from a Short Visit" Examiner, Bombay, Dec. 1968.

19. "An Epistemological Critique of the Knowledge of Christ." Paper presented at the triennial meeting of the Ind. Theol. Association, Ranchi, Dec. 1968, Indian Theological Quarterly, March 1969.

20. "Vatican II and the Church in India," Logos, Ceylon, March 1969.

21. "Secular Values in the Religion of Guru Nanak" Paper presented at the International Religious Conference, Punjabi Univ. Patiala, Sept. 1969. Wardha Medical College Magazine, 1970.

22. Indian Interiority and Christian Theology, Report of the I Christian Colloquy on Hinduism. Bangalore, 1961 pp. 58.

23. Religious Experience, Christian and Hindu, Report of II Christian Colloquy on Hinduism, Bangalore, 1962, pp. 62.

24. "Rasa, the Soul of Indian Art." International Philosophical Quarterly 10 (1970) 44-62.

25. "The Spirit and Orientation of an Indian Theology," Jeevadhara 1 (1971) 452-462.

26. "The Problem of Population Explosion and Traditional Religions" Religion and Society, 19 (1972) 29-34.

27. "Human Suffering and World Religions" Jeevadhara 2 (1972) 377-86.

28. "Faith and Belief in World Religions," Jeevadhara 3 (1973) 412-21.

29. "Image of Man in Religion and Philosophy," Jeevadhara 4 (1974) 353-63.

30. "Problems of Formation for Evangelization, A Theological Perspective," The Living World 81 (1975) 76-89.

31. "Symbolism and Cult in World Religions Today," Jeevadhara 5 (1975) 329-44.

32. "Man's Dialogical Nature and the Dialogue of Religions," Journal of Dharma 1 (1975) 76-89.

33. "Authority in the Hindu Scriptures," Jeevadhara 34 (1976) 380-87.

34. "The Process of Decentralization in the Church," Jeevadhara 28 (1975) 291-310.

35. "Ecumenism Today," Jeevadhara 1 (1971) 463-473.

36. "The Local Church is the Catholic Church," Jeevadhara 1 (1971) 333-40.

37. "Intuition and Reason, An Indian Approach," Journal of Dharma 1 (1976) 391-402.

38. "Meditation, a Discriminating Realization," Journal of Dharma 2 (1977) 164-172.

39. "Man and Feast," Jeevadhara 35 (1976) 405-417.

40. "The Church as the Communion of Churches, according to the Oriental Fathers." Jeevadhara 40 (1977) 358-367.

41. "Theology and Evangelization, Theology for Dialogue and Theology of Dialogue," Jeevadhara 41 (1977) 379-396.

42. "Ministries in the Church in the Context of Interreligious Dialogue" Research and Background Paper presented to the Federation of the Bishops' Conferences of Asia, Honkong, III, 8, pp. 1-11.

43. "Morality Beside and Beyond Religion: An Indian Approach to Morality" Ethical Wisdon East and/or West, Proceedings of ACPA LI, Washington, 1977 pp. 87-104.

44. "The Christian Art of India Today" Catholic Near East Magazine. Summer 1978 pp. 8-11.

45. "Atman and Vishnu: Hindu Insights for Inter-Faith Dialogue," Meeting of Religions ed. Thomas A. Aykara, Rome, 1978, pp. 135-55.

46. "Religions and Law" Journal of Dharma 4 (1979) 373-387.

47. "Towards Renewal in Religious Life-Problems and Orientations" Jeevadhara 1979 pp. 274-284.

48. "Fourteen Years after Vatican II What Have We Achieved?" Jeevadhara 1979 pp. 319-327.

49. "Philosophical Hermeneutics," Journal of Dharma, 1980.

50. "Oriental Pneumatology" Jeevadhara 1980.

51. "Missionary Dimensions of an Indian Theology" Jeevadhara 1980 pp. 270-282.

52. "Four Patterns of Theological Experience," Jeevadhara 9 (1979) pp. 277-288.

53. "Meeting and Scope of an Interreligious Dialogue", Jeevadhara 11 (1981) pp. 319-334.

54. "Religion and Politics: Contrast and Complementarity" Journal of Dharma, 7 (1982) pp. 5-25.

55. "Yoga and Immortality in Samkhya-Yoga", Proceedings of the IASWR Conference 1981, ed. Christopher Chapple, Stony Brook, IASWR 1983, pp. 79-102.

56. "Place and Role of the Aged in the Hindu Perspective", a chapter in Aging, Spiritual Perspectives. ed., Ettore DiFilippo, Lakeworth, FL.: Sunday Publications, 1982 pp. 63-83.

57. "Religious and Pilgrimages" Jeevadhara 12 (1982) pp. 63-83.

58. "Ecclesiology in the Socio-Political Context of India," Jeevadhara 12 (1982) pp. 278-296.

59. "Reflections on Rusurrection, Life and Renewal: Review Article on the book of Varghese Pathikulangara." Jeevadhara 12 (1982) pp. 322-332.

60. "Impact of Science on Religion and Theology", Journal of Dharma, 8 (1983) pp. 5-26.

61. "Liberty of the Person in Society", a chapter in The Human Person and Philosophy in the Contemporary World, Proceedings of the World Union of the Catholic Philosophical Societies, Cracow, August 1978, ed. J. M. Zycinski, Krakow, 1980, pp. 277-289.

62. "Problems of an Indian Christian Theology - A Critique of Indian Theologizing". Ch. 12 in Theologizing in India, ed. M. Amaladoss, T. K. John, & G. Gispert-Sauch, Bangalore: Theological Publications of India, 1981., pp. 195-207.

63. "Towards a World Theology: An Interreligious Approach to Theological Issues," Jeevadhara 13 (1983) pp. 313-335.

64. "Varieties of Orientalism", Jeevadhara 13 (1983), pp. 355-362

65. "The Greek Religious Apophatism", Journal of Dharma, 6 (1981) pp. 69-82.

66. "Religions and Social Change, Some Basic Patterns", Journal of Dharma, 9 (1984) pp. 7-23.

67. "Religious Monograms and Mantras", Journal of Dharma, 9 (1984) pp. 142-149.

EAST IS EAST: ENCOUNTER IN THE EAST

EAST MEETS WEST:
THE STORY OF THE CATHOLIC EXPERIENCE IN INDIA

A. M. Mundadan

Existential religion should be viewed as the result of the confrontation between the revealed Word of God and man in his individual and social context. It is the encounter of the Word of God with contemporary man's views of life and the world. Religion thus considered inevitably raises the question: How far do the form and content of a particular culture or a particular philosophy affect a universal religion? Vatican II has enunciated in its Decree on the Evangelization of Peoples a very sound and at the same time a very dynamic principle:

> The seed which is the Word of God sprouts from the ground watered by divine dew. From this ground the seed draws nourishing elements which it transforms and assimilates into itself. Finally it bears much fruit... If this goal is to be achieved, theological investigation must necessarily be stirred up in each major socio-cultural area.[1]

We know that what the above passage describes happened in the Jewish-Semitic world, the Greco-Roman and Byzantine worlds. Has it happened in India, a country with a very rich culture and high philosophical and religious tradition? Did it happen among the Christians of India before the 16th century? Has it happened since then, among the Indian Christians, both ancient and modern, who have lived in communion with Rome?

Ancient Indian Christians and Their Self-Understanding

Most ancient Christian Churches, whether they were of direct or indirect apostolic origin, had developed an individuality of their own. This individuality is seen in the worship form, Church structure and discipline peculiar to them, and, above all, in the theological and spiritual vision that emerged in each of these Churches in course of time. We are not interested in discovering the reasons for the growth of the individuality of each Church; the individuality is a fact though individual characteristics-liturgical, theological, spiritual, structural or disciplinary-and their expressions in each Church may vary in degree.

23

The Church in India which claims apostolic origin is certainly one of the oldest Churches. It did develop an individuality of its own, with its long tradition and life in India. Naturally one would ask whether it has evolved a distinct theology which serves as a guide and inspiration for theologizing in India today. There is no simple answer to this question. It is often stated that the long dependence of the ancient Christians of India-- the St. Thomas Christians-- on the Persian or East-Syrian Church followed by the domination of the Portuguese and other Western missionaries was least conducive to the emergence of an indigenous theology proper to the Christians of St. Thomas.[2]

Prior to the arrival of the Portuguese, the Christians of India had been living in two worlds-- the geographical, political, and social environment of India (Kerala) and the Christian environment resulting from a long association with the East-Syrian Church.[3] It is this life in two worlds which gave the Christians of St. Thomas a distinctive identity of their own. It is this identity which some writers have characterized as, "Hindu in culture, Christian in faith and Syro-Oriental in worship."[4]

While the socio-cultural environment was fully reflected in the purely social life of the Christians, it does not seem to have touched, except peripherally, the Church-life or the faith-life, especially the worship pattern and the theological and spiritual outlook of the community. From the various reports and letters of the Portuguese in the 16th century, the picture that emerges is that of a Church which not only was ruled by East-Syrian prelates but of a Church which had almost completely taken over the theology, worship form and Church institutions of the East-Syrian Christians of Persia.

We possess a number of Portuguese evaluations of the doctrinal/theological positions of the St. Thomas Christians in the 16th century. Some of these evaluations are derived from general observations which the Portuguese made about the beliefs and practices of the community, and do not go beyond a blanket statement that the Christians professed the orthodox faith. Others are the result of deeper study, especially of the Syriac Books in their possession, and provide evidence that Christians of St. Thomas adhered to the official theological position of the East-Syrian Church.[5]

Taking all this into consideration, the conclusion arrived at by many writers today is similar to the one stated by Robin Boyd who says: "It might be expected that the Syrian Church, with its long Indian tradition behind it, would have evolved a distinct type of theology which could be a guide and inspiration to Indian theologians of other, more recent, traditions. It must be admitted, however, that this has not been the case, and that it is only comparatively recently, and under the influence of Western theology, that theological writers of note have begun to emerge."[6] But a few have taken a very different view. For example, Antony Mookenthottam feels that it is probable that the ancient Church of India had developed some theology of its own and this theology is not written down in books but is implicit in "the life, experience and traditions" of the community.[7]

Today there is no written pre-sixteenth century record of the doctrinal/theological position of the St. Thomas Christians prior to their contact with the West in the 16th century. Even those books which the Portuguese writers of the 16th century examined and used for drawing their conclusions are not available today. Since the Portuguese suspected the presence of errors in the books they all became casualties in the <u>auto-da fe'</u> programme launched by the Portuguese Padroado authorities at the close of the 16th century and later.[8] This leaves us without sufficient data to verify whether the Indian Christians had evolved a theology of their own. Recourse then has to be made to other sources of information, namely "the life, experience and tradition", to derive some idea of the pre-sixteenth century views of the Christians of India. In other words, we have to see what theology is reflected in the general outlook and religious mentality of the community, in their life, customs and traditions.

If you examine the social and certain aspects of the socio-ecclesiastical life the Christians of St. Thomas had been leading,[9] you may come to the same conclusion as Antony Mookenthottam: "Their identification with their socio-cultural milieu was . . . thorough . . . . This oneness with their socio-cultural milieu implies an implicit incarnational theology lived, an awareness that Christ in becoming man assumed everything human and redeemed all social and cultural values."[10]

Another important factor worth considering is their attitude towards the Hindu community in Kerala and their relations with it. The Synod of Diamper of 1599 forbade a number of customs and practices which the Portuguese considered pagan (Hindu).[11] These prohibitions and restrictions imposed by the synod are a witness to the communal harmony and cordial relations that existed between Christians and the Hindus. This communal harmony and spirit of tolerance should be considered a typical Indian contribution to the Christian vision.

In Act III, Decree 4 of the Synod of Diamper we read:

> Each one can be saved in his own law, all laws
> are right: This is fully erroneous and a most
> shameful heresy: There is no law in which we
> may be saved except the law of Christ our Saviour
> . . ." and the foot-note says: "This is a
> perverse dogma of politicians and those tolerant . . .
> Consequently being indifferent they wander very far
> away from the truth.¹¹

It is to be noted that the synod attributes this "error" to contact
with pagans. What is really involved here is the understanding of
the doctrine, extra ecclesiam nulls salus (outside the Church
there is no salvation), by the Portuguese and the St. Thomas
Christians, respectively. The Portuguese came from the West,
where a rigid interpretation of the dictum had prevailed for a long
time and had become acute in the 16th century in the context of
the anti-Protestant Counter-Reformation spirit. They sensed
danger in the more liberal attitude of the Indian Christians
towards Hindus and Hindu religion. Archbishop Menezes and his
Portuguese advisers drew up a decree condemning an error which
they thought was implied in the liberal attitude of the Christians.

The Synod is right in attributing the "error" to the contacts
the St. Thomas Christians maintained with pagans. It would take
centuries before the Europeans would acquire a life-experience of
non-Christian religions, before a theology of the religions of the
world would emerge which would give due respect to the positive
elements in those religions and their providential salvific role for
millions of people. But the Indian Christians had been already
living for centuries in a positive encounter with the high-caste
Hindus and had developed a theological vision of the Hindu
religion which was more positive and liberal. Today, in the light
of modern theological approaches to non-Christian religions, one
must admit that the vision of the Indian Christians was a more
enlighted one than that of their European contemporaries.

Their theological vision was broader and more liberal. But
their position was not that radical and extreme as expressed by
the synodal decree. No Portuguese writers of the 16th century
like Roz, for instance, who had made a rather deep study of the
faith and doctrine of the St. Thomas Christians, attribute to them
such an error. The wording of the decree must have been
dictated by the over-sensitivity of Menezes and his advisers
to a liberal but orthodox approach to non-Christian religions.

The attitude of the St. Thomas Christians towards non-Christians and their religions was an enlighted one and approximates that of modern theology. Their ideas on a local/individual Church agree even more with modern ecclesiology. Act III, decree 7 of the Diamper Synod denounces another "error" of the Christians of St. Thomas.

> the Synod is painfully aware of the heresy and perverse error which is being disseminated in this diocese by the schismatics to the great detriment of souls: There is one law of St. Thomas and another of St. Peter; the Church founded by the one is distinct and different from the Church founded by the other; each is immediately from Christ; one has nothing to do with the other; neither the prelate of one owes obedience to the prelate of the other; those who belong to the law of Peter endeavoured to destroy the law of St. Thomas; for this they had been punished by him.

The words used by the synodal decree are too sharp to be taken at their face value. Those who drafted the decree gave a rather radical and extreme interpretation of the views of the Indian Christians regarding the identity and autonomy of individual/particular Churches. The whole question must be analysed in the particular context in which it was discussed. On the one hand, Archbishop Menezes and his Portuguese associates were out to detect "errors" where perhaps none existed. On the other hand, in the tension-filled atmosphere that preceded the Synod, some leaders of the community including the archdeacon, anxious as they were about the autonomy and identity of their Church, might have criticized in scathing terms the Portuguese action in general and the interference of Archbishop Menezes in particular.

Only twenty years before the celebration of the synod, a Jesuit priest, Francisco Dionysio who had known the Christians rather intimately had written: "They regard the Pope as the Vicar of Christ our Redeemer, on earth, and their Patriarch as subject to the Pope from whom his powers are communicated to him."[12] Even though we do not accept this statement as representing a conscious acceptance of the primacy of the Roman bishop as it is understood in the Catholic Church today, there is no doubt that they showed positive regard to the Petrine office and the Pope's position and believed in the universal communion of all Christians.

Besides, the Indian Christians, as far as history can trace, had all along been welcoming Christian visitors whether from the East or West as brothers in Christ and treating them as such.[13] It was in this spirit of Christian solidarity and cordiality that they welcomed the Portuguese in the beginning. Tension started developing when they felt that the Portuguese unduly interfered in their autonomy and were critical of their customs, practices and beliefs which were indeed marks of their distinctive identity.[14]

The attitude and mentality of the Christians as they emerge from various Portuguese reports and letters deserve mention here. It is clear that the Indian Christians looked upon the customs, practices, and life of the Latin Christians from the West with respect, and expected from the Western Christians a reciprocal regard for their own way of life which had developed with the Indian Church ever since St. Thomas sowed the seeds of the faith in India. The Churches, each one supposed to be founded by one of the apostles, were to be left free to develop their own particular tradition, so that one did not interfere in the affairs of the other while holding on to the same faith in Jesus Christ and being in communion with one another. This did not therefore mean the exclusion of mutual co-operation and deriving profit from one another by remaining in contact. The Christians of India were not averse to learn from the Western Christians in matters relating to clearer doctrinal definition and Church discipline.

But the Indian Christians could never accept the idea that only the Latin form of Christianity was the true form of Christianity. They could, to some extent, appreciate the Latin usages and liturgical and canonical disciplines, but they would not wholly accept them, just as they did not expect the Portuguese to accept their own particular customs and practices in these matters. Their thinking could be described thus: both the Portuguese and they were Christians and both belonged to the universal Church. But each local community had its own customs and usages including Church-discipline, its native customs, etc., probably going back to the times of the Apostles themselves ("Law of Thomas," "Law of Peter," and so on). They could never reconcile themselves to the idea of giving up their customs and practices, both social and ecclesiastical, which had been sacred to them for many centuries. They were prepared to accept from the Latin missionaries what they lacked: instruction, a better discipline; but they would not like the missionaries to occupy the position of their own priests and prelates.[15]

This was, of course, a legitimate theological concept of the individual/particular Church, a concept which is a significant contribution of modern ecclesiology and approved by many official Church documents. To this was added a typically Indian community- or even caste-attitude. The Indian Christians regarded the Portuguese as their own people in friendly recognition of them as Christians and brethren, but this recognition did not mean that the Christians were prepared to admit the Portuguese into the set-up of their own communal life, which was a closed one to which strangers, whether Christian or not (in this sense the high-caste Hindus of Kerala were less strangers to them than the Portuguese), were prohibited entry and assimilation. They looked upon the Portuguese in this exclusive spirit and thus thought of them as strangers and outsiders.[16]

The Church in India, though patterned after the structure of the East-Syrian Church of Persia, was marked by certain peculiarities of its own. It is not certain whether the Indian Christians, since they came into intimate contact with the East-Syrian Church, ever had any prelate of theirs chosen from among themselves.[17] From the existing historical records we know only that bishops came from Persia regularly and administered the Indian Church. The bishops, whether they were Indians or foreigners, were known by such titles as "Metropolitan and Gate of All-India," "Gate of India," "gate" in Syriac parlance signifying "sublime authority" or "sublime and great power." This appears to be a unique position.

The institution of the "Archdeacon of India" was even more unique. His usual title was "Archdeacon of All India." He was not only the alter ego of the bishop but was the national head of the Indian Christian community (Jatikku Karthavian, as he was known in Malayalam), "the prince and the head of the Christians of St. Thomas," as some missionaries have described his position in Kerala.[18]

The Church of India as a whole was governed by the Metropolitan and Archdeacon together with a general assembly (known in Malayalam as pothuyogam meaning "general assembly") consisting of laymen and priests. Each local community had its local assembly (simply yogam) with lay leaders and the local college of clergy as their members and administered the church and directed the local community.

Even in the worship of the community, which, as stated above, in general followed the East-Syrian pattern, seems to have had certain local accommodations. It is possible that rice cakes and palm wine were used in the eucharist.[19] In connection with the sacred rites of baptism, matrimony etc., there were a number of ceremonies which were derived from Indian local social practices common both to Hindus and Christians.[20]

All this points to an identity and an autonomous status of the Church of India marked by a theological vision of its own regarding the particular/individual Churches. If this vision is not written down in elaborate theological works, it is clearly reflected in the life and tradition of the Indian Christians prior to the arrival of the Portuguese. When Roberto de Nobili and his collaborators introduced a way of Christian life well adapted to Indian socio-religious sentiments, they pointed to the life of the Syrian (St. Thomas) Christians as a model, and as justification for their own novel method of evangelization.[21]

Early Western Missionaries and Their Theology of Conquest

The earliest missionaries of the Latin West to work in India for any length of time were a few Franciscans and Dominicans like John Monte Corvino and Jordan Catalani de Severac. Their attitude towards Christians belonging to non-Latin Churches and towards non-Christians could not but be the typical medieval, exclusive, and negative one. When the Portuguese came to India at the close of the 15th century, this attitude and the consequent theological vision had not changed. First I will briefly examine their approach to the Indian Christians who followed a church-life different from that of the Latin West and then analyse their approach to non-Christian religions.

In the West the Eastern Churches were looked upon for a long time as "heretical" and "schismatic." In spite of this, as soon as the Portuguese came into contact with the Christians of India they showed great enthusiasm and willingness to enter into communion with the latter; yet the Portuguese elite, particularly the priests, cherished unhelpful ideas about their form of faith and practices. They considered that the form of Christianity existing in the East including that of the Indian Christians was an imperfect form; for, according to them, the Western Latin form was the only perfect form. The relations of the Portuguese with the ancient Christians of India were governed by their ideas of Christian solidarity and also by a feeling of superiority as they regarded their culture and Christianity far superior to those of the Indian Christians. The Western form of Christianity, which was the Roman form of Christianity, was for them the perfect one not only in matters of faith and morals but in everything else that distinguished a Christian from a non-Christian. Hence every Christian was expected to accept that form. The surest way to achieve this was to bring the Christians under the Portuguese jurisdiction and the Latin rite. The Portuguese apparently had no clear idea of Eastern Christianity. The only thing they probably cared to know about Eastern Christianity was the imperfection of that Christianity, and they probably attributed this imperfection to its divergence from Roman custom.[22] This view of a particular individual Church was quite contrary to the view which the Indian Christians had entertained, as explained earlier.

Our man from Portugal, as a true Iberian of this time, was a typical medieval European and Christian whose faith was strong though sometimes even verging on fanaticism and whose Christianity was a militant kind of Christianity. If this medieval spirit of Europeans had been modified elsewhere in Europe through the influence of more liberal ideas and especially the Renaissance Movement, the Iberian was practically untouched by any such liberal ideas. On the contrary, his age-long war with the forces of Islam--considered both a religious and a patriotic duty--only increased the fervor of his militant faith. As regards the pagan world, the Portuguese had fully inherited the gloomy attitude of the Middle Ages towards it: It was a world wholly under the sway of the spirit of darkness and was to be conquered and converted.[23]

In India, however, where the Portuguese had to operate in territories under Hindu rulers, practical prudence called for the use of moderation. In Goa, which was the only Portuguese territory by conquest, the application of medieval ideas prevailed to some extent. Force was used for conversion indirectly, if not directly. But this means was adopted only after a long time and under pressure from missionaries. Outside Goa the Portuguese showed greater consideration for the religious sentiments of the people, particularly the rulers. There were even instances of the Portuguese adjusting themselves to the local usage. But all this they did not out of any respect for other religions but, being motivated by practical diplomacy, for safeguarding Portuguese economic interests. Their real theological views on other religions found expression in the many reports and books of the Portuguese, especially of the missionaries.

The conquering conception of the mission of the Church was uppermost in the minds of the Portuguese in general and the missionaries in particular when they approached the non-Christian religions. They saw the work of mission and "evangelism in terms of military operations, lines of defence, plans for attack, as if we were waging war against other believers."[24] In many of the missionary reports of the 16th and 17th centuries this attitude is quite evident. The works of Sebastian Goncalves, Diego Goncalves, Paulo da Trindade, Francis de Sousa are good examples. The many letters of St. Francis Xavier and even some of the polemic treatises of Roberto de Nobili are no exception to this. Two mission histories are of special relevance here: one written by a Franciscan in the first half of the 17th century, and the other by a Jesuit in the beginning of the 18th century. The titles of these books themselves are highly suggestive of their contents and the spirit in which they were written. The Franciscan, Paulo da Trindade, described his account of the Franciscan missions in the East under the name, Conquista Espiritual do Oriente, "The Spiritual Conquest of the East." The Jesuit writer, Francisco de Souza was most probably inspired by Trindade's title (perhaps such an inspiration was not needed, the times could suggest the title) when he called his history of the Jesuit missions in the East, Oriente Conquistado a Jesu Christo.., "The East won over to Christ by the Fathers of the Society of Jesus."[25] Though the spirit which moved both the chronicles and the mentality manifest in both of them are more or less the same, it is the Franciscan who employs the conquista vocabulary more frequently and more forcefully.

The scope of Trindade's history is to describe the splendid work carried out by the Franciscan Friars Minor of the Province of St. Thomas in India in the proclamation of the Christian faith and in the conversion of "infidels" in more than thirty countries, from the Cape of Good Hope to the farthest Islands of Japan.[26] The book is dedicated to St. Thomas, the Apostle and patron of India whom the author describes as "the first captain of the conquest" of the East ("o primeiro capitao desta conquista"). The Apostle starting from Socotora moved on as far as China, preaching the Gospel, unfolding the banner of the Cross wherever he went and working miracles all along. The Gentiles abandoned their false and superstitious practices and adhered to the true law of Christ. The Friars Minor were the first to follow in the footsteps of the Apostle to India and convert many to the faith, baptizing many kings, razing many temples of the idols, building many churches, erecting many crosses, and in that way conquering many thousands of souls for God. Trindade prays the glorious Apostle to lead them as the captain and beacon light in this ongoing spiritual conquest.[27]

The conquista was in reality a victory, a triumph over idolatory which reigned in the whole of the East in all glory and splendour with magnificent temples and richly endowed shrines. The religious, armed as they were with spiritual weapons and fortified with divine grace, entered the arena and as true soldiers

of Christ engaged the idols in a fierce battle, stripped them of
their rich vestments, fleeced them of their jewels, razed to
the ground many of their rich and beautiful temples, prohibited
their feasts, obstructed their ceremonies and rites, banished their
priests, deprived them of their revenues, and wrested from their
possession thousands of souls. Always holding aloft the standard
of the cross, the Franciscans scored many a victory over the
idols, the story of which forms the contents of the book.[28]

This highly rhetorical presentation of the mission work of
the Portuguese is not far removed from what actually happened in
the Portuguese colonies, especially in Goa. In 1522 a visiting
Dominican Bishop, Duarte Nunes, wrote from Goa to the
Portuguese King:

> Regarding the people of Goa they have in the island
> temples decked out with figures of the enemy of the
> cross and statues, and they celebrate their feasts
> every year. These feasts are attended by many
> Christians, our own people as well as recent native
> Christians. It is a big mistake to continue to show
> favor to their idolatory. It would be to the service
> of God to destroy in this island alone these temples,
> and to raise in their stead churches with saints.
> And let him who wants to live in the island become a
> Christian, and he shall possess his lands and houses,
> as he has till now done; if not, let him leave the island.

Bishop Duarte's suggestion did not take effect till 1540; then it
was carried out so thoroughly that by 1545 there were no more
temples to be seen in the islands. Decrees were published
transferring the properties of many temples to Christian
institutions; laws enacted by the Church prohibiting the making
and retaining of Hindu religious objects, public celebration of
Hindu feasts, denying public offices to certain Hindu classes, were
carried out by secular authorities. Even banishment of Brahmins
was effected for the Christian cause. Whatever the motivation
behind these moves and the excuses for them, and however
well-known for their concern for the poor and humanitarian
individuals like Miguel Vaz and Diego de Borba who were connected
with these happenings were, such things really happened in Goa.
They were done in the name of "Rigour of Mercy."[29]

Trindade claims that in the Eastern Conquest the Franciscans
assumed the pride of the place over other soldiers of Christ,
religious or not. They had come to India as spiritual conquerors
and followed in the footsteps of "captain" St. Thomas 200 years

before the Portuguese started on their eastward march.[30] Again it was the Franciscans who accompanied the Portuguese captains in their first fleets and started anew the spiritual conquest, which therefore doubly belonged to them by right of prior possession. Some members of a new religious order (the Society of Jesus) failed not only to recognize this fact, but even dared to cast doubts on the competency of the Franciscan soldiers for waging the war. This was too much for a true soldier of Christ and a champion of the past heroes of the Franciscan missions to bear and so he took up his pen to vindicate the prior rights of his confreres in the spiritual conquest of the East and wrote the Conquista Espiritual by the Franciscans in the East.[31]

Not only are the preaching of the Word of God and the conversion of pagans a conquest for Christ, but the very colonial expansion of a Christian nation like Portugal and all the military operations of the Portuguese in Africa and in the East are conquest for Christ. Every true Christian who fought against the enemies of his motherland, who fought for the aggrandizement of his country's territorial possessions, wealth and prestige was a soldier of Christ. In the same way as the missionaries who worked in the colonies were regarded as rendering a service to God and their sovereign, the Portuguese secular personnel in the colonies promoting national interests were to be reckoned as serving not only the king but also God. The very idea of "Padroado" signified a mutual inclusiveness of the secular and the sacred. The whole mentality is to be understood against the background of medieval Europe in general, and of Spain and Portugal in particular. The European was quite familiar for the last five or six centuries with the idea of "Crusade" which was territorial conquest or reconquest as well as a religious undertaking. This task was doubly sacred for an Iberian, Spaniard, or Portuguese: Fighting against Islam had been a religious duty and a patriotic necessity for him for more than seven centuries.

Trindade sees in the discovery of India, for which the Portuguese nation was specially chosen by God, the hand of Providence in more sense than one. The discovery brought to Portugal immense profit, for it established naval hegemony over the followers of Mohammed and wrested from their monopoly the east-west trade in spices and other oriental commodities. Great as these gains were, there were even greater and more valuable advantages to be gained; it facilitated the preaching of the Gospel by the religious so that the true God came to be acknowledged by the "barbarous nations" which were till then adoring the devil. There can be no doubt that God in his Providence employed the Portuguese nation to realize such great things and in doing this

34

fulfilled a promise made by God to the king of Portugal, D. Afonso Henriques! The arrival of the Portuguese in the East saw also the fulfillment of a prophecy made by St. Thomas the Apostle himself!

Many Portuguese soldiers like Christoao da Gama, the illustrious son of the great Vasco da Gama, and many other heroic soldiers who died on the battle-field at the hands of their enemies were really soldiers of Christ. By their glorious death not only did they honor their motherland, Portugal, but showed that it was by divine Providence that the Portuguese came to India, because their arrival was blessed and continues to be blessed with so many and such sublime fruits, reaped for the glory of God.[32]

Roberto de Nobili: A Positive Approach

In all the missionary writings the general outlook was more or less the same as described above though one may find here and there a few positive notes on certain customs and practices of the Hindus. But these are few are far between. With Roberto de Nobili there was a marked change.[33] It is well-known that the Italian Jesuit adopted an Indian sanyasi way of life and studied not only Tamil but the sacred language of India, Sanskrit, and mastered the Vedas and Vedanta. He used Indian philosophy and philosophical language as a vehicle for conveying Christian theological truth. He made an attempt to present Christian theology in a form intelligible to the Brahmins of Madurai. In order to win over India to Christianity he thought it quite necessary to raise a generation of Indian clergy, educated as far as possible according to Indian traditions for which he planned a seminary with a five-year course in Christian philosophy. As Cronin points out,

> He wanted his future priests to present Christianity
> to the Indian people in their own languages, not in
> a jargon in which all religious terms were Portuguese;
> to be well-trained in Christian theology but also
> experts in the religion of the Hindus around him; to
> depend for support and protection on their own countrymen,
> not on foreigners.[34]

It is agreed by almost all writers concerned that de Nobili's methods of work were indigenous and highly original and commendable. Opinions differ on the question whether all this constitutes an experiment in theologizing in the Indian context. Boyd remarks:

We should not imagine, however, that his writings really represent an experiment in "indigenous theology", using Hindu terminology for the exposition of Christian doctrine, for indeed his attitude to religious Hinduism is entirely negative, and he writes to refute. His achievement--and it was a great achievement--is to be seen in his understanding and adaptation of Hindu customs and ceremonies, in his pioneering study of Sanskrit and Tamil and in his initiation of the essential task of evolving a Christian theological vocabulary for Indian languages. For this contribution Indian Christian theology will always be indebted to him.[35]

Others have evaluated de Nobili's theological contribution a little differently. Mookenthottam says:

He was first and foremost a missionary. His principal aim was not to write a theology but to find ways and means to announce the Gospel in a manner intelligible and appealing to Indians and to instruct his converts. He wrote partly to defend his method of evangelization against some of his own confreres and some ecclesiastical authorities who were more intolerant and hostile than the Hindus among whom he worked. In spite of such adverse circumstances, de Nobili did contribute to the cause of an Indian theology.[36]

De Nobili's able defence of his method earned for him the approval not only of his superiors but of Pope Gregory himself for the Indian religious practices he borrowed from the Hindus. The bull of the Pope, Romanae Sedis Antistes, accepts in principle de Nobili's indigenous method of evangelization.

De Nobili, of course, as a missionary followed an apologetic method. But his apology was not merely negative. He wrote to refute, but at the same time he never rejected what he thought was valuable in Hinduism.

He used Hindu scriptures to prove his points; he argues against the outright condemnation of the sciences of the Brahmins as superstitious; he contends that what is also compatible with true religion is found in the Vedas. Hence his approach to religious Hinduism does not seem to be entirely negative.[37]

His concept of Christ as Guru might be considered as a special contribution to an Indian theology. He showed the way towards the development of an Indian theology. Only two or three centuries later some sensitive spirits like Brahmabandab Upadhyaya would be inspired to follow the path let open by de Nobili and advance further.

Brahmabandab Upadhyaya and the Quest for an Indian Church

An ardent nationalist, a great visionary, and at the same time a great activist, a devoted and convinced Catholic, a sanyasin, Brahmabandab Upadhyaya was a pioneer who tried to establish an Indian monastery and worked for an Indian theology and for the socio-cultural integration of the Church in India. But the tragedy is that he was not only persecuted by the colonialist British regime, but rejected and even harassed by his own Church. One of his intimate friends and biographer, Animananda,[38] has called him "the greatest Indian that found his way to Christ." A Catholic missionary Fr. Alfons Vath pronounced a different verdict: Brahmabandab failed -- failed in his attempt to pioneer a new Christian theology, failed even to find a new secular school of purified Vedantic thought.[39]

M. M. Thomas, after briefly analysing the Christology of the Upadhyaya, concludes that his Christology did not deviate from the traditional Catholic position but was a faithful portrayal of it in Indian categories. He then wonders why the Church discouraged him and answers: "Perhaps his boldness in identifying himself with Hinduism and using Hindu categories of thought was too novel for the Church to tolerate."[40] Dr. Heiler describes Brahmobandhab as the Indian Clement of Alexandria, because he regarded Vedanta as "Tutor unto Christ." And in many ways, in the Christian Church, he was a leader for Indian Christian theology as well as for the expression of Christian participation in Indian nationalism. At both these levels, his ideas were "emphatically rejected" by the Church of his time and the life and death of "this great Catholic patriot was a tragedy."[41]

This fiery nationalist and Indian Christian was born into a Bengali Brahmin family near Calcutta in 1861. Various influences, particularly his association with K. C. Sen and the Brahmo Samaj, attracted him to Christ, and finally he took "one step more" than his Brahmo colleague, P. C. Mozoomdar, and was baptized as an Anglican in 1891. Later in the same year he joined the Catholic Church. It was at this time he changed his name from Bhavani Charan Banerji to Brahmabandab (Sanskrit for Theophilus) to which was later added Upadhyaya (teacher). In 1894 he donned the saffron robe and became a Catholic sanyasin. He edited an apologetic weekly journal Sophia. When it ceased publication he started another periodical, The Twentieth Century. Towards the end of his life he edited a daily paper Sandhya which became "the leading nationalist vernacular paper of his time." The theological approach of Brahmobandhab was motivated by his concern for an indigenous expression of Christian faith and life. M. M. Thomas summarizes the four aspects of Brahmabandab's concern:

(a)   an integration of the social structure of India into the Christian way of life;

(b)   the establishment of an Indian Christian monastic order;

(c)   the employment of Vedanta for the expression of Christian theology; and

(d)   the recognition of the Vedas as the Indian Old Testament.[42]

C. F. Andrews wrote in 1912 that the writings of Upadhyaya were "the most striking instances" he had come across up to that time of the use of Hindu terminology by Christians for the expression of Christian truth. It was Upadhyaya's conviction that Vedantic thought could do the same service for Christian faith in India as scholastic philosophy once did.[43]

Brahmabandab's earliest attempt was to construct a Christian theology on the basis of the Vedas. He adopted his own theories already developed by K. M. Banerji, A. S. Appasami Pillai, and others that the Vedas represented original pure Hinduism and that as such they were very similar to the Old Testament and nearer to Christianity. The later introduction of transmigration, pantheism etc., was a sign of deterioration of the original pure religion. Christianity was not the destroyer of Hinduism, but the fulfillment, for "the primitive (Hinduism) and the new (Christianity) are linked together as root and trunk, base and structure, as outline and filling."[44]

Whether Brahmabandab abandoned this "Vedic theology"[45] or not, from the close of the 19th century onwards he turned more to the Vedanta philosophy to interpret Christianity. The result was a "Vedantic theology," a Christian reinterpretation of Maya and application of a Thomistic interpretation of Vedanta to the Christian faith. He evolved a Trinitarian theology in terms of Saccitananda and a Christology based on Cit as Christ.

Brahmabandab's theological attempts were part of his over-all plan to make the Indian Christians and the Indian Church rooted in the culture and society of India. He knew quite well that Hindus like K. C. Sen and P. C. Mozoomdar who showed such keen interest in Christianity remained on the borderlines. They felt it was impossible to join the Christian Church as it existed in India. Indian Christians seemed to them to be denationalized and isolated not only from the Hindu religion but from Indian culture.

Brahmabandab expressed this fact very forcefully when he wrote in an article, "Conversion of India - An Appeal," in 1894:

> Protestantism has created a deep-rooted impression amongst the people that Christianity is synonymous with denationalization. People have a strong aversion against Christian preachers because they are considered to be destroyers of everything national. Therefore, the itinerant missionaries should be thoroughly Hindu in their mode of living.[46]

Brahmabandab is not to be counted among those liberal Indian Christian thinkers like P. Chenchiah who were rather negative in their attitude with regard to a visible organized Church. As against these, Brahmabandab readily recognized the need for a visible, organized Church and for the regular ministry of the Word and Sacraments. It is true that he died very suddenly in hospital, without receiving the last rites of his Church, and his body was cremated by his Hindu friends. The obituary notices which appeared in his own daily Sandhya, however, spoke of him clearly as a Christian and his most intimate friends, like Animananda, never had any doubts about his desire to remain, not merely a Christian, but a loyal member of his own Church. In none of his writings do we find any criticism of the basic "deposit" of the Christian faith as found in the Bible, or even of the Thomist system, which he appears to have accepted without question,[47] and this some consider today as a defect.[48]

What pained him was the Western trappings of the Christian faith in India. It was his determination to reform the Church in a genuine Indian spirit. He made many scathing attacks on the western garb the Church in India was made to wear. He was a born nationalist and was in the forefront of the national movement, one of the first Indians to stand for the complete independence of the motherland and to suffer for it. His uncompromising attacks on colonialism and his biting criticism of the Westernized Church in India were interrelated. H. C. E. Zacharias says:

He was gradually coming to the conclusion that before
India could become Catholic, she must be politically
free and that otherwise it would be impossible to
extirpate the bane of Europeanism which he found so
disastrously rampant in all the missions of the
period.[49]

Difficulties with the Church arose first when Brahmabandab
decided to become a Catholic sanyasin, put on saffron clothes, and
went to church. He was denied admission into the church by his
parish priest. He appealed to the Bishop and the Bishop pleaded
helplessness in the situation. Brahmabandab had to remind the
Bishop about the permission formerly granted to de Nobili. So he
was granted permission to wear saffron clothes.[50]

Upadhyaya did not think there was any incompatibility in
being a Hindu and a Catholic at the same time. This was his
considered view:

> By birth we are Hindu and shall remain Hindu till
> death. But as dvija (twice-born) by virtue of
> our sacramental rebirth we are Catholics, we are
> members of the indefectible communion embracing
> all ages and climes.

> In customs and manners, in observing caste and
> social distinctions, in eating and drinking, in
> our life and living we are genuine Hindus; but
> in our faith we are neither Hindu nor European,
> nor American nor Chinese, but all-inclusive.
> Our faith fills the whole world and is not
> confined to any country or race, our faith is
> universal and consequently includes all truth.[51]

It is these convictions which made this Bengali Catholic and
patriot plan and establish a sanyasi order with two types of
monks: one, yogi type, dedicated to contemplation who by their
experience and thinking would contribute to an Indian theology
and the other, wandering ones, engaged in preaching and social
work. Hardly had such a life started on the banks of the river
Narmada at Jabalpur, in 1899, when the Bishop withdrew
permission because of the intervention of Msgr. Ladislao Zaleski,
Apostolic Delegate in India.

Matters did not end there. In a series of articles,
Upadhyaya attacked the Westernization of the Indian Church. The
Apostolic Delegate intervened again and in a letter warned

Catholics against Sophia and its theological articles in which difficult theological questions were dealt with "by unqualified persons." Brahmabandab offered to publish the magazine submitting to Church censorship to which no answer was given. So he stopped publishing Sophia and began a new periodical The Twentieth Century which was to deal with political and social matters only. Even this was immediately put on the Index. From then on he turned more and more to politics. Thus the lack of understanding and consideration of higher ecclesiastical authorities pushed to the brink one of the Church's most devoted and loyal converts. Here the criticism of Heiler does not seem to be undeserved: "The Roman hierarchy shattered his life's work, paralysed his missionary force and shut his evangelical mouth." The real issue in this case is not the granting of a permission, the closing of a work or a conflict, but the principles involved: the Western apparel of the Church, the purity of doctrine, truth and their relation to ecclesiastical authority.[52]

The end of Brahmabandab was tragic. The British imprisoned him; critics described his attempts a failure; the majority of Catholics were either suspicious or indifferent to his ideas; the Church disowned him. Death came to him unexpectedly and prematurally at the age of 46. Nationalism claimed him; Hinduism owned him up. It is very significant that when a Catholic priest, the representative of the Church, arrived on the scene it was too late. Kaj Baago describes the last scene:

> His body was carried by Hindus to the place of cremation, followed by thousands of nationalists. Brahmabandab was a national hero in the eyes of many and the news of his death spread through special editions of newspapers. When a Catholic priest reached the place of cremation wanting to bury Brahmabandab according to Christian rites, the Hindus had already lighted the pyre. Thus he, who had been born as a Hindu, was also cremated like a Hindu and with Hindu rites. Probably this was in accordance with Brahmabandhav's own thinking, for he was as himself said -- not a Christian, but a Christian Hindu.[53]

Whether cremation was according to his liking or not, the Church was too slow to recognize in this Hindu-Catholic the genuine aspirations of a true Indian Christian. One of his intimate, sanyasi colleagues, Animananda, never had doubts about Upadhyaya's orthodoxy and loyalty to his Church. He paid a glowing tribute to "the greatest Indian that ever found his way to Christ" through his publication of The Blade: Life and Work of Brahmabandab Upadhyaya.

But already before the publication of this book, other Christians like C. F. Andrews, F. Heiler, H. C. E. Zacharias had expressed their great appreciation for the person and the theological efforts of Brahmabandab. It was a Belgian Jesuit, Fr. Pierre Johanns, who was so inspired by the teaching and method of Brahmabandab that he started what may be called the movement: To Christ through Vedanta. The book he wrote under that title and the periodical he and his colleagues published using the same title are a fitting tribute to the cause for which Upadhyaya stood and suffered.

Recent Past and Present: New Horizons

In the last thirty years there has been almost a revolution among Catholic thinkers. Many attempts have been made to develop an Indian Christian theory and an Indian Christian praxis. More and more Catholics began to take active interest in the ashram movement and the Hindu-Christian dialogue. The great services rendered to the Church in India by Roberto de Nobili and Brahmabandab Upadhyaya began to be reappreciated and to give inspiration to many. In the wake of this "revolution" a fairly large body of literature was produced.

Though the new efforts started before the Second Vatican Council, it was during and after the Council that it gained the greatest momentum and thrust. The Council through its various documents, especially the documents on evangelization and non-Christian religions, and more through a new climate of freedom and dialogue it created, gave great impetus to Catholics to enter into a more meaningful encounter with the culture, society, and religion of India. Many regional and national consultations, seminars, and other similar activities gave a boost to the efforts.

In the recent and contemporary Indian Catholic literature[54] one notices various currents and undercurrents, different trends and approaches, to this question of a theology in the context of India. The three major trends appear to be the following: the spiritual-contemplative, the philosophical-theological and the socio-political. Catholic theologians like Rev. Monchanin (Swami Parama Arupya Ananda), Swami Abhishiktananda, Dom Griffiths, and a few others are pioneers of the first trend. Monchanin and Abhishiktananda were the co-founders of the Saccidananda

Ashram (now Shantivanam) on the banks of the river Kaveri in South India. The main purpose of founding this Ashram was the adoration and contemplation of God, One-in-Three, the Saccidananda. In the Indian spiritual context Abhishiktananda has analysed his experiences of Hindu-Christian-dialogue meetings for him. The Christian reading of the Upanishads in the presence of Christ is to rediscover in ourselves the secret place of the Rishi's experience, and, then under the inspiration of the Spirit and by an existential process wholly personal to each one, to allow the Christian expression and Trinitarian culmination of this experience to find its full development in us. For the Christian to do this, he has to put temporarily aside, en epoche, much of the conceptual expression of the Christian faith. He must first of all listen to the witness of the experience itself. He reads the Upanishads so as to enter as authentically as possible into the experience which molded the religious soul of India. The two important conclusions the Swami arrives at are: (1) the Lord is already in India. Our role is to help the holy seed which has been sown by the Spirit in the hearts and traditions of India to germinate. (2) India has received from her Creator a very special gift of interiority, a unique inward orientation of the Spirit.

Abhishiktananda stresses, time and again, the need to receive the message of the Upanishads with the heart of a child--free, open and full of trust--rather than seizing upon what is lacking from a Christian standpoint. The Christian penetrates the Upanishadic experience, and with its help, he sets free the fullness of the treasures contained in the Christian faith experience. According to him, "the mission of the Christian in relation to the Hindu is to transmit to him the fullness of the Spirit given to us in Jesus: to make him realize that there is in man something even more ultimate and profound than the interiority discovered by the sages and mystics, a guha more secret than that of the depth of the heart of man--the abyss of the heart of Christ, into which no one can enter save by undergoing a death of the Spirit. To do this the Christian must begin by himself entering this essential interiority. He must himself die to self and know the Paschal night before he can ask his Hindu brother to enter this death through which he will find resurrection and transformation.[55]

The second trend in contemporary Indian theology is represented by the writings of such scholars as Raimundo Panikkar, J. B. Chethimattam, Klaus Klostermeyer, Antony Mookenthottam, and a number of others. Following the lead given by pioneers like Brahmabandab, and taking into account modern theological approaches to world religions, they are in the process of building up a scientific Indian theology or theologies based on Indian philosophical and religious thought. Their effort may be compared to the pioneering work of the theologians of the Patristic era, like Justin, Clement of Alexandria, Origen, Tertullian, Gregory of Nyssa, St. Augustine, or the Scholastics of the Middle Ages. A few of such Indian theologians are concerned with the sources of non-Christian religions, the Sruti and Smriti literature of Hinduism, to assess their value for developing and Indian theology. Others are interested in the great Indian philosophical systems and schools of thought including the Neo-Vedantic and modern Hindu writers and the relative value of these for an Indian interpretation of Christian revelation. Still others consider the various margas or certain terms such as Brahman, Isvara, and Saccidananda, with the same end in view. Various Christian topics have appeared on the Indian theological scene, namely, Trinity, God and the world, Christ, the Spirit, Church and Sacraments, history and fulfilment.[56]

Perhaps the most popular of the trends is the third one, the socio-political. It emphasizes the common concern of men for the genuine humanization of man's life in the modern world and confronts, in the process, the problems of spiritual foundation and self-transcendence. The writers belonging to this group strongly advocate that the meaningfulness and adequacy of the revelation of God in Jesus Christ have to be made concrete and proved efficacious in the midst of the present social, economic, political and religious ferment within Asia, particularly in India.

In an article entitled "The Kingdom of God and the Mission Field" written in 1925, H. C. E. Zacharias, a Catholic who was a member of the Servants of India Society, Poona, argued that social service work of various kinds must be seen not as preparations for the Gospel but as good in themselves. He drew a sharp distinction between the Kingdom of God and the institutional Church, arguing that the former is primary and that the great end to which the latter is but a means. However, as all religions had as their aim the establishment of the reign of God, and as all people are therefore citizens of that kingdom, we should all work together to bring about the reign of God in human affairs.

R. Panikkar, though not directly interested in the socio-political dimension of Indian Christian thinking, has occasionally referred to the question especially in his book, Worship and Secular Man.[57] Under the concept of total redemption, Panikkar sees the mission of the Church as not primarily one which could be identified with one religion alone, but as an instrument of redemption of the whole cosmos, co-operating with the incarnate Son and the Spirit. He believes that all human activities that have some redemptive value offer a common ground for co-operation between Christians and non-Christians. So the social engagement is neither a means nor a context for making conversions or extending the institutional Church. It is, for Panikkar, a human activity that has redemptive value, to which both Christians and non-Christians are moved by the same Christ.

J. B. Chethimattam also expresses similar views in his Dialogue in Indian Tradition when he says that the center of dialogue should shift "from metaphysics and questions of belief to the secular problems that affect human existence itself."[58] Amalorpavadas understands the great struggle of the developing nations for progress as part of a world-wide upward thrust pursued throughout human history. "If Christ, his Gospel and his Church are to transform the world, orientate history, and lead them to fulfilment; they have to enter into this process, this alternative, this historic movement. The Church must actively be present everywhere with her humble diaconia in testimony to the Gospel and the Kingdom, in her very concern for the contemporary reality and movement in it."[59]

A new understanding of evangelization that has emerged in India is significant in this context. Anto Karokaran in his book, Evangelization and Diakonia,[60] makes an inquiry into this new understanding by a careful analysis of the theological literature and Church documents, and a survey of the views of the missionaries working in the field. He comes to the conclusion that there is a general consensus among theologians as well as missionaries regarding the following points: the positive understanding of other religions; social engagement in the national reconstruction and co-operation with all; understanding of the Church as dynamic and out-reaching into the entire human existence; and, finally, a new form of witness and ecclesial living congenial to the genius of India.[61]

Sebastian Kappen's views on this point are well-known. His article "The Christian and the Call to Revolution"[62] may be taken as an example. He starts with an analysis of the relation of the Kingdom of God to historical teleology which views the Kingdom of God as the future of man. The Kingdom of God is above all else the togetherness of man with God, the indwelling of man in God and God in man. Before God takes man into his heart He personalizes him. This ultimate flowering of man is his liberation from all alienation, but it is not narrow individualization. Man is socialized and is made to exist with others, for others, a definite overcoming of all social alienations and class antagonisms.

The Kingdom is a home of justice, the realization of a classless society. Man will then possess things without their becoming "mine" and "thine." The end of all human development will transcend both collectivism and individualism and usher in the true socialism of being and having, which he identifies as the Kingdom of God. The Kingdom is also already present, as the principle of love that broke into human history in Christ. This love is a dynamic force, a subversive element planted in the center of history. The justice inherent in love seeks to create equality. The new love Jesus introduced in this world is at work to create a new world of justice and equality and it put an end to oppressive elements. Seen in this light all social movements which have for their aims the promotion of God realize God's Kingdom here on earth. The Kingdom also demands an ethical response, a commitment to a constant renewal of the society so that the latter conforms more and more to the eschatological Kingdom though no social system can be absolutized. Thus, like Chenchiah, Kappen sees the Kingdom as the realization of concrete and attainable social goals on earth -- or at least he believes it is possible to achieve an approximation of the eschatological Kingdom on this earth.

Conclusion

If the seed that is the Word of God is to bear fruit, "theological investigation must necessarily be stirred up in each major socio-cultural area." The seed must draw from the ground in which it is sown, "nourishing elements which it transforms and assimilates into itself." We have been trying to see how far this has happened in India, in the Catholic Church in India.

The ancient Christians of India, the St. Thomas Christians, had not perhaps developed an elaborate theology of their own. But a theological vision of their Church in India was implicit in their life and tradition; the autonomy and identity of an individual/particular Church and the relationship of the Christian faith with culture and other faiths and religions were some marked aspects of that vision. This rather liberal and broad vision came into conflict with the more narrow, rigid, and aggressive polemic ecclesiology of the Western Christians. It caused many stresses and strains in the community, which eventually led to division.

The de Nobili experiment and the Brahmabandab story are for me typical symbols of the Indian Church, of its situation in the past as well as in the present. On the one hand, some daring individuals who see far into the future take bold steps to make the Church of India an Indian Church of the Indian people, a Church

46

rooted in Christ and rooted in the rich culture of the country. On the other hand, the majority of Christians who do not grasp the real significance of the daring attempts remain indifferent, if not hostile; the Church authorities often, in the name of orthodox doctrine and orthodox praxis, stifle the attempts. Both the movements, of Brahmabandab and of de Nobili, ended tragically. That of the former was simply nipped in the bud at the intervention of the Papal delegate in India. De Nobili's movement survived for some time because the powerful Society of Jesus backed it. But finally it also met with a tragic end; the highest ecclesiastical authority formally suppressed it.

If we glance at the happenings in the Indian Church in our own days, it would appear the story is being repeated in one way or another. Vatican II adopted very dynamic principles and created an atmosphere conducive to creative thinking and creative action in each cultural context. The pronouncements of the Popes gave further encouragement.[63] The Indian Church showed eagerness to snatch the opportunity to give shape to a real Indian Church.[64] Agencies like the National Biblical Catechetical and Liturgical Centre initiated various programs to achieve fully the Indianization goal.

Everything changed soon. Fear and anxiety began to be expressed in the highest circle of the Church: perhaps the Vatican spirit has gone too far; some restraint is quite necessary. At this critical juncture the more conservative elements in the Church which had been lying low after the Council began to raise their head. The Roman synod of 1974 reflected the confused situation.[65] In the next year (1975) the Indian bishops received a letter from Cardinal Knox of the Sacred Congregation for Divine Worship forbidding liturgical experiments and the use of the Indian anaphora. The confusion and embarrassment into which the Indian hierarchy was thrown was obvious in the CBCI meeting held at Hyderabad in 1976. B. M. Aguiar wrote an editorial in The Examiner (1976, p.37) under the caption "behind the Closed Doors." He commented: "It was a perfect picture of pre-Vatican siege mentality: the bishops locked in the hall, talking to each other in hushed tones, afraid that secrets would leak out to the world outside, represented by three religious and three members of the Catholic press."[66] All this had a stifling effect on the great Indianization movement enthusiastically launched after the Vatican Council. There are symptoms everywhere to proclaim that the Church today is led by a conservative group which is determined to wipe out whatever has been undertaken so far.

The observations made above are equally applicable to all the Catholics of India whether they belong to the Latin rite or to the Oriental rite. In the case of the Oriental Catholics there are other factors which act as obstacles to their growth into an Indian Church. Ever since these Christians, the St. Thomas Christians, confronted the Christians of the Latin West in the 16th century, they had be engaged in continuous struggle to retain or to restore their autonomy and the individual character of the Church. Basic autonomy was granted them towards the close of the 19th century and it matured during the early decades of this century. In the wake of this autonomy the Church made tremendous progress. But two factors continued to obsess the community and progressively retarded its growth. One is the restriction put on their freedom to work in the whole of India as Oriental Christians, and the other, a tension within the community created by a polarization of views on the identity of their Church.[67]

Once the Church of the St. Thomas Christians was "The Church of All India." In the course of the last four or five centuries (since the arrival of the Portuguese), they were forced to confine themselves within very narrow limits in the South. The rest of their motherland is "Latin territory" where Oriental Catholics have no right to work by remaining within their own rite. Sixty to ninety per cent of the missionaries, men and women, working in those Latin dioceses hail from the St.-Thomas-Christian-Oriental-rite community. But they had practically to give up their rite. Large groups of St. Thomas Christian laity live in various centers of India, but they are not permitted to have a single pastor to cater to their spiritual needs in their maternal rite. The community whose Church was "the Church of All India" had to wait till 1962 to get a "mission" in India to evangelize people in their own rite (later six more missions were given to them), and that too thanks to the generosity of a Latin bishop! A gnawing and desperate feeling is brewing among the thinking members of the community; the Latin Church is higher in status than the Oriental Church; the former has higher rites and in the exercise of these rights the latter could be sacrificed; the growth of the Latin Church in India could and should be safeguarded at the expense of the Oriental Church. A very discerning person has aptly captioned the situation: "A Church in Fetters."

The second factor, the tension within the community, also need a brief explanation. The Church of the Catholic St. Thomas Christians enjoys a measure a autonomy within the Roman communion. This means the Church is independent not only of any intermediary Latin jurisdiction (Padroado/Propaganda) but also

48

of any intermediary Oriental jurisdiction (East-Syrian). Now arises the question: how far is the Indian Church bound to retain or restore the East-Syrian character? In the wake of the recent Indianization movement this question has become all the more acute.

Two strong views began crystallizing within the community and tended to create a tension: 1) Only the Latin elements are foreign and as such they alone need be eliminated, and, after the process of de-Latininization is complete, the question of adaptation or Indianization may be taken up; 2) Both the Latin and the Chaldean elements are foreign and both must be eliminated or retained as far as it is necessary for the emergence of a truly Indian Church. At present the first group appears to be impeding the growth of an Indian Christian form of worship and an Indian Christian way of life. It is a well-known fact that in the past too much dependence on the East-Syrian Church was detrimental to the development of the Indian Church.

NOTES

[1] Ad Gentes, 22.

[2] R. H. S. Boyd, Introduction to Indian Christian Theology, (Madras, 1975), p. 88 gives a few other reasons.

[3] Cf. A. M. Mundadan, C.M.I., The Arrival of the Portuguese in India and the Thomas Christians under Mar Jacob, 1498–1552, (Bangalore, 1967), p. 1–34. (Hereafter it will be referred to as A. M. Mundadan, The Arrival).

[4] Cf. Placid Podipara, The Malabar Christians, (Alleppey, 1972), pp. 27 ff.

[5] Cf. Jonas Thaliath, T.O.C.D., The Synod of Diamper, (Rome, 1958), pp. 12f., 15f.

[6] R. H. S. Boyd, op. cit., p. 8.

[7] A. Mookenthottam, Indian Theological Tendencies, (Berne, 1978), pp. 23f.

[8] In accordance with a resolution of the third provincial synod of Goa (1585), Father (later Bishop) Ros had started scrutinizing the books and marking the "errors" before the synod of Diamper (1599). The synod itself decreed not only the correction but the burning of the books which the Portuguese authorities thought contained "errors." See Act III, decrees 14, 15 and 16. The original Portuguese Acts of the synod were published in 1606 together with the Jornada (diary of the visit of Archbishop Alexis de Menesis to Kerala in 1599) written by A. de Gouvea, Jornada do Arcebispo de Goa Dom Frey Aleixo de Meneses..., Coimbra, 1606. See also Jonas Thaliath, op. cit., p. 31.

[9] A. M. Mundadan, C.M.I., Sixteenth Century Traditions of St. Thomas Christians, (Bangalore, 1970), pp. 118–55. (Hereafter referred to as A. M. Mundadan, Traditions.)

[10] A. Mookenthottam, op. cit., p. 24.

[11] The synod of Diamper which was dominated by the Western "exclusive" theological outlook of the Middle Ages thought it necessary to prohibit certain customs and practices of the community in order to distinguish Christians from the Hindus. It noted with regret that in social life there were no external signs to distinguish Christians from the nayaras (the chivalry class of

Kerala); in dress, hair style, in everything they followed the same pattern. Hence the assembly decreed that Christians desist from boring ear-lobes (IX, 17); at least that would be a distinguishing sign! It prohibited a number of other items: observance of legal impurity by women after child-birth (IX, 7); use of "non-Christian names" (IV, I, 16 & 17); practice of ordeals and omens (IX 4 & 6); Hindu musicians singing in Christian churches (V, II, 14); certain ceremonies connected with marriages, child-birth, death; selection of auspicious days for certain functions (VII, II, 15); sending children to schools run by Hindu panicars (teachers) and Christian panicars keeping Hindu idols in their schools for the sake of the Hindu children attending lessons (VIII, 36; III, 13); the clergy eating with the Hindus (VII, I, 11). The synod recommended strongly that the Christians live together remote from the "danger" of communication with non-Christians (IX, 23). It encouraged conversion of low castes to Christianity though separate churches might be built for the low cast converts (VIII, 36).

[12]Antonio da Silva Rego, Documentacao para a Historia das Missoes do Padroado Portugues do Oriente, India, Vol. 12, (Lisbon, 1958), p. 399.

[13]Just to give an example: John de Marignoli, O.F.M. came to Quilon in the   14th century. He was received by the Christian community of Kerala with all respect and consideration. See A. M. Mundadan, The Arrival, p. 151f.

[14]A Portuguese priest, Alvaro Penteado wrote from Kerala to the Portuguese king c. 1518: "The Christians of St. Thomas do not care for communication with the Portuguese, not because they are not happy that they are Christians as we are, but because we are among them as the English and the Germans are among us. As regards their natural customs, their will is corrupted by their priests who say that just as there were twelve Apostles, even so, they founded twelve customs, each different from the others." A. M. Mundadan, ibid., p. 83. Though the Portuguese clearly understood this mentality of the Indian Christians, they were not prepared to tolerate it because it was "wrong and unchristian mentality." They would bluntly ask the Christians to conform to the Portuguese way of life. Cf. ibid., p. 93.

[15]Ibid., pp. 82f., 151-54.

[16]Ibid., p. 83.

[17]There is reference in a letter of Patriarch Timothy I (A.D. 780–823) to bishops in India choosing and ordaining their metropolitan. But no clear evidence is available for deciding whether the bishops and the metropolitan were chosen from among Indian Christians. Cf. Jacob Kollaparambil, _The Archdeacon of All-India_, Kottayam, 1972, p. 80.

[18]Ibid.; A. M. Mundadan, _Traditions_, pp. 123–25; J. Kollaparambil, _ibid._

[19]A. M. Mundadan, _ibid._, pp. 165f.

[20]Ibid., pp. 172, 174.

[21]A. Mookenthottam, _op. cit._, p. 189, foot-note 28.

[22]A. M. Mundadan, _Traditions_, p. 157.

[23]Ibid., p. 154.

[24]Murray Rogers, "Hindu and Christian – A Moment Breaks", _Religion and Society_, 12 (1965), 37.

[25]Paulo da Trindade, O.F.M., _Conquista Espiritual do Oriente_, ed. by Felix Lopes, O.F.M., 3 vols., (Lisbon, 1962–67).

[26]See the full title of the book.

[27]P. da Trindade, _op. cit._, p. 3 (dedication of the book).

[28]Ibid., p. 82ff.

[29]See Antony D'Costa, S.J., _The Christianisation of the Goa Islands, 1510–1567_, (Bombay, 1965), pp. 29–35. While documenting the various ways the policy of "Rigor of Mercy" was carried out by the Portuguese authorities, both secular and ecclesiastical, the author makes it a point to indicate always the mitigating circumstances as excuses for the actions.

[30]The allusion obviously is to the medieval Franciscan missionaries, John de Monte Corvin and others who worked in India for short periods on their way to or from the Mongol missions in China in the 13th and 14th centuries.

[31]P. da Trindade, _op. cit._, Prologue.

[32]Ibid., pp. 29ff.

[33]Before de Nobili the English Jesuit, Thomas Stephens, realized the hold that the popular vernacular Puranas had on the minds of the people and composed a Christian Purana in colloquial Marathi with an admixture of Konkani, cf. R. H. S. Boyd, op. cit., p. 12.

[34]Vincent Cronin, A Pearl to India: The Life of Roberto de Nobili, (New York, 1959), p. 168.

[35]R. H. S. Boyd, op. cit., pp. 13, 14.

[36]A. Mookenthottam, op. cit., p. 27.

[37]Ibid., p. 28.

[38]He published the biography probably in 1947: B. Animananda, The Blade: Life and Work of Brahmabandab Upadhyaya, (Calcutta, n.d).

[39]Alfons Vath, S.J., Im Kampfe mit der Zauberwelt des Hinduismus (Upadhyaya Brahmabandhav und das Problem de Überwindung des hoheren Hinduismus durch das Christentum), (Berlin and Bonn, 1928), p. 216.

[40]M. M. Thomas, The Acknowledged Christ of Indian Renaissance, (Madras, 1970), p. 112.

[41]Ibid., p. 113. Thomas quotes H. C. E. Zacharias, Renascent India, (London, 1933), pp. 25, 27.

[42]M. M. Thomas, op. cit., p. 104.

[43]C. F. Andrews, The Renaissance in India: Its Missionary Aspect, (London, 1912), Appendix VIII, p. 289; M. M. Thomas, op. cit., pp. 104f.

[44]Kaj Baago, Pioneers of Indigenous Christianity, (Madras/Bangalore, 1969), p. 35.

[45]Baago seems to think so; ibid. M. M. Thomas is of the view that he never gave up Vedism, though he now turned more to the Vedanta for a Christian synthesis (M. M. Thomas, op. cit., p. 107).

[46]Kaj Baago, op. cit., pp. 119f.

[47]R. H. S. Boyd, op. cit., p. 83.

[48]M. M. Thomas, op. cit., p. 113f.

[49]Ibid., p. 112f. where Thomas quotes, H. C. E. Zacharias, op. cit., p. 27.

[50]A. Mookenthottam, op. cit., p. 41.

[51]Kaj Baago, op. cit., p. 124.

[52]Cf. A. Mookenthottam, op. cit., pp. 41f.

[53]Kaj Baago, op. cit., p. 49.

[54]See a survey of this in A. M. Mundadan, C.M.I., "Hindu-Christian Dialogue", Jeevadhara, 65 (1981), pp. 375-94.

[55]See especially his following works: Hindu-Christian Meeting Point within the Cave of the Heart, (Bombay, 1969); Saccidananda, A Christian Approach to Advaitic Experience, (Delhi, 1974); The Further Shore, (Delhi, 1975).

[56]See A. Mookenthottam, op. cit., pp. 167-81; R. H. S. Boyd, op. cit., pp. 228-64.

[57]R. Panikkar, Worship and Secular Man, (London, 1973); see also "Evangelization, Dialogue and Development", in Monumenta Missionalia, 5 (Rome, 1972), pp. 195-218.

[58]J. B. Chethimattam, C.M.I., Dialogue in Indian Tradition, (Bangalore, 1969), p. 94.

[59]D. S. Amalorpavadass, Theology of Development, (Bangalore, 1972), p. 16.

[60]Anto Karokaran, C.M.I., Evangelization and Diakonia, (Bangalore, 1978).

[61]Ibid., p. 250.

[62]Sebastian Kappen, "The Christian and the Call to Revolution", Jeevadhara, 1 (1971), pp. 29-45. Kappen's book, Jesus and Freedom, (New York, 1977) has lately become target of severe criticism. See a critique by T. Kottukapilly in Vidyajyoti, 46 (1982), pp. 128-37.

[63] See statement of the council similar to the one quoted at the beginning of this paper; see also the pronouncement of Pope Paul VI, quoted in A. Mookenthottam, op. cit., pp. 113f.

[64] See the final declaration of the All India Seminar: Church in India Today, Bangalore, 1959, (New Delhi, n.d.), pp. 241f., 262f. See the declarations of the Catholic Bishops Conference of India in 1974, quoted in A. Mookenthottam, op. cit., pp. 117f.

[65] A brief discussion of this synod may be found ibid., pp. 115f.

[66] Quoted by A. Mokenthottam, ibid., p. 251.

[67] See A. M. Mundadan, C.M.I., Quest for an Indian Church and the Thomas Christians, STAR Documentation, No. 3, (Alwaye, 1981). See also an article by the same writer: "19th Century 'Autonomy' Movement among Syrian Catholics", Indian Church History Review, 8 (1974), pp. 111-30.

BEING A HINDU IN INDIA

Raghava Nand

I am in the process and some day may become and be a Hindu.

I can't say that I was born one; I was like every baby else that comes Wailing into the world, just a bundle of flesh and bone, struggling in the new-found atmosphere, to survive. I had hardly any identity, but each successive year has chiselled me into something different, recognizably and palpably of a different mould. In my childhood I used to play about, and every boy, who shared his delights with me, was just like me and a frank communion welded me to him with rivets of affection but, on the occasions of Dashehra,[1] Holi,[2] and Deepavali,[3] I used to be a good deal sorry to find my Muslim and Christian friends wearing their soiled everyday clothes while I, being the son of a doctor, and, therefore much more prosperous, wore the finest I had. That, of course, occasioned a glee in the heart, which, however, ill-suited the sorrow at the joylessness of my friends as far as dress goes. However, the sorrow was soon extinguished by the zest they took in the crackers at Deepawali, in the spray of the colors on Holi, and in watching how Rama killed the deca-headed monster Rāvana on Dashehra. After the Dashehra, for a week or so, we, children, Christians and Muslims included, indulged wholeheartedly in the display of our histrionic skill, wielding the bow and the arrow like Lord Rama and flashing our bamboo-sticks for a sword in the right honorable fashion of Ravana, muttering dialogues, we had heard at the Ramlila,[4] mostly haphazard and improvised versions of Rāvana's gasconade. Someone of us, having a sturdy physique and the knack for mischief, would put on his back a stick for a tail and romp about with great eclat like Lord Hanuman.[5] We never bothered ourselves about the historical veracity of the myths as we were agog with imagination and tried to turn myths into palpable realities. Even my Muslim friends felt that Lord Rāma was good as he killed Rāvana and Lord Hanuman could be a fact. Why not, if aeroplanes could be?[6] Till I was eight I was cheerful like a lark and sang with the big throng of larks every morning, and withdrew into my nest, of course, with a sad heart every even-fall.[7]

But all this was not to continue long. Custom fell with a heavy weight, blasting the tender nurslings of sympathy and love for my Muslim and Christian friends. It came all of a sudden with a terrible vengeance, with a bang, not a whimper. Our house with all its furnishings and paraphernalia was burnt down to ashes by irate Hindu mobs, who, blind in the frenzy of communal

hatred, punished my father, a genuine Hindu, for the very
Hinduesque magnanimity and charity, at whose suggestion he had
to shelter a group of Muslims, seventy-five strong, pale,
awestruck, flabbergasted, and bearded faces; they had been his
friends of yore. We turned refugees.[8]

That was an agonising experience, and it led me to intense
broodings, albeit childish. Questionings of the self and the
society it was placed in loomed large, and such questions as why
my house was burnt, why Hindus hated Muslims, occurred to me
with agonising frequency. Whenever I put them up to my Hindu
elders, they sought to enlighten me by suggesting that the
Muslims, throughout history, had been hostile to Hindus, had
demolished many a holy Hindu shrine, had tried to convert Hindus
to Islam by coercion in the past, were anti-national and had
shaken hands with the British just to dispossess us, Hindus, of
our birth-right.[9] But, like Huck Finn,[10] I had little faith
in the omnipotency of the past and, to my childish fancy, past was
just past, dark backward abyss of time, which could have but
little effect on the present, unless resuscitated by the living
interest of living men and women. The answers I received acted
as soporofics on my curiosity and, gradually, it was increasingly
blotted out by the tides of time and the constant erosion of the
mind's focus by whatever happens around. Unable to tackle the
questionings and not finding much in whatever others told me on
them, I felt a kind of mental, even spiritual security
in the current assumption that Muslims were despicable people and
did many a thing contrary to the Hindu fashion just on purpose to
tease us. That they killed the cow,[11] our Mother, and lived on
beaf happened to be the nucleus of my narrow-minded communality
vis-a-vis the Muslim community.

My father, who was himself a staunch Hindu came to be
disillusioned of the Hindu non-violence after the traumatic
experience. While refugees, under his guidance, we seriously
thought of turning Sikhs as Sikhism could brook putting on and
wearing arms, at least a sword, and we could put up a show of
bravery fighting in self-defense. We put on the Sikh iron bangles
and my brothers, even the father, stopped having the daily shave
they were hitherto accustomed to. I wondered to myself why my
father preferred to turn Sikh and now, when I am grown up, and
have known Hinduism quite enough, I am able to attribute a reason
and that follows from the fact that Sikhism is the only sect among
Hindus, that permits of violence in self-defense on theological
grounds.[12] Of course, some other sects such as the worshippers
of Goddess Kali, Lord Shiva, and goddess Durga[13] might resort to
violence under force of circumstances and might even shine forth

at that, but they do not necessarily put on arms. In practice, even the Vaishnavites[14] cannot abjure violence. But my father was too much of an idealist and would calm down the qualms of his conscience before he would do a thing.

But as is the case with all expedients, our expedient Sikhism had but a month's long spell and, when peace began to touch the skies after the communal frenzy preceding the declaration of India's Independence in 1947, we reverted to our own Hindu creed, Polytheistic Vaishnavisism, a strange amalgam of contradictory beliefs, practices, and rituals, which might seem to neutralize one another to a petty-fogger, mounted as he is on the stilts of logicality and rationality. Under the serener glow of our political independence, we set ourselves to the observance of the Vaishnava mode of life with a fresh gusto.

What is Vaishnavistism? It is a pertinent question to ask at this juncture of my spiritual story and I will try to answer it as clearly as I can. I may not be able to define it, for definitions per se are products of reason and Hinduism or Vaishnavitism like many another religion teases one out of rational thought. Falling short of a suitable definition, I will make an attempt to describe it. When did it begin? I can't say. It is Sanātan, (from the beginning), whatever was, ever has been, ever will be, like the anir-vachaniya (beyond description) Brahman, which monistically unites in the vastness of its conception, Spirit and Matter, the seer and the seen, the doer and the deed, the creator, the creation and the creatures. Etymologically, it may suggest devotion to Vishnu, and his avatārs (incarnations) such as Lord Rama and Lord Krishna, but, in practice, it does not exclude the worship of such Gods as Shiva, Brahma etc. and of such Goddesses as Kāli, Durga etc., which have no kinship with Vishnu. A Vaishnavite respects and adores all of them, extending his worship to rivers, mountains, trees, birds and beasts and looking upon them as venerable manifestations of the anādi ātma (eternal spirit).

My father, though an enlightened medical practitioner, cherished faith in all the Gods. I do not remember even a single occasion when he spoke even a word in dishonor of any of the Gods. That was so despite his deep faith in the Vedānta and the Upanishads[16] and of his philosophic devotion to Shankaracharya's[17] conception of the Advaitavāda.[18] His was a curious blend of polytheistic worship and monistic philosophy[19] a paradox characterising Hinduism. He would practise Prānayāma[19] and meditation and yet read the Rāmāyana[20] every day, recommending it very strongly to all of us. I am referring to the diversity and multiplicity of my father's beliefs, because, now that I am grown up, I find that, unconsciously, I have imbibed the complex religious patterns, I found in my father. Being a Hindu in a way involves inheriting the pattern of worship and faith, current in the family. There is a thick core of primitivism, even tribal conservatism in Hinduism in the sense that religious patterns pass on from the father to the son and are not necessarily prescribed or sanctioned by a communal church. If you are a Hindu, you have no church; you, of course, begin to have it as soon as you look upon yourself as belonging to a Kula (family or clan) and there are as many churches as there are Kulas.

I feel myself unconsciously inclined to have faith in the many Gods my father believed in and have also a share of his faith in the Advaita. Strangely enough, my worship of the household Gods does not come in the way of my association with the other Hindus, having a different faith. For I believe that faith is a matter of one's Kula or Vansha (family or clan). They have as much a right to believe in something for their spiritual salvation as I have, but their belief may be quite different from my own. Nor am I conscious of my faith ever hindering or perverting my response to the non-Hindus. The large freedom of faith that Hinduism sanctions breeds religious tolerance. A Christian attending his church or a Muslim praying at a mosque readily comes within the purview of my sympathies, just because there are Hindus, who differ from me in faith almost antipodally and yet are my brothers. The early experience of the multiplicity of faith and worship a Hindu invariably has so conditions his mind that he looks upon religion more as an individual realization-experience than as a consistent social organization.

Now that I am grown up, I am able to appreciate that the communal tension which sway my country off and on, have their origin in political pressures and maneuverings. To a large extent, they are unleashed by the very system of democracy, combined with certain other conditions, for example, the need of coming together under communal denominations in the absence of any other sharply felt pattern of social organization, just to make one's voice heard or capture attention at the national level. The various communal sections of the Indian Society are not pitted against each other in a battle because of conflicts in faith and beliefs, but because of their need to assert themselves as distinct communities in order to survive and flourish. I have seldom come across a Hindu treating a Muslim as his enemy and vice-versa at an individual level, and that is so in spite of the occasional mutual bloodletting that takes place in India. So in the process of being a Hindu I practice a tolerance for all other religious sects.

This religious case-history of mine would remain incomplete unless I mention two potent influences over my faith. Somehow, Ram Krishna Paramahansa's[21] gospel of the Iṣṭa Devata,[22] (the beloved is the God) has restrengthened my faith in the validity of the multiplicity of faiths. What a man needs to be at peace with himself, at peace with other men, and at peace with the universe is an undying firm faith, a faith that extinguishes doubt and duality and breeds conviction and confidence in one's own self. The other influence was exerted by Mahatma Gandhi, by the faith he had in a song which says that those who wish to be the followers of Vishnu must feel the pain and misery of others.[23] That has acted as a moral corrective on my sensibilities challenging me, if I want to be a Hindu, to use every moment of my life in allaying the suffering of mankind. But that is a big order and a number of lives will pass by before, absolved of my karma,[24] I will look upon others' pain as my own. Meanwhile I have necessarily to rest content with the realization that I am just a sprout of Hinduism and not the ideal follower of the Hindu religion: "Passing the hues and objects of the world/The fields of art and learning, pleasure, sense/To glean eidolons." (Whitman).

Apart from the spiritual ramifications of Hinduism in my consciousness, I have traced above my attitudes molded by religious experience and, as such, possibly distinct from those of others. I cling to my kith and kin despite the bitter alienation from personal ties the economics of a fast-developing India is increasingly forcing on us Hindus. When I happen to meet a distant uncle of mine, I get conscious of a bond with him and treat him with traditional Hindu hospitality and wish that he should reciprocate it if an occasion arises. Whenever I hear that somebody belonging to my caste has come to stay in my township, I make it a point to contact him and look after his comfort. I can be accused of casteism for this by men of modern international sympathies. However, the idea of the caste is a convenient key to the Indian social build-up and is practically helpful in so far as it facilitates the exercise of choice in social relations and, thereby, lessens the strain of civil association. It also, eventually, mitigates the sense of alienation and aloofness, the sense of being an individual, leading naturally to a happy recognition of the claims of society over the individual and that perhaps explains why democracy has been successful in such a vast country as India.

As a Hindu I cannot even think of divorcing my wife, nor she her husband. Marriage is a life-long bond and breaking it, whatever may be the strain of living together to the partners concerned, appears to me to be a sacrilege. Hence the greater security Hindu women experience. The Rakshābandhan,[25] a festival celebrated by Hindus all over the continent, is a cultural recognition of the obligation man owes to woman as woman, not as a beloved or a wife. It is an assertion of the fundamental fraternity of the two sexes, the male vowing to protect the female because he is the stronger of the two. Of course, owing to a number of politico-economic pressures, practices that degrade woman, such as the dowry-system, have cropped up, but, fortunately enough, they are not sanctioned by the Hindu dogma and ought to be viewed as expedient compromises made by a culture with the changing economic facts. Belief in predestination is so much ingrained in the Hindu mind that in the right Hindu way, boys and girls first marry and then love; I did not want to see my wife before marriage and I don't think I could have come across a better life-partner for all my fastidious hard search. I share the Hindu belief that both pleasure and pain are the gifts of God to us. "A destiny shapes our ends, rough-hew them how we will"- that is the unshakeable conviction of a Hindu from the very beginning.

As a Hindu I am overburdened with a sense of responsibility towards my children. Not only do I worry about their up-bringing and education, but also think hard on the question of their marriage. Finding them a suitable life-partner is a responsibility I cannot shirk. As a father, I am busy securing their happiness; not even icy death has muted the unending concern of a parent for the welfare of his children. I share wholeheartedly the Hindu will of amassing and leaving a fortune, howsoever small, to my children. I am living not for my own sake but for my children's and quite frequently think of myself as a sacrifice on the altar of life. A Hindu by tradition has to learn to surrender to his obligations, whether to individuals or to society and thereby develope detachment to work (Nishkāma Karma). The surrender of the self that a Hindu is inevitably obliged to make to the world and the self-effacement which such a surrender entails must be viewed as a befitting prelude to the selflessness enjoined upon him by the provisions of the Vānaprastha and the Sanyāsa Āshramas.[26] Occupied as I am with worldly cares as a house-holder, I look upon my life as a steady endeavour and preparation to obtain Mōksha (salvation), freedom from desire and, thus, form the cycle of "birth and death, from the infinite travails our soul has to undergo during this earthly sojourn. A man deserves to be called a Hindu, only when he has obtained Mōksha(salvation).

NOTES

[1] Dashehra is a Hindu festival lasting for ten days in which Ramalila (a dramatisation of the life of Lord Rama) is played all over India.

[2] Holi is another Hindu festival associated with the myth of Hiranya Kashyap, the atheist king who ordered his theist son, Prahlad to be burnt alive, seated in the lap of his aunt, Holika. It is a festival of colors and commemorates how Prahlad survived the ordeal of fire.

[3] At Deepawali festival all the Hindus illumine their houses to commemorate the return of Lord Rama to his hometown Ayodhya.

[4] Ravana is the deca-headed monster who ruled over Sri Lanka in the days of Lord Rama. He kidnapped Rama's consort, Sita, and was slain by Rama after a long and fierce battle.

[5] Lord Hanumana – A monkey-shaped God, ever devoted to Lord Rama. He is a legendary image of valour.

[6] Lord Hanumana could fly through the air.

[7] There is no ban on children mixing with those of another community in Indian Society, and children of different faiths play together.

[8] The reference is to the communal fury that swept India in the wake of her Independence in 1947.

[9] The various grounds of the Hindu prejudice against the Muslims.

[10] Huck Finn is the boy-hero of Twain's The Adventures of Huckleberry Finn.

[11] The cow is worshipped and honoured by the Hindus as a mother is. The Hindu community strictly proscribes the eating of beaf.

[12] Sikhism is a sect of Hinduism, established by Guru Nanak in the Punjab to boost the love of Hindus for themselves as a nation.

[13] Goddess Kāli, Lord Shiva and Goddess Durga are Deities associated with war. Lord Shiva is one of the three eternal gods,

the other two being Lord Vishnu and Lord Brahma. The three symbolise the three functions of nature: Brahma, creation; Vishnu, preservation; and Shiva, destruction. Kali is the most monstrous of deities; she wears a wreath of skulls and symbolises war, fury, and bloodshed. Goddess Durga, symbolising valour, is pictured as riding a lion.

[14] The Vashnavites are followers of Lord Vishnu and his several Avatars such as Lord Rama and Lord Krishna and are strictly non-violent in creed particularly as Lord Vishnu symbolises preservation.

[15] Vedanta means the final sum of philosophy which the Vedas amount to.

[16] The Upanishadas are the concluding part of the Vedas.

[17] Sankaracharya is a philosopher – saint of the south of India, who preached his philosophy of the Advaita in the 6th century A.D.

[18] The Advaita – The Advaita Darshana implies non-duality. It affirms that the final reality is one and the same, against the other philosophies that believe in three eternal essences – Prakriti (Nature), Purusha (the Individual soul) and Ätma (The Eternal soul).

[19] Prånåyama is the science of so regulating the breathing that concentration on the self becomes possible.

[20] The Rämåyana is the life story of Rama and was versified by the greatest of the Hindu poets, Tulshi Dass of the 16th Century A.D.

[21] Ram Krishna Paramhansa – A 19th-century saint of Bengal who obtained the same vision of the Divine by following the religious practices, prescribed in different religions and sects. Thus, he tried to prove the validity of all of them.

[22] The Ista Devata is the God loved by a man and beloved to him. The principle holds that a man can obtain salvation by following any of the faiths, any of the forms of worship, with devotional intensity.

[23] "Vaishnava jan tin tene kahiye prita pari jane jo" which means "The followers of Lord Vishnu are only those that can feel the misery of others."

64

[24] Karma: The Hindus have strong faith in the idea of Karma (the bondage the soul contacts from deeds). They believe that not only the deeds done in this life but also those done in the past lives affect and determine the destiny of a man. The Theory of Karma implies faith in the idea of the transmigration of the soul, its birth, and rebirth. It affirms that Rebirth is due to the effect of the bondage of the soul to Karmas.

[25] Rakshābandhan is a Hindu festival at which sisters tie a thread round their brothers' wrists and in return brothers promise to safeguard their interests.

[26] The Vānaprastha and the Sanyās Āshrama: Life has been divided by Hinduism into four stages or āshramas. The first is Brahmacharya (the state of absolute celibacy) lasting till one is twenty-five. It is a period of self-education. The second is Grahasthya i.e., life as a family holder. The third is Vānaprastha, when husband and wife after having discharged all their worldly obligations, try to detach themselves from their family and with that intent in view keep their habitation changing. The fourth is Sanyās, a life of complete alienation from the world of man and retreat into the peace of a forest ever endeavouring to realise the self.

CHRISTIANITY AND THE INDIAN CULTURE

T. M. Thomas

Since India is known for its Hindu religion, the important place that Christianity occupies in that nation is not usually well recognized. The significance of Christianity in India is found not only in its long history of nearly two thousand years but also in the valuable contributions it has made for Indian culture over a long period of time. The Christian presence in India is greatly recognized during modern times when foreign powers from the West have found their way to this country.

Christians in India form part of the land, sharing common values and maintaining the same traditions with the rest of the people in that country. Christians feel at home in India and they find their identity as Indians just as their friends in Hinduism or other religions. Their experience as Christians is not in any way diminished by their belonging to the Indian culture. In a country where the majority of the people are Hindus, about 85 percent, the presence of Christianity, consisting of nearly 3 percent of the population, and the role it plays in the culture form an interesting phenomenon for study. Christianity as part of Indian culture is being shaped by the latter while at the same time supplying new elements or traits for the surrounding culture. An understanding of the dialectic between Indian Christianity and its surrounding culture is essential for our study of the growth of Christianity in the Indian culture.

Christianity and the Surrounding Culture

The religious life of a group can be studied by an understanding of the surrounding culture which exerts influence in the formation of a certain style of living. Accordingly, we look to the Indian culture in which Christianity has grown for many years. However, Christian life or any other style of living is not just the product of the environment. In recent years many behaviorists adhere to a simplistic approach of explaining human behavior in terms of the determining forces in the environment, both physical and social. Different from this explanation many others believe that the fulfillment of the Christian life is achieved by transcending the environmental forces and by identifying with the universal elements of Christianity. Religion, in the estimate of Emile Durkheim is concerned with the transcendental, calling it the "sacred" and separating it from the "profane" or the ordinary. This transcendental aspect cannot be ignored while admitting the environmental forces that shape any religion.

Indian culture is enriched by several religions. Starting with Hinduism we see them flourishing in India one after another, Buddhism, Christianity, Islam, Sikhism and others. People became Christians at two periods in history, one during the first century or early centuries with the arrival of St. Thomas or Christians from Syria, and the other during modern times with the arrival of Western missionaries. The early Christians of India maintained contacts with Syria and Persia for centuries. The name "Syrian Christians" expresses a sense of pride based on the long history and an upper class position in society. For several centuries the church was orthodox in nature. Later, Western missionaries came and worked among Christians as well as non-Christians when Catholic and Protestant divisions emerged in India. The large number of people who became Christians from the Lower Hindu Castes during this time brought new social issues to Indian Christianity.

Prior to the contact with the Western missionaries during modern times, Christianity does not seem to have acted as a missionary religion. Christians in the early centuries were treated as one among the upper castes in a society organized on the basis of caste. While maintaining the social privileges, they ignored the evangelistic task of Christianity found in other lands. The tolerant orientation of Hinduism allowed Christians to exist in India enjoying their privileges and adhering to their faith. However, Christianity was not absorbed into Hinduism as it had happened to some other religions.

Christians in India, while maintaining the distinct faith of their religion, identified themselves with the local culture by following the rituals and practices of the area religions. I shall present some examples, keeping in mind that the diversity of Indian culture is so great that we cannot select the practices that are applicable everywhere. Hence in these examples I shall focus on Kerala where Christians claim the origin of their religion with the arrival of St. Thomas in the first century. The distinct faith of Christians in India is not discussed here. The basic elements of religion, discussed by Emile Durkheim are; 1) belief system related to the sacred, 2) a worshipping community, and 3) rituals and practices. Among these we shall discuss only the last element found among Kerala Christians.

Some Social Practices of Christians

During the long history of their existence in Kerala, Christians observed many ceremonies connected with birth, marriage, and death. The expectant mother is brought to her parents' house by a group of ladies usually seven in number. The child is born in her parents' house. The birth of a boy is announced with a sound Kurava, a shrill call. This practice is taken from Nambudiris and Nairs. Immediately after the birth the horoscope of the baby is taken. The child is given a few drops of honey into which some gold powder is added. This custom, shared with Nambudiris, is claimed to ensure prosperity. After seven to ten days, the husbands' family visits the baby, and a gift of gold is made to the child. About two months later the mother with the child returns to her husband's house, taking with her the gift of jewels, clothes, and household equipment. Many of these practices are still followed in Kerala.[2]

During the marriage ceremony, the most important part is the tying of Minnu or Tali. This is a small pear-shaped or pipul-leaf-like ornament of gold worn on a thread round the neck. The tali used by Hindus is decorated by a tiny image of a goddess, and in the minnu used by Christians there is a cross made of tiny gold beads. This practice is maintained today and all married women wear minnu throughout their life, even after the death of their husbands.

There are two ceremonies relating to death; they are Pulakuli and Sraddha. When there is a death, the family is considered under pollution until a feast called pulakuli (pula means "pollution" and kuli means "bath") is observed on the tenth day. During the days under pula, the family attends church daily. The family cannot move freely with one another and they are expected to avoid oil baths, betel, ghee, milk, meat, fish, beds, and sexual intercourse. On the morning of the feast everyone takes a bath. All the people in the neighborhood, especially the poor, can come to the feast. The priest conducts a service of prayer and chants for a considerable time and the sextons go around with incense, offering everyone the fragrance. All attending the feast would place a coin in a vessel before the priest and receive blessing (kaiyassuri) from him.[3]

On the anniversary of death each year, the chattam or feast, derived from the Sanskrit word sraddha, ceremony is performed. The Hindu Nambudiris also perform a sraddha ceremony. Many special dishes have to be prepared and the married daughters of the house are supposed to come home with neyyappam, a kind of deep-fried cake. After the morning Qurbana (Syrian term for Eucharist) in the church, a candle is lit on the grave and the

sons and relatives bow to the grave before each one departs.
Later they return to the house where a meal is served. The poor
in the neighborhood are also given food and alms.[4]

To this point, we have described social practices related to
the birth, marriage, and death. Christians have assimilated many
other practices, and we will continue to describe them. The Hindu
influence is evident in many churches and festivals associated with
them. There were church buildings with carvings similar to those
of the temples. The flagstaff is still a prominent feature of both
church and temple. Very tall stone lamps of Hindu type can be
found in church precincts. In the chancel of a Syrian church
there is the large brass lamp which is known as nilavalaku.[5] It
derives its name from the tier or steps of light. In its design the
lamp is similar to those used in the Hindu temples. All the
paraphernalia of Hindu religious processions were also used by the
Syrians--various kinds of ceremonial umbrellas, drums, and musical
instruments.[6] Zachariah concurs when he remarks: "The flag-
hoisting ceremony, the public procession of the members of the
congregation, the community feast, the cultural programs, the
fireworks display etc., of a church festival had many similarities
with the Hindu pattern of festivals."[7]

In day-to-day living also Christains were influenced by their
Hindu neighbors. They both shared certain superstitions.
Christians were strong believers in omens (sakunam) and they
thought it is important to see the right objects when setting out
on a journey or any important business. The sight of a cow or
lighted lamp being carried were considered as lucky signs. It was
a bad sign to see a widow, a woman without ornaments, a priest,
or a Brahmin. As noted before, Christians also had the habit of
casting horoscopes for a new-born child. Astrology was firmly
believed in and it was very common to consult with the astrologer
or (kaniyan) before fixing the day for a marriage, building a new
house, or transacting any important business. Important
undertakings were attempted only at an auspicious hour or
subhamuhurtam.[8]

Christians also accepted more practices from Hindus though
only of minor importance. They followed the convention of
sleeping with the head to the east and feet to the west and not
north-south. In many ceremonies the mother would bring a lighted
lamp which was a relic of agni worship. Christians, like Hindus,
would never blow out a flame with their breath, as this would be
an insult to the firegod. Instead they used Tavikkuga or a small
laddle to extinguish the fire.[9] Among the Syrian Christians a
bishop is called Thirumeni, a term used to address Nambudiri, and
it implies reverence. A Hindu calls his father achen and the same

70

term is used by the Christians in addressing their priests. After studying the social life of Christians, Zachariah concludes: "Living in the same local communities among the Hindus and Muslims, sharing the same culture, wearing the same dress, speaking the same language, the Christians were active participants in the social life of the local communities. The difference in faith and forms of worship did not differentiate their social life."[10]

Though Christians accepted several Hindu practices, they maintained their identity as a separate Christian group. Their identity is mainly based upon faith and is quite different from other religious groups'. While sharing with the rest of the people in their customs and practices, Christians took pride in the distinguishing features of their religion.

Christians did not deviate from their central belief in God as seen through the Incarnate Son, Jesus. The liturgy which they used for their worship expressed the meaning of God's acts in Christ. The center of community life was the parish church where they gathered on Sundays and other important days. Though they could not fully understand the words of service, being in Syriac, they were interested in redemption and Christ's reign in glory. The people lived through the events of Christ's life as the special ceremonies of the Christian year were observed in cycle, and all the great occasions of their lives were celebrated in the church.[11]

Brown, after studying the distinctions of Christians and adapted practices from Hindus, states: "The Christians of St. Thomas appear to have lived in two worlds at the same time, but with no consciousness of tension between them or disharmony within themselves. They were Christians of Mesopotamia in faith and worship and ethics; they were Indians in all else. In church they professed belief in one Almighty God, out of church they observed omens and propitious days and were content to recognize the existence of Hindu gods, though they did not worship them."[12]

Christian Contribution to the Indian Culture

As noted earlier, Indian culture is enriched by several religious groups over a long period of time. The impact of Christian contribution on Indian culture is recognized during modern times after the arrival of Western powers in India. We shall point out a few areas where such an impact is felt.

The existing system of education in India reveals the influence of Britain as well as of missionaries from Europe and America. Many leaders of independent India openly recognize their indebtedness to mission schools; without these schools their chances for higher education would have been slim. The learning of English taught by the missionaries has brought the nation together, where one common language is lacking for communication.

The mission schools established in various parts of the country and the British rule in India paved the way for a new system of education which was established by the 19th century. The British system of education transformed Indian society for greater acceptance of modernization and the new values that agree with this process. In this context the Christians of India found a new social role and became pioneers in education by establishing schools and colleges. Since more Christians live in Kerala state compared to other states, this state became a leader in the matter of education, a lead it maintains even today. Since the Christian schools were open to youngsters of all religions, the level of the education of people across the country improved during the Nineteenth and Twentieth centuries. In this way the Christians played a significant role in the improvement of education in India.

When people are educated we can anticipate some fundamental changes in the organization patterns and values of society. Such changes in the Indian culture during the past two centuries may be summarized under the concept modernization. What is "Eastern" in the Indian culture has diminished with the growth of the "Western" style of life in India. The new sense of equality and justice which emerged in India as a result of the contact with the West has shattered the traditional stability of a caste-ruled society. The mobility of educated people and the freedom that goes with it have challenged many age-old practices of society. People confined to traditional roles, especially women, find greater opportunities for expression and the exercise of freedom. In the freedom struggle for an independent India, women came to assume a significant part. In short, there have been a greater sense of equality and freedom, and society has changed from its caste-dictated roles to new roles that education has opened up.

This emerging situation is best used by Christian women. They received not only general education but also specialized training in technical and professional fields such as nursing. The number of women receiving nursing education is extremely high among the young women of Kerala. These nurses moved out to other states in India as well as to many other countries, especially to the United States of America.

The above-mentioned "Western" style of life has become the core of modernization, a process that earns greater acceptance in India along with most other nations of the world today. Modernization means change toward the type of society found in advanced industrial nations. It has become the popular term to refer to changes brought about in a non-Western country by contact with a Western country. Some scholars, such as M. N. Srinivas, prefer the term "Westernization" because it is ethically neutral[13]; while others, such as Mandelbaum, prefer the use of "modernization" because it avoids the unwarranted implications of Westernization.[14] I believe that this process, however we call it, is hastened in India by the presence of Christians who feel at ease with the Western ways of living. Also, we shall admit that Indian spirituality is broad enough to absorb the material treasures that modernization brings with it. Singer agrees when he says that the "traditionalism of Indian civilization is not opposed to innovation and change, to modernity, to the foreign and strange . . . India's traditionalism is rather a built-in adaptive mechanism for making changes."[15] In short, the special nature of Indian culture and the presence of Christianity, in my view, are the two major factors that have enabled the traditional society of India to enter into the process of modernization.

This process assumes a liberal orientation, different from a traditional outlook. While rooted in its traditionalism, Christianity in India shifts to liberal views through the efforts of progressive Christians. The discriminatory practices that have prevailed in society for centuries have been seriously challenged by a considerable number of Christians throughout India though some of the churches are slow in such efforts. Several church leaders, by denouncing social evils, try to promote the creation of a just society which the country needs today.

The creation of a just society by eliminating social and economic inequalities is perhaps the most urgent need of the country today. It is achieved when people become aware of the problem and when they seek the political means to solve it. In promoting greater awareness through formal and informal education, Christians play a significant role. Further, the political involvement of Christians is also on the rise. In some states Christians undertake organized efforts to support and control political parties. When the Church does it as an institution, it may violate the principle of the separation of religion and state. But, as citizens, Christians can be involved in political activities. In our view it is done at a satisfactory level though there is room for growth. Christians cannot simply ignore the creation of a just society.

Christians resort to organized political activities when their freedom and interests are threatened. Changes in educational policies by state governments were strongly opposed by Christians in the past when their interests were at stake. Recently a bill was presented in the Indian Parliament to restrict Christian missionary activities, but the bill was withdrawn when Christians all over India made organized efforts to block its approval in the parliament. This was an occasion when Christians themselves recognized their strength during their struggle at the national level.

Though Christians form only a small portion of the population, a little less than three percent, their impact on the Indian scene is much more than their number indicates. In all major cities, New Delhi, Bombay, Calcutta, Madras and others, the Christian presence is felt through many church steeples, schools, colleges, and hospitals. In Kerala state a visitor is surprised by the large number of churches which are found only in Christian countries. The importance placed on education has enabled the community to climb the ladder of social power and prestige. Educated Christians occupy important positions in various walks of life across the country and they exercise much power in society.

In short, Christianity has grown in the country over the last two millenia as part of Indian culture. During their long history, Christians have followed many practices in common with the people of other religions, especially Hinduism. Christians, on their part, have made valuable contributions to Indian culture, and that at a remarkable level during modern times. The Christian impact on Indian education is significant. The process of modernization is being quickened by Christians. In the social hierarchy Christians are placed high. Though a minority, they are likely to exert significant influence on the future course of India, too.

NOTES

[1] Emile Durkheim, The Elementary Forms of Religious Life (1912) trans. Joseph Ward Swain, (New York, Free Press, 1965).

[2] S. G. Pothan, The Syrian Christians of Kerala (New York: Asia Publishing House, 1963), pp. 61-62.

[3] P. P. Philip, "A Comparative Study of the Funeral Rites of the Syrian Christians and Nambudiri Brahmins of Kerala" (Unpublished Master's Thesis, Hartford Seminary Foundation, Hartford, 1970), p. 24.

[4] Pothan, The Syrian Christians, p. 26.

[5] "Nila" means step, "valluku" means lamp.

[6] L. W. Brown, The Indian Christians of St. Thomas, (Cambridge: At the University Press, 1956), p. 172.

[7] Mathew Zachariah, "Whither Kerala" (Unpublished doctoral dissertation, University of Minnesota, 1968), p. 61.

[8] Pothan, The Syrian Christians, p. 95.

[9] Brown, The Indian Christians, p. 173.

[10] Zachariah, "Whither Kerala", p. 65.

[11] Brown, The Indian Christians, pp. 4-5.

[12] Ibid.

[13] M. N. Srinivas, Social Change in Modern India (Berkeley: University of California Press, 1966), p. 52.

[14] David G. Mandelbaum, Society in India: Change and Continuity (Berkeley: University of California Press, 1970), p. 467.

[15] Milton Singer, When a Great Tradition Modernizes: An Anthropological Approach to Indian Civilization, (New York: Prager Publishers, 1972), p. 404.

75

THE TRIBAL RELIGIONS OF INDIA AND THEIR FUTURE

Zacharias P. Thundy

Introduction

Conversion of Harijans and tribals to Islam and Christianity is a highly controversial issue in India these days. On the one hand, the freedom of religion protected by the Indian Constitution stipulates that one be free to practice and propagate his religion, which implies that a person is also free to embrace the religion of his choice. The various Congress administrations of the Central Government have consistently upheld the right of religious freedom. On the other hand, conversion is often perceived as "forced" and therefore "unfree." The argument goes that a person is induced to change his religion with the promise of material benefits like money, jobs, and food and that the impoverished tribals become Christians or Moslems just for the sake of obtaining these benefits. To prevent the abuse of forced conversions and to protect religious freedom, some states have been contemplating anti-conversion legislation, and Arunachal Pradesh has enacted legislation which forbids conversion. The intent and purpose of such legislation is to discourage the conversion of tribals or Harijans to Islam and Christianity from Hinduism. The implication is that all Harijans and tribals are Hindus, which is not true. First, I shall define the tribes and describe their place in the Indian society. Second, I shall discuss the distinctiveness of tribal religions by examining one tribal religion, the religion of the Santals; it is not practical or feasible to discuss all the different tribal religions of India in a few pages; the Santal religion is, however, representative of the tribal religions of India. Third, I shall point out the gradual conversion process the tribal religions are going through, again by examining the Santal religion. The final part of this paper is a speculation on the future of the tribal religions.

Tribes of India

The tribals are the indigenous people who had been settled in the country long before the arrival of the Aryans. Many of them were absorbed as castes into the mainstream of the mixed race of the Aryans by being Sanskritised or Brahminized or Hinduized. Most of the Brahmins and the rest of the Hindus belong to one of the many castes that make up the Hindu society and Hindu religion. But there are still other groups of people in India known as tribals who have not been integrated into the mainstream of the Indian society and Indian religions like Hinduism, Islam,

Sikhism, Buddhism, and Christianity. Geographically speaking, these tribes live in seclusion and isolation on the hills and in the forests. Most of these aboriginal communities, though not all, have been identified as "Scheduled Tribes" in the Constitution of India.

There are 256 Scheduled Tribes--I include the Cholanayickar of the Nilambur forests in this figure; they were "discovered" only in 1973--in all the states and union territories. According to the 1971 census--the 1981 census figures were not available when I wrote this paper in October 1981--the total population of India was 549 million of which the Scheduled Tribes accounted for about 38 million. That means they are 6.94% of the total population. In the northeastern states and the union territories they are the majority population. Thus Nagaland has 88% tribals, Maghalaya 80%, and Arunachal Pradesh 70%. But half of the country's tribal population is found in the three states of Madhya Pradesh, Bihar, and Orissa. Madhya Pradesh has over eight million tribals, that is, 20% of the state's population: Bihar has about five million or about 8.75% of the population. The numerically dominant tribes are the four-million strong Gonds of central India (Madhya Pradesh, Maharashtra, and Andhra Pradesh), the four-million strong Bhils of western India (Rajasthan and Gujarat), and the three-million strong Santals of eastern India (Bihar, Orissa, and West Bengal).

The Indian tribal population was never considered as absolute aliens or total outsiders, but as part of the body politic; nor were they originally considered as the first inhabitants of India. It was the English who gave rise to the concept of the aborigines, which notion was readily accepted by the educated Indians whose Dravidian and Aryan ancestors, like the English, came from the outside. Most Indians today consider the tribals who live in isolated and self-contained communities as culturally and ethnically distinct groups. On account of about two thousand years of isolation, these tribals have become culturally distinct; ethnically, however, most of them are hardly distinguishable from the other dark-skinned and brown-skinned Indians. Politically and legally, the tribals are supposed to enjoy the same rights and privileges like the other Indians with no discrimination whatsoever. In spite of all this, most Indians consider them not as their own kin but as strangers in the house.

The heart of the matter is the caste system, the structural principle of the Hindu society. All members of the Hindu religion belong to one of the numerous castes. If an Indian is not a member of one of the castes, he cannot fully and truly be a Hindu. Imagine Hinduism as a concentric circle. In the past, years ago, at the center of the circle stood the Brahmin and the political establishment; various castes stood at a distance, but in mutual dependence, from the center. The outermost circle was made up by the lowest class. Beyond them almost outside the sphere, but not totally outside, still live the tribals and other untouchables. Some fifty years ago, there took place the most spectacular conversion attempt of these millions of untouchable castes and tribes. Mahatma Gandhi with the best of intentions christened the untouchables as Hindus by calling them Harijans. Since then many Hindu leaders without further questions have considered the Scheduled Castes and Tribes as Hindus. The 1961 census even reported that ninety percent of tribals were Hindus. H. N. Bahuguna recently wrote in the popular Sunday magazine (September 13, 1981, p. 27): "If they [the Harijans] were unhappy with the Hindu system, improve that system; but leaving it would not be a solution because they too were part of the system." However, a verbal declaration by the great Gandhi is not capable of bringing about a change of heart and a change of conviction for the tribals or the caste Hindus with eventual social acceptance. So the tribals still lead a peripheral existence which affects their entire life--social, political, economic, and especially religious. Tribal religions are different from Hindu religion just as Islam and Christianity are different from each other. I shall briefly dwell on one representative tribal religion, the Santal religion, to show the distinctiveness of tribal religions.

Religion of the Santals

Religion is generally understood to describe man's relations to the supernatural powers and various organized systems of belief and worship in which these relations are expressed. Religions differ from one another according to the gods or objects of worship, belief systems, and various rituals.

Like the other aboriginal tribals of Chotanagpur and central India, the Santals believe that their universe is inhabited by supernatural beings and powers. In fact, the Santal social structure is influenced by their religious universe. The Santals have this religious world, which is not necessarily consistent and uniform.

The supreme deity of the Santals is Thakur Jiu, which word is probably derived from the Sanskrit Thakkura. The most common Santal term now used for the supreme deity is Cando, which means the Sun. They do not mean that the Sun is the supreme deity, but that the Sun is supreme manifestation of the divine activity, power and splendor. Because of this view, the east, the direction of the rising sun, is important in their rituals. They face the east when they worship and take solemn oaths. The Thakur Jiu is the creator and sustainer of the universe. He is invoked on all important occasions such as marriage, death, oath-taking, droughts, deaths, and disasters though there is no specific ritual according to which Thakur Jiu is worshipped.

The Santals also believe that they are surrounded by bongas or spirits who intervene in human affairs all the time. The Santal folklore shows that the bongas often intervened in their behalf in critical situations and helped them. These bongas are regularly worshipped, appeased, and kept satisfied; if offended, they may cause harm and tragedy. It does not mean that all these bongas are malevolent spirits; it only means that these spirits are intimately associated with the life and destiny of the Santals who cannot do without the bongas. The Santals do distinguish between the manita bongas or the benevolent spirits and the banita bongas, the evil ones.

The various bongas can be divided into ten categories without the implication of any hierarchy among the categories or among the bongas of these divisions: (1) Village tutelary deities consisting of Maran Buru, Moreko Turuiko, Jaher Era, Gosae Era, Pargana Bonga, Manjhil Haram Bonga. (2) The Abge Bongas or sub-clan spirits. (3) Household spirits or Orak Bongas like the Lares and Penates of the Romans. (4) The spirits of ancestors or Hapramko Bongas. (5) Saket Bongas or the tutelary spirits of the Santal ojhas or shamans. (6) The Jom Sim bongas. (7) The Deku Bongas or the Hindu deities. (8) The village boundary spirits (Sima Bongas), the spirits of the village outskirts (Bahre Bongas), the mountain and hill spirits (Rongo Ruji), and water spirits (Baghut Bongas). (9) The spirits who, through ojha-divination, are found to be the cause of disease or other mischiefs and who are to be exorcised by the ojha himself. These include Naihar Bongas, Kisar Bongas, Thapua Bongas, and bonga husbands of witches. (10) The wandering spirits who have to be chased away through divination and magic. They are the malevolent Curins, Bhuts, Ekagudias, and Rakas.

Of all the bongas the most important and powerful one is Maran Buru who taught the first Santal couple--Pilcu Haram and Pilcu Budhi--the purpose of sex and the method of brewing handi (rice beer). The Santals offer him rice beer and propitiate him at all festivals and rites of passage.

Jaher Era is the lady of the sacred grove (sarna); she is a genial spirit who is always looking after the needs of all people; the Santals offer her a fowl at all festivals.

The ancestral spirits (Hapramko Bongas) are worshipped in each household. During festivals the dead are given their small offerings.

In the recent past some Santals have adopted Hindu deities as their Orak Bongas. These gods are Kali, Dibi (Durga), Ganga Mai, Lakshmi Mai, Siva, Parvati, Rama, and Krishna.

The dominant element of the Santal religion is a belief in supernatural spirits who, they believe, guide the destinies of the tribe and the individuals. They personify these spirits, identify their names, and ally themselves with the benevolent bongas to protect themselves from the evil bongas.

The Santals also have strong faith in community solidarity, express it, and maintain it through collective feasting, drinking, singing, and dancing. They sometimes make sacrificial offerings to the bongas on behalf of a social unity like a family or a whole village. Thus their belief in the common bongas and collective worship of them strengthen the Santals' social unity.

The Santals surround their life with seasonal religious rites and festivals which constitute the Santals' public worship. The Santal life cycle coincides with the agricultural cycle. For the success of agriculture, religious beliefs and magical practices are indispensable, for a drought or blight could mean hunger for all. They believe that the bongas guard over their economic activities. The seasonal festivals in honor of the bongas mark the different stages of the agricultural year. They hold rites at the opening of the season and at the end of the season and pray to the benevolent bongas for their continued protection and appease the evil spirits in order to ward off their wrath.

The main festivals are the following: (1) Baha: it is held in January-February; it is the offering of the first fruits and flowers. (2) Erok Sim: it is held in July-August when the rice seeds sprout. (4) Iri Gundli Nawai: it is held in August-September with the offering of the first millet crop. (5) Janthar: it falls in November-December when the first fruits of the winter crop are offered to the bongas. (6) Sohrae falls in December-January after rice-harvesting. (7) Magh Sim: during this festival, which falls in January-February, the Santals cut grass for thatching house roofs. The annual hunting, Karam, Jom Sim, and Mak More are other important Santal festivals.

All these celebrations are social events accompanied by collective rituals, dances, and banquets. During the Sohrae festival the Santal moral code tolerates sexual excesses; so Christian Santals are forbidden from taking part in these festivities; instead, they celebrate Christmas with great gusto.

Some individual Santal households also celebrate Chata, Pata, and Jatra which are festivals of Hindu origin. Though many Santals attend these festivals, they do not consider these as their religious festivals. Nor do the Santals invite Brahmin priests to officiate at the important rites and ceremonies of the individual's life cycle like the critical occasions of birth, initiation, marriage, and death.

Conversions to Hinduism

It is a fact that the tribals of India have been influenced considerably by India's dominant religion, Hinduism, and that they have borrowed extensively from the ideas and institutions of the Hindu religion. It is also true that a certain tribe like the Ezhavas of Kerala has become absorbed into the Hindu social order as a caste. But it is not true that the tribal religion is a backward form of the Hindu religion or that the distinction between the tribal religion of the Santals and Hinduism is meaningless. N. K. Bose argues:

> One might indeed say that tribes can be regarded as being fully absorbed in the Hindu fold if Brahmin priests perform Brahminical ceremonies for them during the three critical events of birth, marriage, and death. If the latter are still celebrated by tribal rituals, then the communities are still true to their own faith in spite of the fact that in the outer fringes of their culture, they participate in some of the ceremonies of their Hindu neighbors.[1]

Though the Santal and the other tribal religions do not invite Brahmin priests to officiate at religious rituals and are thus distinct from Hinduism--to apply Bose's criterion--, the growing influence of Hinduism on tribal religions should be recognized. For over two thousand years Hinduism has had an impact on the various aspects of tribal life--material, social, economic, linguistic, and religious. It should also be admitted that the tribal deities have been adopted by the Hindu religion. For instance, among the majority community of the Khasas of Uttar Pradesh and Madhya Pradesh the numerically insignificant high caste Hindus have accepted the beliefs and ritual practices of the tribal people.[2]

In the case of the Santals, the following points of contact between their religion and Hinduism are worth mentioning. The name Thakur, the current Santali designation for the supreme God, is of Hindu origin. Siva, Parvati, Ram, Kali, Durga, and Krishna are today part of the Santal pantheon. The Santal festivals of Chata, Pata, and Jatra are believed to be of Hindu origin. Today Durga-puja is a major festival for the Santals. The institutions of Ojha or the medicine man was also influenced by Hinduism; the words ojha and mantar are of Sanskrit and Hindi origin. The marriage and funeral ceremonies are very similar to their Hindu counterparts. The failure of the Santal Rebellion--the leaders Sidhu and Kanhu claimed that God wanted the Santals to revolt against their oppressors--shook their faith somewhat in the power of their own bongas. Hinduism offered an alternative path toward better economic conditions, and the Santals increasingly began to turn to Hinduism. The Kharwar Movement, started in 1871, encouraged the Santals to adopt Hindu deities, festivals, customs, and concepts. But the Jharkhand Party, started in 1938 by the Oxford-educated Jai Pal Singh, exhorted the Mundas to demand a tribal state, to renounce Hindu Gods, and to continue eating beef. The Vaishnavas, since the 1920's, have encouraged the Santals to join the Hindu fold by undergoing sudhi or purification ceremony. The Arya Samaj still actively campaigns to convert the Santals and tries to persuade them to declare themselves as Hindus. Of course, quite a few Santals were converted to Hinduism, but most of these converts refused to break completely with their ethnic and religious traditions. The belief in the bongas is still strong. They still practice their traditional festivals and rites of passage in the Santal way. In short, the Santal religion is still alive and well in spite of missionary attempts at converting them to Hinduism and Christianity.

The attempts to convert the tribals to Hinduism have taken today an active form. Militant Hindu organizations believe that anyone can become a Hindu; this form of conversion is taken from a page of Christianity. The newspaper Hindu on October 21, 1981 reported that forty Harijan Christian families numbering over 200 members embraced Hinduism at Belthangady Taluk near Mangalore in Karnataka. On the other hand, according to the Amritabazar Patrika, October 9, 1981, 200,000 Harijans became Budhists near Patna. Note that the normal Hindu conversion process is one in which the movement is from below, from the community of the untouchable tribe to the status of a caste above. This change of religion is not imposed from above by an edict or declaration like when the Mahatma declared that all untouchables were Harijans and therefore Hindus. Conversion is an evolutionary process which usually takes years; it is not a revolutionary act, an instant act of free will; conversion is not accomplished simply by request and with an act of commitment. The complete absorption of conversion of any group of people into the Hindu fold is indicated by their becoming a caste. Sociologist M. N. Srinivas who calls this conversion process "Sanskritisation" writes:

> The caste system is far from a rigid system in which the position of each component caste is fixed for all time. Movement has always been possible, and especially so in a generation or two, to rise to a higher position in the hierarchy by adopting vegetarianism and teetotalism, and by Sanskritsing its ritual and pantheon. In short, it took over, as far as possible, the customs, rites, and

beliefs of the Brahmins, and the adoption of a Brahminic
way of life by a low caste seems to have been frequent,
though theoretically forbidden. This process has been
called "Sanskritisation."[3]

By means of the conversion process of Sanskritisation, the
tribals were absorbed not into the intellectual Hinduism of the
Upanishads, the Bhagavadgita, the Philosophical Systems, and the
Sanskrit language and rituals, but into the ordinary, local
Hinduism. The local Hinduism is made up of feasts, fasts, vratas
(rites and austerities performed to obtain certain ends),
pilgrimages, visits to temples, and beliefs in some Puranas and
Itihasas. This form of Hinduism can be called Sanskritic to a
certain extent since it shares many gods and myths in common with
Brahminic Hinduism. Yet it is also non-Sanskritic since in it there
is a vast and ever-growing mythology, the worship of trees and
mountains, and the association of deities and epic heroes with local
spots all over India. Thus the dual nature of Hinduism in a way
encourages the tribal religions to seek assimilation into Hinduism.
As Srinivas again points out, "the pantheistic bias in Hinduism
also contributes to the Sanskritisation of the deities and beliefs of
low castes and outlying communities. The doctrine that everything
in the universe is animated by God, and that all the various
deities are only forms assumed by the same Brahman, makes the
process of absorption easier.[4]

The Future of Tribal Religions

The eventual result of this Sanskritisation process is the
absorption of almost all minority religions into the major civil
religion of India, which is popular Hinduism which admits an
infinite variety in its component castes and religious manifestations
and which will also tolerate the rise of newer forms of religion as
long as the new forms do not threaten the status quo of society.
Here, however, a few distinctions and qualifications are in order.

First, large minority religions like Islam, the Christian
Churches of South India, Goa, and Bombay, and the large Santal
religion can and will retain their individualities because they are
too numerous and powerful to be swept away, with little
proselytizing, without gaining new converts, and without losing
many faithful.

Second, the small pockets of ethnic Parsis or Anglo-Indian
Christians, and Jews will be tolerated because they are too few to
be a threat to the vast majority of Hindus. Their numbers will
considerably decrease in the years to come. The Christian
communities of North India will survive in the urban environment
because of their relatively higher affluence, professional

qualifications, and educational institutions. The Christians of the rural environment will gradually languish and finally vanish for lack of economic support from the institutional Churches. This is especially so because the ranks of these Christians are not being replenished and re-inforced by new converts and because large-scale conversions are a phenomenon of the past. No amount of social work on the part of Christian missionaries, who are to a certain extent competing with the powerful government agencies, will be capable of spreading the Christian faith in most parts of northern India.

Third, tribal religions are in the same bind that the Christian religion in the north is. The tribals who have moved to the cities have already given up their tribal, ethnic, and religious identity for all practical purposes except for the purpose of securing government employment within the quota system guaranteed by the Indian Parliament. Those who remain behind are also being gradually absorbed into the mainstream of popular Hinduism through the process of Sanskritisation. Though their religions are still distinct, when questioned about their religion today they would reply that they are Hindus and would talk about the Hindu gods and Hindu festivals as their gods and as their festivals. This process of Sanskritisation--many people call it "Indianisation"--can easily be detected in the names by which many of them are known today. The names like Santhosh, Satish, Joshy, Sheila, Supriya, Anu, etc., which abound in Christian and tribal communities indicate that these people are gradually renouncing their traditional, ethnic, religious identity and adopting the pan-Indian civil religion, which is another word for the modern variation of popular Hinduism.

Conclusion

The scenario I have sketched is the logical outcome if the present situation and present public policy hold good for the next twenty-five to fifty years. It is more than likely that the current process could be accelerated. The Hindu-dominated Janata Party's brief rule shows that the ideal of Ramarajya or Hindu India is still the dream of many Indians, especially of powerful militant minorities like the RSS. On the other hand, the rejection of the Janata rule by the vast majority of the people of India indicates that Indians are still capable of religious tolerance. However, the anti-Moslem, anti-Christian, anti-Harijan, and anti-tribal rumblings heard in the streets, coffee-houses, and legislatures indicate that Indians are also capable of the ruthless fratricidal violence committed by Hindus against Moslems and by Moslems against Hindus during the partition of India in 1947. Reports of the mass conversions of Harijans to Islam have provoked the people to demand strong government action to stop all conversions. The India Today opinion poll of October 15, 1981, p. 19, shows that the majority (57%) want the Government to intervene to stop conversions; only 27% want the Government to stay out; Bhopal (78%), Lucknow (72%), Jaipur (64%), and Delhi (69%) are overwhelmingly in favor of Government intervention. I forsee more violence between Moslems and Hindus; I also forsee the looting and burning of more Harijan and tribal villages in Bihar, Orissa, and the Uttar Pradesh. Only an enlightened political leadership can prevent another major religious tragedy in India.

NOTES

[1]N. K. Bose, Tribal Life in India (New Delhi: National Book Trust, 1971), p. 66.

[2]See S. L. Kalia, "Sanskritisation and Tribalisation," in T. B. Nail, ed., Changing Tribe (Chindwara: Tribal Research Institute, 1961).

[3]M. N. Srinivas, Religion and Society Among the Coorgs of South India (Delhi: Asia Publishing House, 1952), p. 30.

[4]Ibid., p. 227.

BEING AND NON-BEING:
A PHENOMENOLOGICAL ANALYSIS OF LIMITATION AND LIBERATION FROM INDIAN AND WESTERN POINTS OF VIEW

Cyriac Kanichai, C.M.I.

As affirmation precedes negation, so Being (sat) precedes non-being (a-sat). Being, as it is its own fullness and finality, cannot comport with non-being. It is therefore absolute existence by dint of non-existence. As altogether different and distinct from non-being. Being is compresent to itself, and this self-compresence renders it consciousness through and through (cit). It is complete lightness, complete translucency. As light and self-diffusion, Being is not encompassed by non-being or limitation. It is therefore infinite (anantam). It is thus reality, consciousness, and infinity (satyam, jnānam, anantam).

That Being precedes non-being implies that the former is always in front of the latter. Such priority and precedence of the Real over the unreal renders Being a transcendent Reality, existing before the unreal, yet not bound or comprehended by it. But existence designates the spontaneity of consciousness to be realised, in this case, not in some sort of nihilating reduction, but through the self-introjection of the Real into the unreal. Thus, because of the Real, the unreal is made a complement of essence (complementum possibilitatis) to be actuated, liberated and integrated into the Real. Such self-introjection of the Sat-Cit (the Real-Conscious) into the unreal resolves the radical or primary self-reflexion of the former into a secondary reflexion of the unreflected, enabling the latter to be induced into being, illumined by consciousness, and integrated into infinity. Basically, this is the liberation of the limited because of the Unlimited. Between the Real and the unreal, the Infinite and the finite, a new relation is entered into -- relation not of dialectical anti-polarity, but of dialogical complementarity.

There exists, therefore, no antithetical opposition or nihilating difference between the Real and the non-real. The non-real being the boundary line of the Real, is affixed to it from without as its potential complement. As existing face to face with the Real, the non-real is certainly factual but not actual. Being devoid of a radical logos (paramārtha) of its own, the non-real is for the Real an era for self-introjection (pratibhāsa) and self-positing (vyavahāra).

89

The non-real is, therefore, no mere void without ground. It is grounded in the Real from which it is born, by which when born it is sustained, and into which, on deceasing, it is reabsorbed.[2] The Chāndogya Upaniṣad expresses this idea by characterizing the ultimately Real as Tajjalan.[3] It is a cryptical expression brought out by the syllables ja, la and an, which stand respectively for the verbal roots jan, li and an denoting origination, reabsorption and sustenance of existence. The Real, as the true Transcendental, is thus the source, ground and terminus of the non-real. The Real and the non-real are, therefore, inter-related between each other, as meaning and manifestation (paramārtha and pratibhāsa). The limited shines because of the light and logos of the Unlimited; by the light of the Supreme the relative shines multiformly.[4] The non-real being an essential adjunct of the Real, any fundamental ontology, i.e., an ontology of the foundation of foundation, would demand that we ascend to the Real through the non-real. This Indian insight reminds us of Martin Heidegger's contention that fundamental ontology leads us to an ontology of non-being, into a meontologie. Since the radical logos (paramārtha) remains hidden in the phenomenon (pratibhāsa), the phenomenological method should be a method of making us see what it is otherwise concealed, of taking the hidden out of its hiding and of detecting it as "un-hidden," i.e., as truth, (a-letheia).

Martin Heidegger's view that truth is apparently not given without any concealment is anticipated in the Upanishadic doctrine that the Real exists in the non-real, as the unmanifest in the manifest. The Taittirīya Upaniṣad, for instance, speaks of Brahman as the logic concealed in and by the ontic, or the phenomenal, since the former exists as encompassed by the five concentric sheaths of matter, life, will, consciousness, and bliss.[5] Truth has an ontological tendency to hide and to withdraw. For it, as the principle of principles (antaryāmin), "creates all, wills all, smells all, tastes all; it has pervaded all, silent and unaffected."[6] Heidegger's interpretation of truth is based on a literal dissection of the Greek word a-letheia as "un-hiddenness" or "openness". As a matter of fact, this resembles very much with the apophatic methodology of the ancient Madhyamika philosophers of India, who maintained that only by disclosing the silence or hiddenness of being (samvriti) the supreme truth (paramārtha) is attained to.

As Being reveals itself through self-introjection into non-being, the revelation of Being in its truth is its own doing. It has, therefore, to be regarded more as an action than as an event. Being is thus self-determining. It is very striking that

Heidegger uses the German intransitive verb ereignen (to happen) in a new transitive manner to indicate that Being makes things happen. On the part of Being it is an act of letting Being-be. Heidegger's thematization of the activistic self-introjection of Being into non-being, and the consequent letting-Being-be in a plane of plurality and finiteness to be sustained by and integrated into Being (as the spider ejects and retracts the threads – to use an analogy of the Upanishads), could be taken for a rational critique of an Indian insight found in the Taittirīya Upanishad: "The Self wished: 'Let me be many; let me be born.' Through a deliberation it energized itself. Having energized itself through deliberation, it created all this that exists. Having created that, it entered into that very thing. And having entered there, it became the formed and the formless, the defined and the undefined, the sustaining and the non-sustaining, the intelligent and the non-intelligent, the true and the non-true. Truth became all this that there is. They call that truth."[7] The dialectics of the finite and the infinite is here worked out on a conception of the self-introjection of the Logic into the ontic, because of which the Logic (Ātman) becomes the Sat-Cit (inner Cause-Consciousness) of the ontic which, as belonging to the phenomenal plane of names and forms, is an essential adjunct (upādhi) of the Real totally relative to it, non-existent except in and by it, yet not affecting its transcendence. The fact that Being remains hidden in non-being, in negation, multiplicity and change, and that truth is attained to only through disclosing Being, would necessitate what Husserl calls apophantics (i.e., a logical investigation of the meaning of the given or the phenomenal) to be the epistemological method proper to a formal ontology or the science of the Real.

Towards a construction of such apophantics and ontology, some of the Indian systems through their analysis of appearance and reality seem to have made lasting contributions. To begin with, Nagarjuna's logic of the Void deserves mentioning as a specific instance of systematic apophantics in the Indian tradition. In unison with the general Buddhistic doctrine of the impermanence and momentariness of reality, the Madhyamika or the Sunyavada School, to which he belonged, held that all things were of a non-essential and indefinable character and void at bottom. But the void in question does not mean pure nihilism or negation. It only means that none of the appearances possesses any intrinsic nature of its own. This is clear from Nagarjuna's treatment of the phenomenal world as samvriti, i.e., its truth is concealed or veiled. For in regard to the phenomenal world, all things are in process (nirmāṇa), and therefore, have only empirical validity devoid of ultimacy (paramārtha). The phenomenal world is thus called prapanca, because it is only an elaboration through concepts and conventional entities. Consequently, the phenomenal cannot be said to be either existent or non-existent.[8] This is the reason why this doctrine is called The Middle Doctrine (mādhyamika). The implication is that, with regard to the phenomenal, existence and non-existence have only a relative and concealed truth (samvriti-satya).

It is not very easy to determine the exact meaning of the term sunyata or void in Nagarjuna. From a general survey of his philosophy of reality it would seem that he could not find a way of reaching the Unconditioned from what is conditioned and contingent, since every reality is in process, and all our knowledge about it is conditioned by concepts and conventions. This might have made him directly pass over from logic to ethics without the aid of a formal ontology. Such liquidation of ontology, by its being converted into ethics, resulted in his equating the ultimately Real with Void or śunyata. Void, however, is no mere passive emptiness. In reference to Paramartha, the ultimately true nature of things, śunyata means the non-conceptual, non-phenomenal, undivided, indeterminate nature of the absolute, ultimate reality, the full, the complete.[9] This is evident from his identification of śunyata with dharma-dhātu. In dharma-dhātu, dharma stands for nirvāṇa, which is Void eternal and unborn, as it is beyond the phenomenal categories of existence and non-existence. Dhatu conveys the sense of the essential, intrinsic, all-pervasive, inmost nature, the fundamental, ultimate essence. The basic fundamental source of all things is called dhātu. It is the primary aim of the wayfarer to realise the dhātu-dhātu.[10] However, śunyata is not only the ultimate end of man but also the means to that end. For it means also a religious method of understanding the nature of things, which is nothing short of a fundamental moral attitude arising as the result of non-clinging, i.e., not clinging to the determinate as ultimate in its determinate nature nor clinging to the ultimate as anything specific. The Ultimate is therefore Void, the Beyond, which, as it stands above all actual and imaginable categories of existence and non-existence, has to be realised in an ethical attitude of Void or non-clinging.[11]

Such a view of the Void, however, does not imply that the conditioned has no role to play in our ascent to śunyata. The precise import of the conditioned is its dependent nature, its deriving its nature from an "other," a "beyond" which is not itself dependent. This seems to be the purport of Nagarjuna's analysis of the tathata or the true nature of things in three steps:[12] the first one, the inferior tathata, consists in the given suchness of things. In this form, things are conditioned by their substance, qualities, capacities, causes, conditions, consequences, nature (essence), limitations, and communication. Therefore, they in their phenomenal givenness cannot claim any ultimacy. All such factors ultimately make things return to change and extinction. That is the middle tathata. From there one has still to rise to the sphere of the Void where things are neither existent nor non-existent, neither arising nor perishing, where all things are in their ultimate nature purity itself, where all determinate modes of knowing become extinct. This is the supreme tathata, the ultimacy beyond existence and non-existence, the Void.

Nagarjuna's apophantics is thus worked out in strict neutrality toward both idealism and realism. With his middle position, he does not seem to admit any ground for a deduction of the ideal from the real or vice versa. His direct leap from logic to ethics is, at certain points, reminiscent of Nicholai Hartmann's taking emotionally transcendent acts, i.e., acts characterised by the ingredients of activity, energy, struggle, involvement, risk, suffering, and being affected, for a base to transcend or step beyond into the Ultimate. However it may be, Nagarjuna with his Buddhistic distrust in metaphysics, could not ground the noumenal in the phenomenal. For the phenomenal is nothing but a conglomeration of conditions, and when conditions are removed, the phenomenal will cease to be, leaving only emptiness or void to remain. Phenomenal reality comes into existence and goes out of existence. Void, however, is beyond the categories of existence and non-existence. For it never comes into being, is not sustained by anything, nor absorbed into anything. Hence Void, the Supreme, is not something to be postulated as an ontological explanation of the phenomenal, but something to be realised through its elimination and extinction.

Philosophers of nothingness seem to overlook the fact that negative terms have no independent meaning, but are merely syncategorematic. There is no good reason to think that Nagarjuna's nihilism can be absolved from this charge of faulty semantics. As a matter of fact, he is not the only one to take up the phenomenology of the negative. In our own times Martin Heidegger, for instance, has attempted to show that the nothing has a status independent of negations, on a par with Being, even though he did not credit it with the same type of existence but with a particular mode of being which he called "naughting" (nichten).[13] The views of Nagarjuna, in this respect, bear some striking similarity with those of Heidegger that, for both of them, it is primarily through the experience of suffering and anxiety in extreme worldly situations, that nothing is manifested. All the same, for Heidegger as well as for the Western phenomenologists in general, in an ontology of nothingness the real issue involved is ultimately one of an excursus from nothingness to being. Nagarjuna, on the contrary, has undertaken to revert it by seeking the solution in a flight to nothingness from being. By absolutizing the Void as the ultimacy existing beyond the categories of existence and non-existence, he purports to have eliminated the problem of the contingent and phenomenal. But eliminating a problem is never explaining it.

For Nagarjuna, therefore, what is implied in the question of being is only a possibility for thematizing the absoluteness of nothingness as a situation which transcends the world of birth and death, of existence and non-existence. The primordial concreteness of existence is arrived at, not through one's being-in-the-world, but by being blown out of the world into an indefinable Nirvāṇa. This view does not only regard the finite and the phenomenal as devoid of any meaning and value but also takes them as an obstacle to the attainment of the eternal and the infinite.

It was in the attempt to overcome the shortcomings inherent in the nihilism of the Buddhists that the Advaitins stressed the need for taking a more positive look at the problem of the finite versus Infinite. For them, what is latent in the question of being is not a nihilating difference between being and non-being, but an ontological bipolarity between them.

To begin with, the Advaitins assign a double role to our empirical human consciousness in regard to the knowledge of the particulars. The human empirical consciousness, while revealing the particulars of what-is (upādhis or adjuncts), does also conceal in the same act, the Being of what-is. An epistemological analysis will reveal that the particulars of what-is are only the dissimulated appearance of Being (Brahman). For the empirical human consciousness exists in three conditions, namely, waking experience, dream state and dreamless sleep. All these three do reveal Being in some degree, for through them all there runs the consciousness of a persisting substratum. Otherwise, it would not be possible to remember them and co-ordinate them. Therefore the Buddhist contention that there is only becoming, no being, is not admissible. In this respect these modes of consciousness are said to be revealing reality or Being. But the Buddhist principle that satya (true) and nitya (eternal) are convertible, is also incontestable. On this basis, it has to be admitted that the Being revealed in such modes of consciousness cannot be real; for, as manifested in such states, truth has a beginning and an end; what they project cannot therefore be Being, but only the dissimulations of Being, or the particulars of what-is. As such, they necessarily point to the Being of what-is, which is attained to in the fourth state of bliss (tūriya). The particulars of what-is, do thus act as pointers to the concealed Being of what-is, which is itself self-subsisting, immutable, and eternal.

Such an analysis of the particular or the limited will unfold two important aspects of the Advaitic view of the finite. In the first place, the dissimulation of the Being of what-is, takes place in the human consciousness. The different noetic levels, waking, dreaming, and dreamless, by concealing the Being of what-is, do, at the same time, raise our human consciousness to a point of self-projection into the infinite and the eternal as the ultimate horizon, to which every consciousness, as a search for the Real, is converging intentionally. In other words, our phenomenal consciousness by eclipsing the Being of what-is through the particulars of what-is, renders the latter an intentional medium in cognition to dive into the former. Secondly, the phenomenal world, being not entirely unreal nor fully real, functions, on the one hand, as base for the Infinite to hide itself (pratibhāsa), and, on the other, as a ground for the human consciousness to uncover the Real through our being-in-the-world (vyavahāra). This will bring home to us a striking similarity between the view of Sankara and Heidegger that human existence (Da-sein) is, in the sense of being-there for Being, a horizon for its dissimulation and appearance as the particulars of what-is as well as for our discovering it from the particulars as the Being of what is.[14]

The self-introjection of Being into the phenomenal or finite gives the latter a historical mode of existence, which the Advaitins call the world of vyavahāra or human actions. This view seems to corroborate the contention of Martin Heidegger that "the world has an historical kind of Being because it makes up an ontological attribute of Dasein."[15] Viewed in this manner, it can be seen that the Advaita view is not a denial of the historical world of actions but an affirmation that Being is and can only be sought within the compass of human historicity.

Because being exists as thrownness (vikshēpa) in the particulars, it is concealed (āvaraṇa) as a mystery (māya) to be unveiled through consciousness, which is Being-present-to-self. But the worldly man of historical actions, because of his care for and involvement in the particulars of what is, is always in danger of forgetting the Being of what-is. For in the phenomenal world, the Being of what-is, remains hidden as the inmost logos (paramārtha) of the particulars of what-is. The consequent unawareness of Being causes the fundamental error (avidya) from which human existence is radically suffering, which error leads man to a misery of dread, suffering and anxiety (dukha).

At this stage there is an important point of departure between Heidegger and the Advaitins. For, unlike Heidegger, the Advaita philosophers do not think that such unveiling process can be done within a compass of mere historical anthropology of being-in-the-world. The Paramārtha or the Supreme Logos resides within the phenomenal or the pratibhāsa as its antaryāmin and sākṣin, i.e., the inner controller and witness. The descent of the Timeless into the temporal (avatār) makes the temporal an abode for the Timeless. The logic is thereby made incarnate in the ontic. The Infinite operates in the finite without however being conditioned and controlled by the latter. The consequent redemption and re-integration of the temporal into the Infinite, through self-introjection of the Logic into the ontic, is what is meant by the concept of vivarta in the Advaita philosophy. What it denotes is not a material evolution of the Infinite into the finite, but only an historical actuation of the non-real by the Real. The Infinite acting as the total controller of the finite from within raises it into being, sustains it in existence, and re-absorbs it into infinity. Such incarnational and cosmic descent of the Infinite into the finite, and the consequent inducing of it from its abysmal nothingness into the apex of being, makes redemptive activity not merely a matter of pure anthropological history but of sacred history.

In regard to the phenomenal, the Paramārtha or the Supreme Logos, in addition to being the antaryāmin or inner controller, also acts as the sākṣin or the inward witness. This arouses the receptivity of human nature to divine speech, which is actuated only by man's passing from mere historicity to sacred history. Absolute consciousness, which is Being-present-to-self, by entering into the finite and making itself present there as the Being and Logos of beings, actuates the latter's receptivity to the inner speech of Being. Residing as the antaryāmin or the inner controller of beings, the Logos inwardly testifies itself to non-being, in which Being is concealed and by which is set simultaneously a forum for man to be a hearer of the Word (śruti). The Infinite is thus revealed in the finite, the Real in the non-real. The revelation of Being in non-being, the Timeless in the temporal, makes it necessary that the Word be heard only apophatically in silence and negation (nēti,nēti).[16] The non-being is thus a medium both of concealment and revelation of the Word. By the Word the non-real is brought into being through a kenotic self-introjection of the Real into it; it is sustained in existence by the Word which remains hidden in it, as meaning in manifestation; by the same Word, the non-real is re-integrated into the Real, through self-consciousness aroused in the non-real as a result of the former's being present to it as its inner self and support.

Thus the non-real is not merely the negation of the Real. Being the abode and area for the real to posit itself in time and space, the non-real is more than even a mere shadow or reflection of the Absolute. As a potential complement of the Real, the non-real adds names and forms to it, and is as such raised to actuality by the Real -- an actuality which is totally relative to and dependent of Being, existent in, by, and for it. The non-being, with its own individuality and specific nature, thus constitutes a realm of empirical validity, from which it has to rise to the ultimate horizon of the Real, the One without a second, through the transcendental realisation of the Real as the inner soul and support of the non-real. The compresence of Being in non-being, as its soul and witness, arouses in the latter an amor aeternitatis, inspiring it to a metaphysics of ascent to Being, as the reality of reality (satyasya satyam) and meaning of meaning (paramārtha). At the same time, because of the availability of Being in non-being, which is due to the "thrownness" of the former into the latter, the possible danger of forgetting the human origins of the radical temporality of metaphysics is also averted. The creative descent of Being in non-being, its dwelling in it as its logos through time and space, and the final restoration of non-being into Being -- all these are processes taking place in sacred history, i.e., the history of the Transcendent in time because of the letting-be of the Being in beings.

Through the dynamics of the Logos, interiorly possessed and listened to as the Self of his self (paramātman) and verbally articulated in religious scriptures, man is drawn from within to the Absolute, from the phenomenal plane of being and becoming, suffering and sorrow, death and decay. With the aid of religion does he thus ascend from the finite and the limited to the Absolute and the Infinite through the Logos, which is his origin, ground and terminus. Thus, because of the Unlimited the limited is liberated. Such a liberating process of the limited by the Unlimited calls for, in the first place, a descent of the Logic into the ontic of the Divine into the human, of the Logos onto the flesh. This involves the becoming of Being, the passion of the

Actual, the kenotic self-effusion of the Full into the void. And, religiously, this constitutes the first basic truth about suffering: suffering is a religious technique employed by the Divine in the sphere of sacred history, whereby the human and the finite is redeemed and re-integrated into the Infinite, through a kenotic process of total self-emptying of the Divine into the human. The Full and the Unlimited is thus enfleshed and made present and available in the limited and the human.

Such self-positioning of the Word in the void, on the other hand, demands of man a definitive choice of and response to the Logic and the Transcendental, which can ultimately be made only at the cost of a non-clinging to whatever is outer phenomenal, which, as devoid of ultimacy, is intrinsically unstable and transitory. Such intrinsic instability of the outer and the consequent necessity to break oneself off from the given and the phenomenal is what lies at the bottom of every human suffering. In this perspective, suffering acquires a new meaning: through it, one is educated to earnestly and resolutely express one's unshaken determination to affirm the primacy of the Logic and the Transcendental, as the true Self and Goal of life and action, to be sought after in a determined mood of non-clinging to all that is plural, phenomenal, and divisive. Such a renunciatory process of non-clinging, to be constantly experienced and consolidated through dread, suffering and, ultimately, death will prove to be the unassailable test of one's total determination to leap into the Full and the Unlimited, to the complete elimination and extinction of all that was incomplete and transitory. This is the second truth about suffering, the culmination of which is death; man enters into mukti or liberation, having been definitively freed from all that was limiting, divisive, and decaying in him. Such total evanescence of the limited and phenomenal is not, however, a suppression and the liquidation of it, but an induction and integration of it into the Infinite and the Unlimited through the Logos, which has been all along existing in it, as its source, soul, and goal.

NOTES

[1] Taittirīya Upanishad, II, I.

[2] Taittirīya Upanishad, III, I.

[3] Chāndogya Upanishad, III, 14, I.

[4] Mundaka Upanishad, II, 2, IC.

[5] Taittirīya Upanishad, II, 2-5.

[6] Chāndogya Upanishad, III, 14, 4.

[7] Taittirīya Upanishad, II, 6, 8.

[8] cf. K. Venkata Raman, Nagarjuna's Philosophy (Delhi: Motilal Banarsidas, 1978), 338-339.

[9] Venkata Raman, p. 339.

[10] Ibid., p. 261.

[11] Ibid., p. 339.

[12] Ibid., pp. 256-258.

[13] H. Spiegelberg, Phenomenological Movement, Vol. II (The Hague: Martinus Niihoff, 1965), 504.

[14] G. Srinivasan, The Existentialist Concepts and the Hindu Philosophical Systems (Allahabad: Dayananda Publications, 1967), p. 230.

[15] Martin Heidegger, Being and Time, trans. John Macquarrie and Edward Robinson (New York: Harper and Row, 1962), pp. 432-33 (381).

[16] Veermani Prasad Upadhyaya, Lights on Vedanta (Varanasi: Chowkhamba Sanskrit Series Office, 1959), pp. 79-81.

YOGA AND CROSS-CULTURAL RELIGIOUS UNDERSTANDING

Christopher Chapple

Yoga has spread far from its home in India, yet its message has remained the same: there is a way of life by which one can experience freedom and spontaneity. This philosophy has a long history in North America, beginning with the discussion of the Upanisads by the Transcendentalists. In later years, the Theosophists popularized their interpretations of Indian religious practice, and finally in 1893, an authentic Indian teacher, Swami Vivekananda, introduced Indian philosophy to the Parliament of Religions, held in Chicago. During the early part of the twentieth century, Indian philosophy proved very popular, particularly due to the efforts of the Ramakrishna-Vivekananda Mission and the Self-Realization Fellowship of Yogānanda. Both these organizations continue their work at centers throughout the country.

During the past fifteen years, there has been a resurgence of interest in yoga, but with a difference. No longer are Americans at the mercy of third-hand accounts of yoga, relying on translations given through the medium of translators who rewrite texts extensively to make them comprehensible to the Judeo-Christian mind. Nor is the spectrum of teachings available limited to the Neo-Vedāntic syncretism which captured the imagination of the masses in the 20s and 30s. Philosophers, Sanskritists, and a new wave of yoga teachers have enriched our interpretations and brought a new understanding of this ancient discipline. Speculation, discourse, and worship characterized some of the early moments of yoga's transmittal to the West. In more recent times, yoga teachers are exacting radical transformations in their students, requiring extended periods of serious sadhana and study. In some cases, neo-yogis undergo a phase of "Hinduization," wherein the Indian mindset is rehearsed, recited, and embodied. In other cases, some Indian gurus in the West have "modernized" their teachings and tolerate behavior which would not be found in India. However, whether Hinduized or not, the New World followers of yoga have, for the most part, questioned their fundamental needs in life. The superiority of Western advances in science are no longer taken for granted; the horrors of chemical pollution, increased cancer rates, and rampant stress have soured the comforts brought by technology. Due to a number of cultural changes enacted in the late sixties and early seventies, the notion of progress and development is no longer seen as ultimately healthy or even worthwhile.

The taking-on of "Eastern" sensibilities has not gone unnoticed by social scientists and theologians. Two recent studies have been devoted to this phenomena: Turning East by Harvey Cox[1] and The Light at the Center: Context and Pretext of Modern Mysticism by Agehananda Bharati[2]. The former is written by a Christian theologian; the latter by an Austrian-born Hindu monk and professor of anthropology. Cox investigated a number of Eastern meditation techniques. He talked with members of the International Society for Krishna Consciousness; sat with a Zen Buddhist meditation group; lived and taught at Naropa, a Buddhist education center established by Chogyam Trungpa. Ultimately, he found peace in the company of Benedictine monks and pointed out, correctly, that the West has its own systems of worship and pathways for meditation. However, he fails to recognize that the background of most young Americans is not that of his generation; religious education does not play a prominent role in the upbringing of the "television" generation, whose imagination is captured more by superheroes (or supervillains) than by Biblical tales. For those who do attempt to make a connection with their mythic origins, quite often the exotic is the most appealing.

Agehananda Bharati, on the other hand, lived the life of the sixties a generation early. His early training in Indian languages and cultures opened avenues to the exotic for him long before discount airfare made India accessible to the masses. In some respects, he seems reluctant to accept the legitimacy of the new, Americanized meditation movements, preferring to lend credibility to the more Hinduized groups such as ISKCON. However, towards the end of his analysis he sees that America is ripe for the freedom which successful meditation produces, and predicts that yoga will wane in India, just as Buddhism and Christianity disappeared from the places of their origin.

In their analyses, both Cox and Bharati address the sociological implications of Westerners embracing Asian philosophies. Cox approaches the various groups with the naivete of the young Americans who prompted his initial curiosity. Unfortunately, he does not delve into the presuppositions which initially gave rise to the movements. Turning East is more travelogue than indepth investigation. Similarly, although Bharati regards himself an insider of the Hindu tradition, he insists that his work is social science. Professionally, he leads two lives, that of the anthropologist and that of the mystic. Although willing to describe his encounters with the "zero experience," he declines from drawing philosophical or theological conclusions. As Roman Catholic Modernist George Tyrrell has pointed out, religious experience includes affective revelation and its explication[3]. Both impression and expression are required. Cox's affective experience is somewhat limited, and is prompted best in a Christian environment. Bharati is well qualified in the affective realm, and explains it well, but does not seem to relate this experience on a "public" level; his revelation is exclusively private, and he implies that all such experiences are inherently private.

The purpose of theological and spiritual speculative thought is to express clearly the mechanics of intimate spiritual experience so that others may follow, experience, and understand. A language is needed which demythologizes the esoteric and/or exotic and in some way humanizes it. Throughout history, several avenues have arisen to achieve this end, such as the many developments of the early Christian church, the discussion of the two levels of truth in Buddhism and Vedanta, the model of the dark night of the soul, etc. In each of these seemingly unrelated traditions, religious insight gained through meditation is explained without sacrificing its power. With such a tool, Bharati's zero experience or Cox's Buddhist breathing insight can be rendered intelligible and integrated into the overall fabric of human experience.

The Yoga Sūtra of Patañjali, (ca. A.D. 300) is a text that helps to bridge many of the chasms which are apparent in the discussion of meditation practices of the East and their transmittal to the West. Yoga deals explicitly with states of affective experience (samādhi), listing several varieties and diverse means to achieve them. For crosscultural purposes, its emphasis on practice is extremely useful, as it discusses process, not doctrine or belief. Fundamentally, yoga explains how and why we hold beliefs and feelings, it does not dogmatically dictate <u>what</u> to believe, feel, or do.

Yoga regards life as a continuing relationship between two fundamental experiences, <u>prakrti</u> and <u>puruṣa/ātman</u>. The ātman or "true nature" is amply described in the Svetasvatara Upaniṣad:

Than whom there is naught else higher,
Than whom there is naught smaller, naught greater,
The One stands like a tree established in heaven.
By Him, puruṣa, this whole world is filled.
That which is beyond this world
Is without form and without ill.
They who know That, become immortal;
But others go only to sorrow.   SU:3:9-10[4]

In reading this or any other text describing the highest nature of man, it is important not to regard the self as a thing. When reified or objectified, the concept of self loses its dynamism and its existential appeal. The self is an experience, a body-feel, a state of utter absorption, not an ideal to be obtained in some external fashion.

The state of absorption, wherein the separation between subjective and objective breaks down, is referred to in the Bhagavad Gita as the "higher self." Although this contrasts with the "lower self," both are necessary for human life; their relationship is reciprocal, not mutually abnegating.[5] The cause for the lower forms of embodiment rests in a fundamental misidentification. The seer (puruṣa/ātman) is always a witness, always neutral and inactive (SK19). However, due to lack of discrimination, the seer (puruṣa) becomes identified with the seen (prakriti): draṣṭr-dṛśyayoh samyogo heya-hetuh (YS II:17). This attribution of consciousness to an aspect of the non-conscious prakrti results in suffering and must be somehow overcome. Within prakrti, the culprit is the finite, limited self-sense (ahamkara, literally, "I-maker"). The ahamkara erroneously claims experience to be its own and fixes the world as seen from its own limited perspective. The lower self elevates itself to the status of highest priority: all that matters is what relates to the "me." Arjuna's distraction in the first chapter of the Bhagavad Gita serves as a perfect example of this dilemma. With this attitude in control, a damaging rigidity arises, and the pain of samsāra continues. With each action a seed for further action is planted; as these seeds mature and flourish, strengthening selfish motives, the primal, pure puruṣa mode of detached witnessing becomes concealed. The breath of life is constricted, and the threefold suffering continues.

In such states, puruṣa and prakṛti no longer interact in reciprocity; only prakrti is apparent. The antidote for this "disease" is found through meditation, during which the non-selfish, purusa state may be engaged and embodied. To achieve this goal, the Yoga Sutra prescribes many different paths, all aiming to effect citta-vṛtti-nirōdha, the suppression of mental modifications (YS 1:2). The mental modifications, which comprise the play of prakṛti, are five in number: cognition, error, imagination, sleep, and memory (YS I:6). When these are held in abeyance and the play of the guṇas is supended, the highest self gains ascendancy and the freedom of detachment is made present.

Essentially, yoga is technique. It does not describe experience for the sake of description; the elaborations on the means to knowledge and the causes of suffering (kleśa) are important only in that they provide a conceptual framework, ultimately to be transcended through meditation. The system is not metaphysical or ontological: it does not posit entities or explanations of how "things" are. It is, however, a phenomenological investigation of suffering and its transcendence, its sole presupposition being that each person has the ability to reach a state of liberation. Furthermore, yogic liberation is given no embellishment; there are no dogmatic limitations placed upon moksha. The closest "definition" is dharma-megha, a beautifully metaphoric and appropriately vague term which lends itself to a variety of interpretations, including "cloud of virtue."

How can yoga, a tradition steeped in Indian culture and atmosphere, be translated for application by Westerners? Have the attempts made by various Indian teachers been at the sacrifice of yoga? Or can yoga be applied universally to enrich non-Asian religious practices? In order to answer these questions, the basic presupposition of yoga must be examined, to see if the needs which gave rise to yoga are also relevant in the post-modern, technological era. Along with virtually all systems of Indian philosophy, yoga is predicated on the supposition that humankind is plagued with discomfort and suffering (duhkha) and that this suffering can be alleviated. The Yoga Sutra states "the pain of the future is to be avoided" (heyam duḥkham anāgatam II:16). To the extent that this analysis holds true, yoga can be applied by any individual seeking self-fulfillment of a spiritual kind. If someone has perceived a degree of suffering in life, yoga practice offers a means to transcend that suffering. Unless one shares the basic intent of alleviating pain, the suitability of yoga would be questionable. (I recall the experience of one individual who, after three years of graduate studies in Buddhism abandoned the field, primarily because he did not see life as inherently painful.)

All over the world, yoga and systems related to yoga are being practiced; discontented people are searching for viable paths of transformation. Part of the appeal of yoga lies in the many diverse means it prescribes. Patanjali offers the practitioner an abundance of practices. The student of yoga is told that the liberating suppression is achieved through well-cultivated practice and detachment (YS I:12-14). One who applies faith, energy, mindfulness, non-dual awareness, and insight (śraddhā, vīrya, smṛti, samādhi, prajña), is said to gain success (YS I:20). Another way is to devote one's meditation to the primal teacher, īśvara, who remains untainted by the ravages of change inflicted by association with prakṛti (YS I:24). This teacher defies objectifcation as an external deity, being also identified with the recitation of the syllable om, a self-generated vibration within the body of the practitioner. Appropriate behavior in interpersonal relationships is seen to be another tool for self-evolution: "One should cultivate friendship with the joyful, compassion for the sorrowful, gladness toward those who are virtuous, and equanimity in regard to the non-virtuous; through this, the mind is pacified" (YS I:33). The emphasis here is on flexibility, being able to recognize a situation and act as called for. Goodness does not suffice in all circumstances; at times, the best lesson is provided by restraint, as in the cultivation of equanimity among those who are non-virtuous (apuṇya).

Breathing is seen as a means to achieve the peace of nirodha (YS I:34). By recognizing the most fundamental of life's processes, a closeness to self is achieved. The word ātman is in fact derived from the verbal root āt, breathe. The Chāndogya Upaniṣad tells the story of a contest among the bodily functions of speaking, seeing, hearing, thinking, and breathing. Each respective faculty takes a turn at leaving the body and remaining away for a year. When speaking leaves, the body becomes dumb; when the eye leaves, blindness results; upon the departure of the ear, deafness follows; and when the mind leaves, a state of mindless sets in. But when the breath begins to go off, "as a horse might tear out the pegs of his foot-tethers all together, thus did it tear out the other Breaths (speaking, etc.) as well. They all came to the breath and said 'Sir! Remain! You are the most superior of us. Do not go off!'" (CU, V:1:12).[6] Of all bodily functions, the breath is the most fundamental, without which life is not possible. In gaining control over the breath, the yogin masters the other senses, including the thinking process (YS I:34, II:49-53).

Other practices prescribed in the Yoga Sūtra include directing one's consciousness to one who has conquered attachment (vita-raga), or meditating on an auspicious dream experience, or centering the mind in activity, or cultivating thoughts which are sorrowless and illuminating, or by any other means, as desired (YS I:35-39).

The purpose of these various practices is to diminish the influence of past actions which have been performed for selfish or impure motives (kleśa). These motives are five in number and catalogue pitfalls in the path. The first, non-wisdom (avidyā) is seen to be the cause of the other four. Patanjali describes this kleśa as "seeing the atman, which is eternal, pure, and joyful, in that which is non-atman, non-eternal, impure, and painful" (YS II:5). The "I" mistakes its limited experience for the ultimate reality, and life is pursued through combinations of the other four klesas: from the attitude based solely on self-orientation and self-gratification (asmitā), or clinging (rāga), despising (dveṣa), or because of an insatiable desire to hold on to life (abhiniveśā) (YS II:6-9). These influences, which color body-felt experience, must somehow be lessened in order for the experience of freedom to take place.

The yogic process of transformation begins at the ethical level. Through the adherence to particular behavorial practices, the yogin begins to erode the bank of past impressions which have bound him to a life of rigidity. In recent times, freedom has been equated with an ability to do whatever one wants. For the yogin, freedom is found through disciplined action. By restraint from violence, stealing, hoarding, and wantonness, and through the application of truthfulness, the influences of the self-centered past are lessened. Cultivation of purity, contentment, forbearance, study, and devotion to a chosen symbol (isvara-pranidhāna) establishes a new way of life, deconstructing the old, painridden order and constructing a new body of free and responsible action. Yama and niyama, although listed first among Patanjali's eight limbs, are not to be seen as preliminary practices. As Feuerstein points out, "it would be quite wrong to interpret these 'members' as stages, as has often been done. Rather they should be compared with functional units, which overlap both chronologically and in their activity."[7]

The world is intended and constructed through personal behavior, and the world created by the practitioner will continue to operate, even when the state of kaivalyam is reached. The Sāmkhya Kārikā states that even when the highest wisdom has been attained, and prakrti has displayed herself and retreated, the force of past impressions causes the body to continue to operate, just as a potter's wheel spins on even after the kick of the potter ceases (SK 67). Similarly, the state of dharma megha, so tersely mentioned in the Yoga Sūtra, does not seem to imply that life evaporates. Rather, this may be seen as a cloud wherein the totality of the non-dual experience is made apparent, and all distinctions of "grasper, grasping, and grasped" dissolve (YS 1:41). In conventional consciousness, the world stands against and apart from the experiencer. Through yoga, self unites with circumstance, and the ground of all possibilities is laid open. Life does not cease, but is freed from the constraints of a limited perspective.

The system of yoga, which has been only briefly considered here, presents various avenues by which the pettiness of self-centered orientation may be overcome and the fullness of human potential may be realized. It is not explicitly theological, yet it is immensely practical. The notion of deity is suggested as an expedient means for entering meditation; emphasis is placed on the iṣṭa devatā, the idea that the object of meditation is chosen by the practitioner according to his or her desire (YS II:44). This non-doctrinal, non-dogmatic approach is Hinduism at its best, and even defies the label "Hindu." In fact, the same practices and closely related philosophies spread throughout Asia with Buddhism. In both Hinduism and Buddhism, the human condition is regarded in much the same manner. Two pathways are open to humankind, kliṣṭa (associated with ignorance) and akliṣṭa (oriented towards enlightenment). By continually generating kliṣṭa behavior or "worlds," one is bound to misery. By cultivating the opposite, the practitioner of meditation builds a life of responsible freedom.

Given the basic thrust of yoga as practice, not belief, it has served as a bridge between cultures and diverse religious forms for millenia. At the beginning of this paper, Vivekananda was mentioned as a great bringer of Eastern truths to the West. He was certainly far from the first Indian to transmit Indian philosophy to foreign places. Bodhidharma took Zen to China (the Sanskrit word for meditation (dhyāna) became transliterated as Ch'an in China, and Zen in Japan). Padmasambhava introduced Buddhist meditation techniques in Tibet. Closer to the Western world, major texts on yoga such as the Yogavāsiṣtha were translated into Persian during the 13th century. At even earlier times, Indian influence on Greek and Roman thinking through various trade routes is well documented.[8]

This dialogue between India and the world has not been a one-way street. Mughal rule greatly influenced large sectors of the population. British rule in India led to a new cultural and philosophical exchange. A sizeable group of respected English scholars held the native philosophies of India in high regard. Concurrently, Indians began imbibing in European traditions. Ram Mohan Roy, partly due to his exposure to and exchange with Christian missionaries in Bengal, contributed greatly to the revitalization of Hinduism, incorporating some dimensions of church services into the meetings of the Brahmo Samaj. This in turn influenced later Hindu movements, and undoubtedly made Vivekananda's message more easily understood during his lecture tours of the late 19th century and early 20th century.

Since 1967, yoga has again caught the imagination of thousands, perhaps hundreds of thousands of Americans. Numerous swamis and yogis have formulated teachings which appeal to an almost exclusively non-Indian audience. What explains the success of Swami Satchitananda, Swami Prabhupada (A.C. Bhaktivedanata), Yogi Bhajan, Sri Chinmoy, Swami Rama, and Amrit Desai? Much of their success is due undoubtedly to a sense of alienation which pervaded the youth of the West during the sixties and seventies; gurus from India offered a new sense of identity through which they could "find themselves." Many have been disappointed, discovering what Harvey Cox refers to as the Orient which is "a myth that resides in the head of Westerners."[9] And although he surmises that the answers to life may be found on "the horse we have been riding all along,"[10] others have found a new way of life through Asian religious practice, whether yoga, Tibetan Buddhism, or Zen.

If genuinely presented, meditation does not strive to create a new cultural--or cult--identity, but provides the occasion for insight into the very presuppositions which determine the need for personality. Yoga does not require an identity crisis wherein a better self-image is sought; rather, yoga has as a prerequisite a desire to examine and overturn all notions which perpetuate clinging to self-identity. If yoga is to be effective in bridging cultural sensibilities, it must be divorced from popular psychology, from limited religious views, and from the charisma of its proselytizers. Yoga, in itself, is cross-cultural; it requires no further embellishments or ornamentation. It can be used by Hindus, Buddhists, Christians, Sufis, and Sikhs, but the practice remains universal, not bound by the symbols chosen or the language used to convey its teachings.

As never before, Americans and Europeans are intellectually and spiritually prepared to benefit from Asian meditation techniques. However, unless the needs spoken to by the traditions are the needs motivating practice, the would-be practitioner runs the risk of self-deception and, perhaps, a few wasted years. Education about yoga must accompany education in yogic techniques, to ensure that the remedy suits the illness. Yoga is a cross-cultural tool for cultivating religious insight, and has demonstrated a universal applicability. Its effectiveness rests on a desire to transcend suffering; for one who shares this desire, yoga offers a way of release.

ABBREVIATIONS

SK   Sāmkhya Kārikā

YS   Yoga Sūtra

SU   Śvetāśvatara Upaniṣad

CU   Chāndogya Upaniṣad

NOTES

[1] Harvey Cox, Turning East: Why Americans Look to the Orient for Spirituality -- And What That Search Can Mean to the West (New York: Simon and Schuster, 1977).

[2] Agehananda Bharati, The Light at the Center: Context and Pretext of Modern Mysticism (Santa Barbara: Ross-Erikson, 1976).

[3] George Tyrrell, Through Scylla and Charybdis, or The Old Theology and the New (London: Longmans, Green, and Co., 1907).

[4] Robert Ernest Hume, The Thirteen Principal Upaniṣads (London: Oxford University Press, 1931), pp. 400-401.

[5] Antonio T. deNicolas, Avatāra: The Humanization of Philosophy Through the Bhagavad Gīta (New York: Nicolas Hays, 1976), p. 269.

[6] Hume, p. 228.

[7] Georg Feuerstein, The Essence of Yoga (New York: Grove Press, 1974), pp. 71-72.

[8] C. L. Tripathi, "The Influence of Indian Philosophy on Neoplatonism," in Neoplatonism and Indian Thought, R. Baine Harris, editor (Norfolk, Virginia: International Society for Neoplatonic Studies, 1982), pp. 273-292.

[9] Cox, p. 149.

[10] Ibid, p. 156.

GOD AND THE WORLD IN AN INDIAN HYPHENATED CHRISTIAN THEOLOGY

Christopher Duraisingh

It is highly appropriate that a Festschrift that honours Fr. Chethimattam has as its central thrust reflections upon religious experience and realities in the context of an increasing coalescence of the heritages of the East and the West. For, one of his major concerns has been to theologise at the intersection of the Indian and Judaeo-Christian traditions as both coalesce in the Indian-Christian experience. The following is a tentative exploration in theologising in the context of a conscious appropriation of the religious heritages of both East and West.

The Locus of Indian-Christian Theology as Doubly-Determined.

The locus of Indian-Christians and our "inner-history" include distinctly new elements than that of our fellow Christians in Euro-American and Third World countries. Simply put, we are not Christians who happen to be also Indians by accident of birth; nor are we Indians who have somehow come to be also Christians either by choice or birth. We are Indian hyphenated Christians, hyphenated wholes, wherein both the realities, "Indian" and "Christian" equally operate in our mental constructs. In a sense we are doubly-determined by two traditions, strands of the pan-Indian and particular components of the Judaeo-Christian according to our time and place. My own analysis of the imaginative writings of several lay bhaktas and lyrics of rural Christians tend to confirm this affirmation that the structure of religious consciousness as well as the reflective modalities of many Indian-Christians are co-constituted by the simultaneous operation of one or more strands of the pan-Indian religious heritage and one or more strands of the Judaeo-Christian heritage.

Perhaps this was best expressed by Mark Suder Rao, a lay theologian:

The idea of the confluence of two streams of thought and faith, sangam, of East and West, in the heart of the Indian Christians had then taken firm grasp of my thought and life...Supposing some thing has indeed happened in the religious consciousness...what would be the consequences for an Indian Christian theology?...In the mental constituents of an Indian Christian, somehow both the living ideas of the West and of the East had converged, each side retaining its distinctions and yet conjoined in a new configuration.[1]

If strands of the pan-Indian religious heritage--be it Islam, tribal religion, popular village bhakti or particular schools of Vedanta--are related to us in the way suggested above, then the shape of the question of the relation between the Christian Scripture and other Scriptures of the pan-Indian heritage will have to be raised differently. Scriptural texts belonging to those strands of Indian tradition that are constitutive of our linguistic, cultural, and mental constructs will form decisive elements of our 'inner-history.' They are not merely external to us as objects that we can objectively behold, examine and obtain conceptual mastery over; but rather they will be in an "effective" historical relation to us; that is, they will effectively determine our context of theology and interpretation.

If the relation is as dynamic and determinative of our perceptual and conceptual processes as I have described above, then the act of theologising is not what is often described as "indigenization," indigenizing something that is alien and external to us.[2] Instead, theologising begins with a discovery of the indigenous emerging within the context of a coalescing and a growing-together of strands of the two traditions in the private and corporate inner history of the Indian-Christian faith community.

Our memory out of which we understand in the present is thus doubly determined; our praxis as Indian-Christians is to be identified the praxis of other fellow Indians, members of larger pan-Indian traditions; our hopes and anticipatory awareness are shaped also by the same forces that shape the hopes and aspirations of other Indians. I do not think that much of the theologising that goes on in India has yet taken seriously this doubly-determined locus of our theological existence in India today. The dominant mode or approach to non-Christian heritage hitherto has been to reduce it as the necessary indigenous form for the expression of the unchanging core of the Christian faith. But if one accepts the doubly-determined character of Indian-Christian theological existence, then I believe that we are called upon to reject every form of essentialist approach to theology, an approach that is committed to a historical understanding of an allegedly unchanging core of a faith which needs only to be clothed, from time to time, in thought forms created by the contingencies of varied historical settings. If we do not accept a clear-cut and universally valid conceptuality for Christian theology, then Indian-Christianity is better understood as an emergent process, a continuous confluence, which comes to be what it is as the two traditions--their specific strands in particular time and place--dynamically act and interact shaping the thought and praxis of Indian-Christian communities; and it is through that operation of dual traditions that authentically indigenous perceptions of God, world, Christ, humans, and their inter-relationships take place. What happens in this process is not a mere cognitive comparison of a concept from the Indian tradition with another from the Judaeo-Christian heritage. Rather, as the two traditions operate upon the Indian-Christian perceptual processes, authentically indigenous and primordial images and root metaphors <u>emerge</u>.

Illustrating such a process of indigenous image formation, Raimundo Panikkar compares two ways of learning a language: "One proper to adults and foreigners; the other peculiar to children and natives....The first way proceeds by comparing 'words' with 'words'..., but the child and the native learn by discovering relation between words and things..."[3] The difference is between a process of "inward integration" and external "assimilation." Is it too much to claim that Indian-Christians are natives and children in both traditions?

The following is a tentative exploration of the implications of the above description of Indian-Christian doubly-determined life for theology. The particular strand of the pan-Indian heritage that is determinative for me is the viśiṣṭadvaita of Śri Ramanuja[4]. Of the Western Christian strands of theological thought, it is Process theology, particularly influenced by Charles Hartshorne[5], that has been more determinative in shaping these reflections.

<u>Toward An Indian-Christian Understanding of the Relation Between God and All-Else</u>

"Then therefore the enquiry into Brahman:"[6] these are the opening words of <u>Brahma Sūtras</u>, the most important composition of the essence of <u>Vedanta</u> in the form of aphorisms. They express, in no uncertain terms, that "knowing" <u>Brahman</u> is the most decisive quest of the Indian religious world. Everything that is said, done or thought is "for the purpose of originating such knowledge," says Ramanuja.[7] Therefore, he spends about one-hundred and fifty-six pages of packed prose in expounding the need, the conditions, the mode and the fruits of the knowledge of <u>Brahman</u> in his commentary on the first <u>sūtra</u> in his <u>Śribhāṣya</u>. Every other orthodox commentator on <u>Brahma Sūtras</u> does almost the same.

But no sooner does the Indian seeker begin to enquire into <u>Brahman</u> than he comes to realize that this enquiry invariably is accompanied by an enquiry about the world. For the very second sūtra raises the question, "...from whence the origin... of this," where "'this' denotes the entire world with its manifold wonderful arrangements, not to be fathomed by thought, and comprising within itself the aggregate of living souls... in definite places and definite times."[8] That is to say, any discourse about God immediately raises also the discourse about all-else that is. The compound problem of God and all-else is then the problem of the theologian's enquiry. Whether the conclusion is that Brahman is the only undifferentiated Consciousness as we find in Samkara or the Brahman is "that highest Person...who possesses infinite auspicious qualities...supremely merciful...from whom the creation, subsistence and reabsorption of the world proceed,"[9] as we find in Ramanuja, it seems that the discourse about God and the world are very closely related.

An Indian-Christian theologian who claims such a quest as his heritage, cannot but start with the same sort of questions. But more often than not both in the theology and preaching of the Indian Church, the emphasis has been upon the remedial work of Jesus saving one from guilt and sin. Acknowledging this predicament of the Indian Church, Bishop Appasamy states:

> A distinguished missionary thinker who, convinced of the weakness of the Hindu ethical sense, has tried by many arguments to deepen it has confessed that his efforts in this direction have not been of much avail. My own conviction is that a more effective way would be to begin with God and not with man. The Hindu has a real passion for God. He is willing to suffer the utmost in order to realize God. Here we have a very useful point of contact with him.... The Hindu should be first helped to understand the wonder and the depth of God's love.[10]

An Indian-Christian theology that does not begin with Brahma vidya or at least present Christa vidya primarily as that which has to do with God's essential manifestation of God's proper and perfect relation to all-else in space and time is bound to be unintelligible in the Indian context.

It can also be argued that discourse about God even within the Judaeo-Christian tradition involves a discourse about the world. Gordon Kaufman demonstrates both in his God the Problem[11] and in An Essay on Theological Method[12] that any speech about God within the Judaeo-Christian tradition "also implies a definite conception of the world within which man lives

114

and of man himself,"[13]   In his Essay he points out that the concept of God "stands in tandem" with the concept of the world.[14]   At any rate, for an Indian-Christian who consciously acknowledges that Ramanuja's theological tradition as well as the personalistic theistic affirmations of the Judaeo-Christian tradition constitute his heritage, the problem of the relation between God and the world is the central theological problem.

Right at the beginning of an Indian-Christian's reflection upon the problem, the theology and tradition of Ramanuja place before the theologian a central text from the Brhadāraṇyaka Upaniṣad:

> He who dwells in the self, who is in the self, whom the self does not know, whose body the self is, who rules this self from within, that one is your Self, the inner Ruler, the Immortal (III,7,20)[15]

The Judaeo-Christian tradition distinctly places before the theologian its central affirmation as follows:

> God so loved the world that he gave his only Son that whosoever believes in him should not perish but have eternal life (John 3:16).[16]

Here then, as the Indian-Christian attempts to understand the reality of God's relation to the world, he is faced with two different manners of conceiving the relation.

His Indian heritage presents God as the Self whose body is all-else. God is the all-including One and not simply the Other. Therefore in knowing the One, one comes to know all. Or in relating to the one true Self of all in love and devotion one relates to all. Besides, the self-body analogy is to some extent qualified by terms of interaction between the Supreme Self and the finite selves. For the Self is also spoken of as controlling, ruling and indwelling other selves.

The basic affirmation of the Judaeo-Christian tradition that we have uses the analogy of an inter-personal relation. God loves the world; he give his Son. The world thus stands in a relationship of God's love even though it has not recognized it and is at present in a state alienated from the love of God.[17]   This text also assumes the biblical picture that this world is a creation of God and that it has been given a certain amount of autonomy and freedom. The Creator God now takes the initiative for its salvation. It is God's purpose that the world be restored to its proper relation to its Creator. God's love is expressed by his Son, meaning God's self-initiated and self-enacted manifestation and execution of this love in time and space. The possible lack of immediacy within a social model is overcome by reference to loving and responding. Elsewhere in the tradition, in particular in the Gospel of John, this loving relation is taken to its climax and is described as a mutual abiding in one another. Reflecting upon this relationship of love, Bishop Appasamy says, "the religion of Christ is essentially a communion between God and the human soul."[18]

As the two traditions coalesce in the process of understanding in the Indian-Christian theologian, he is led to affirm that God is the One who includes all-else and at the same time acts and inter-acts with them in the most intimate love. His is an understanding of the relation between God and the world that emerges at the inter-play between an organic model, which holds that God relates to all-else as a self to its body, and as an inter-personal model, which holds that God and all-else are in a relation of love initiated by Jesus.[19] In other words, the basic analogical structure of such an Indian-Christian understanding of God's relation to all-else is a self-body relation radically qualified and interpreted by inter-personal relation (or vice versa). But Ramanuja recognizes that descriptive terms that arise out of a self-body analogy are not adequate in themselves to describe his understanding of God's relation to all-else; and, therefore, terms of social interaction are used even though these are not adequately brought together. In the following pages, then, and Indian-Christian understanding of God's relation to all-else is presented in terms of what can be called a socially-qualified self-body model.

Such a qualification is essential. For neither of the models in itself is adequate to articulate all that one's understanding about the reality of God's relation to the world entails. While each helps us to focus on some aspects, each can distort and misrepresent others. Therefore as R. H. King suggests qualifying a particular mode of discourse about God with other models is important to "make up for the limitations" and to help "correct for tendencies which might otherwise lead to misunderstanding."[20] For example, while the self-body analogy can help us to focus better on the immediacy and inclusiveness of God's relation to the world, it cannot adequately express the relative autonomy and freedom of the world of things and persons. This can be done only when the self-body analogy is radically qualified by inter-personal relational terms.

Let us first consider the role of the self-body analogy as it is theologically applied to express an understanding of God's relation to all-else. This will then be followed by an attempt to show how such an analogy, qualified by the terms of inter-personal relation, affects one of the central Christian motifs, namely, creation.

The particular use of a socially interpreted self-body analogy in this study is different from some of the standard ways in which mind-body relationship is conceived in modern thought. Leonard Levin in his unpublished dissertation "Deriving Theological Position from Mind-Body Interaction"[21] suggests twelve distinct possibilities; but only four of them are of any interest for the theistic understanding of God's relation to all-else. It is claimed here that even these four are inappropriate to our task and therefore they are distinguished from the particular use in this study.

First, let us consider the view that mind or mental properties and body or aspects of physical properties are identical. Surely this is inappropriate for describing God's relation to all-else. For both the traditions that we inherit insist upon the fact that there is a radical distinction between the nature of God and the nature of the world. God is affirmed to be omniscient and omnipresent and is not dependent upon anything outside himself for his being. But the world is entirely dependent upon God. Its contingent nature in all its parts would prohibit any such identification in a Christian theology.

Secondly, there is the mind-body parallelism according to which the mental and physical properties take place in two distinct parallel causal chains without any interaction. Occurrence in one causal chain may correspond to another, such as a physical event and the feeling of pain, but there is no causal interaction between them. Insofar as we affirm that God is directly involved with the world of things and persons through creating, recreating, and sustaining it, such a way of conceiving mind-body relation is inappropriate for our theological application.

Nor can the epiphenomenalistic conception of the relation between mind and body be appropriate for a theistic discourse about God's relation to all-else that we are proposing here. For such a view holds that mental aspects in themselves have no causal efficacy. It is rather the physical occurrences that determine the mental events. A theology that insists upon the radical

117

superiority and independence of God over all-else is totally incompatible with this notion.

Finally, there is the view known as mind-body interactionism. This is more attractive to many theologians, particularly to those who are influenced by Charles Hartshorne's development of process philosophy. However, the Indian-Christian who takes seriously the theological insights of Ramanuja as well as the classical Judaeo-Christian theologies would insist on the basic difference between the Christian notion of God all-else interaction and the modern notion of interactionism. The basic distinction is two-fold. First, while the theologian recognizes some form of interaction and mutuality between God and the world, there is a radical distinction in the basis of their relating to each other. In the theological view proposed here, finite selves respond to the supreme Self out of their need to do so; for they are entirely dependent upon God for their very existence. But this cannot be said about God. Even though God is in an inseparable relation (aprthaksiddhi) to all-else, he is in no way dependent on them for his being. Secondly, with the Judaeo-Christian theologies, it is affirmed here that the initiative for a responsive relation or mutuality comes solely from God. As Saint Paul says, "God shows his love for us in that while we were yet sinners Christ died for us."[22] A little later in the same passage the term sinners is replaced by the term enemies.

What is important to point out is that in this study, the term body is used to help grasp the nature or the relation that the world has to Brahman and not the nature or the properties that constitute the world of things and persons. Both the analogy and the analogate are relations and not entities. What is claimed here, therefore, is simply that the relation between God, the Supreme Person, and all-else is analogous to the relation of a self to its body. Even such a relation is qualified by relational terms from social relations. If we bear this in mind, objections to the analogy such as that the world is not physical or a single unified organism become irrelevant.[23]

Since it is the relation that is significant in the analogy, the primary conception of the body in this study has to do not with the property of the entities that constitute the world but rather with their functional role in their relation to their Self. Ramanuja consistently attempts to avoid the physical notion of God's body. At one place his reference to the body as deśa (field) is highly suggestive. Deśa is defined as the place or the focal point in and through which something like light or heat manifests itself and lets its influence be felt.[24] Expanding on his insight in terms of contemporary experience, we can state that the body is that field or region in and through which a self organizes its experiences, acts and expresses itself directly and immediately. In this sense, the self is the foundational center that integrates all activities and feelings in, around and through the body, the field. Therefore, the identity, the purpose, the value, and even the being of the body are dependent upon its relation to the self. For, without a relation to an organizing center, there can be no field.

Body, in this sense, may be constituted by many different entities and at times some parts may conflict with some others. But it is in and through the center that they find their cohesiveness, and common identity constituting them together as the body of a self. Thus, the self serves as the "one beyond the many" in which the many become one. Analogously, in spite of the plurality and disharmony that characterize the world, it is only in so far as the plurality of the entities in the universe contribute directly to the purposes of God, the "One beyond the many," that they can find their unity. It is in this sense that God is the Self of all-else, the center of being and interpretation. For in the words of H. R. Niebuhr, by the term "Self of the world" we refer not to some "one reality among the many but to the One beyond all the many, whence all the many derive their being, and by participation in which they exist."[25] As Christians, we can affirm that it is the eschatological hope that in spite of the present disharmony in the pluralities of God's body, there will be a perfect recentering of all in the Self, their only center; and then in the words of Saint Paul, "God will be everything to everyone."[26] This hope is founded on the belief that the Self of all provided a self-enacted pattern of such cohesiveness and purpose for all plural entities of the body in Christ Jesus and that in and through him a potency is at work in the whole body bringing into being restoration of harmony and purpose. The reality of the Church is the sign of the process of a recentering of disjointed members of God's body, the world, to the Self. Hence Saint Paul can say, that it has pleased the Self "to reconcile to himself all things" through Christ in whom "all things hold together."[27]

To sum up, our primary concern in the use of the analogy of the relation between self and body to describe the relation between God and all-else has to do with the relation and not necessarily with the nature and properties of the human self and the human body. In the latter sense, our analogy of the body to the world would have to be stretched beyond the breaking point. The primary significance of our reference to God as the Self of the universe is because of the fundamental theological understanding that God is the principle of being, purpose, value, unity and identity of the world of things and person. It is in this sense that God is the One in whom the many are integrated. But this statement has to be qualified by terms of social relation in such a way that the One also relates to and interacts with the members of its body.

Now we shall briefly consider the motif of creation in the light of what we have described as a socially qualified self-body bhava in the context of the Indian Christian Church.

An Indian-Christian Understanding of Creation.

An Indian-Christian concept of God would want to insist upon the following as they are suggested to the Christian from both the traditions that are inherited:

In the light of the contribution from the Indian heritage, it is affirmed that God cannot be conceived as external to and separable from the world and, therefore, the idea of God without a world is unthinkable and, at best, is an abstraction. At the same time, God is not identifiable with the world for the reality of God is qualitatively different from that of the world. God is the source of being, purpose, unity and value. In brief, God is the Self of the world; and the world as God's body is entirely dependent upon him for its origination, maintenance, and transformation.

The Judaeo-Christian tradition insists that the reality and the plurality of the world must be maintained; the world has been given relative autonomy though God as its Creator is its ultimate source of being and meaning. The world is brought out of nothing by the will of God. It is purposive, for it is the creation of a purposeful Creator. God as the Creator transcends the world both in its entirety and in its parts. God loves his creation and has taken the initiative in relating to it in love and in recreating it.

The Indian-Christian doctrine of creation is formulated at the intersection of these basic presuppositions and theological affirmations of both the traditions.

We start with the affirmation in both the traditions that God is the source of everything that has come to be. The Judaeo-Christian tradition has developed a concept of creatio ex nihilo. Insofar as the Judaeo-Christian tradition takes this concept not as

120

a description of the "how" of creation, its theological intention is primarily to deny that God depends upon something other than his own being, independently of his being to bring the world to be. The Indian heritage presents the world of things and persons as having always been co-eternal with God. But Ramanuja radically qualifies this by saying that the world prior to creation is in so subtle a stage that it is right to speak as though it was not. Further, anything that is or was other than Brahman is so radically dependent upon Brahman and inseparable from him that it is legitimate to say that it has no being other than the being of Brahman. When both the theological concerns are qualified in this way, creation is God's self-expressive free and volitional act out of which a world of plural entities comes to be which does not have its origin in anything except the being of God. In this sense, creation for an Indian-Christian is neither a simple bringing to be, that is, a process by which a Creator-God suddenly brings about something from nowhere or nothing at his will and power and sets it over against him nor is it a self-projection or self-transformation of Brahman or part of Brahman into a new form. It surely is not Brahmaparinama, a transformation of God. Rather, it is primarily a divine self-expression, an act in which the being of God is involved fully and not merely his power or purpose. But it is meaningless to speak of an act without some form of embodiment. Hence, creation is that volitional and purposive act of God through which a real world of pluralities come to be out of nothing but God's own being which includes an utterly dependent, inseparable, and indistinguishably subtle body. God's purpose and volition are so direct, immediate, and effective that they bring out of his subtle body, the manifold world. As Nicholai Berdyaev puts it, "Creation of the world implies movement in God; it is a dramatic event in the divine life."[28] Insofar as the divine body has no being of its own, the act of bringing the world to be is a creation out of nothing-other-than-the-being of God. Insofar as what has come to be is relatively independent of the being of God and distinguishable from him, it is a creative act, a srsti. For the created order of finite selves and things now comes to have a reality of its own and in some sense stands in interaction with its Creator. But at the same time, insofar as the manifest world is still related to God as his body and it has no ultimate meaning or being apart from him the process can also be spoken as a new sthiti, state. It is a transformation from an earlier state of utter lack of any identity to one of relative self-identity. It is because of this new state of distinction and identity that a contrast of the world as creation to God as Creator is possible. But this new state should not be misunderstood merely as a relocation of an exactly the same entity from one location into another in space and time. It has a new state in that

121

it is now relatively autonomous through Brahman's willing act. It has now a new identity of its own and, in some sense, can assert itself over against its true Self. Therefore, for an Indian-Christian theology proposed here, neither the term "creation" nor the term "transformation of state in itself" is adequate to describe the process of the manifest world coming to be. It is both; it is God's volitional act of creative transformation.

Furthermore, in this act of creative transformation, it is God who chooses what is to be and how it is to be. Ramanuja's theology has radically qualified a traditional notion of creative process in the larger Indian tradition. For, according to that view, the notion of creation is simply an initiation of another phenomenal process in which the law of karma could work itself out. Ramanuja introduces into such a scheme the notion of divine grace and will; the Judaeo-Christian tradition strengthens one's perception of God's purposiveness in the world process. The result is that creation is construed both as a transformative state as well as a creative act, an expression of God's will, purpose, and self-involvement.

In God's continuing creative act in the world, i.e., God's providential act, the past has an important part to play. But here again insofar as saṃsāra is not simply a process where the law of karma works its way, God cannot be conceived simply as the overseer of such a process. Rather, in grace and through his active will, God provides particular finite selves, particular effects of their past acts. In the place of the law of karma, it is the divine grace and intention for the liberation of his creatures that serve as determinate factors in mediating the effects of the past in the present and in bringing into being a new future in terms of the acts of the present. In this sense, the present world process is a purposive one conditioned by the grace and will of God for the salvation of his creatures. The past is significant for the present and the present for the future, but only insofar as their potency is mediated through God. Therefore, as the Judaeo-Christian tradition insists, time and the process of history become important; for history itself is now the locus of God's working out his purpose of grace. The self-body relation, through the Judaeo-Christian tradition, is radically temporalized. Past, present, and future are no longer determined by a principle apart from the ultimate Principle of world's being and purpose, namely, God, the Self of all.

Within a socially qualified understanding of self-body relation, God does not function merely as Creator or the agent of providence, but he also functions as the indwelling controller or guide (Antaryāmin). He inspires, checks, and guides the jīvas without totally determining the outcome. For the finite selves are relatively free and autonomous. They are also agent-selves. With the aid of the indwelling and inspiring Self within, they work out their future. The Self within conditions the context and inspires the process, but the determinate shape of the outcome is also partly dependent upon the response of the finite selves to their indwelling Self.

NOTES

[1] "Christa Darśana: A Christian Vision of Reality," Religion and Society, 14 (1967), 6.

[2] See my "Alternate modes of theologising now prevalent in India," Religion and Society, 27 (1980), 84ff.

[3] "Indian Philosophy and Christian Doctrine," Frontier, I (1958), 271-272.

[4] Of the many works of Sri Ramanuja the most significant ones are Vedārtha-samgraha, Commentary on the Bhagavad Gita and Commentary on the Vedanta Sutras. The edition of the latter used in this essay is the Translation by George Thibaut, Sacred Books of the East, vol. 48.(Oxford: Clarendon Press, 1904). Sri Ramanuja is an eleventh-century thinker belonging to the Sri Vaisnava tradition in the Tamil speaking part of South India. The best secondary work on his theology of J. B. Carman, The Theology of Ramanuja,(New Haven: Yale University Press, 1974). References to Ramanuja's Vedanta-Sutras tr. by Thibaut are shown below as SBh.,(T).

[5] Man's vision of God, (New York: Harper and Row, 1941)

[6] SBh.,(T), p. 3.

[7] Ibid., p.16.

[8] SBh., (T), p. 156.

[9] Ibid.

[10] The Gospel and India's Heritage, (Madras: SPCK, 1942), pp. 98-99.

[11] (Cambridge: Harvard University Press, 1972)

[12] (Missoula: Scholars Press, 1975).

[13] God, p. 105.

[14] Ibid., p. 28.

[15] This text is central in Ramanuja's theology. He introduces it in the opening section of his very first work, the Vedārthasamgraha: it is also one of the few texts that he

repeatedly refers to in the Sribhasya. It is significant that Appasamy who uses Ramanuja's theological writings identifies this text as crucial for understanding the Hindu theistic affirmations.

[16] Archbishop William Temple says that it is in this verse, "we come to the central declaration, more central for Christian faith than even the Word became flesh;. . . here is the whole great truth . . . This is the heart of the Gospel." (Readings in St. John's Gospel, First and second series, (London: Macmillan and Co., Limited, 1945), p. 48. Or again as A. J. Gossip puts it in his exposition of this verse in the Interpreter's Bible, "In the whole Word of God there must be few if any scriptures which have appealed so irresistibly to so many as vs. 16." vol. 8 (New York: Abingdon Press, 1952), p. 509.

[17] John 15:1-17; 17:26.

[18] What is Mokṣa, (Madras, 1931), p. 36.

[19] The phrase is from Austin Farrar referred to by R. H. King, The Meaning of God (Philadelphia: Fortress Press, 1973), p. 111.

[20] The Meaning of God., p. 88.

[21] Unpublished Ph.D. dissertation, Brandeis University, 1973, pp. 5-10.

[22] Romans 5:8.

[23] Several of these objections can be met. For example, let us take the objection that the world is not a simple homogeneous physical property or an organism such as the body and that therefore the world cannot be analogous to the body. First, it can be argued that even the human body is not simply a homogeneous entity or a simple physical thing as we used to understand it. Rather, we are increasingly becoming aware of the fact that it in itself is a complex world or a process of internal action and interaction. Secondly, in so far as our referent in a theological discourse is the body of God, in the words of William James, "the particular features of our body are adaptations to a habit so different from God's that if God have (sic) a physical body at all, it must be utterly different from ours in nature." Cited by William J. Wainwright, "God's Body," Journal of American Academy of Religion, 42 (1974), 476.

Wainwright addresses three other objections to the notion of the world in its entirety or in its physical or mental aspects being said to be the body of God; see particularly pp. 476-479.

[24] SBh., (T), p. 564.

[25] Radical Monotheism and Western Culture (New York: Harper, 1960), p. 32.

[26] I Corinthians 15:28.

[27] Colossians 1:17, 18.

[28] Cited in C. Hartshorne, Man's Vision, p. 230.

WEST IS WEST: DIALOGUE IN THE WEST

THE TWENTIETH-CENTURY ENCOUNTER OF THE CHURCHES

Kuncheria Pathil

After centuries of separation, when the Churches met together in the Ecumenical Movement of the 20th century, they were surprised to discover the unity of their faith and the richness as well as complementarity of their diversity. In fact, the historical divisions in the Church happened as a result of the insistence on uniformity to the extent of condemning the diversity of the theological and doctrinal formulations. The insistence on uniformity was the consequence of the alliance between the Church and the State. Uniformity was necessary for the political stability of the Empire, and the Church had been used by the State as a tool for uniformity and political power. The forces that led to the condemnation of the so-called Nestorian and Monophysite Churches in the fifth century and to the separation of Eastern and Western Churches in the eleventh century were more political and socio-cultural than doctrinal. Similarly, the sixteenth-century Europe was politically and culturally very much divided, and it influenced to a great extent the Reformation and the subsequent divisions in the Western Church. Today, in the ecumenical movement the Churches have learned that unity is not uniformity, but unity in diversity, unity in faith and diversity in faith-expressions.

In the following pages we shall briefly outline how the different Christian Churches met together in the contemporary ecumenical movement in search of their visible unity and what the different stages of this encounter were. A gradual but radical change in the attitude and self-consciousness of the Churches is clearly visible, a change from self-righteousness and self-absolutization to repentance, self-questioning and mutual recognition. We believe that the history and development of Christian ecumenism can teach several lessons to the wider ecumenism or to the encounter between the different religious traditions which is one of the major concerns of this volume.

Historical Background of the Contemporary Ecumenical Movement

To understand the phenomenon of the contemporary ecumenical movement and its impact on the Churches, one has to start with the historical background of this new quest for the visible unity of the Churches. Evangelical Awakening of the 19th century and the subsequent missionary movement was the birthplace of the ecumenical movement. German Pietism, English

Methodism and American Revivalism were all inspired with great missionary zeal. Personal piety, spiritual experience and fellowship were the common characteristics of these movements. And, naturally, this revivalism was coupled with the desire to share the spiritual experience and thus to extend the fellowship. Thus, several missionary societies and organizations were formed, and missionaries were sent all over the world to preach the Gospel and to convert all peoples to the Christian faith. When the missionaries from the different denominations met together in the mission lands, they realized increasingly that division among them was a scandal to the non-Christians and an obstacle to the success of missionary work. The native Christians from the mission lands also realized that the divisions in Christianity imported by the missionaries had no meaning for them in their land. Why should they who are united as Hindus or Tribals be converted into the different brands of Christianity and thus be divided. So the plea for One United Church and the search for the rediscovery of the visible unity of the Churches came first from the mission field.[1]

The Evangelical Awakening and the Missionary Movement inspired and contributed also to the formation of several Voluntary Movements which were interdenominational or ecumenical, like the Young Men's Christian Association (YMCA), the Young Women's Christian Association (YWCA), the Student Christian Movement (SCM), and so on. All these late Nineteenth-century movements, although their primary objective was not the restoration of the visible unity of the Churches, in fact, united young men and women and students from all Churches in prayer, discussions, Bible studies and common missionary and social action. The young men and women as well as the students were convinced that denominational differences should not prevent them from coming together on the basis of their fundamental unity as Christians. On the other hand, they realized that they could be loyal Christians only if they live faithfully in their own denominations or traditions. Thus, in these movements or associations the great ecumenical principle or a new method for ecumenical conversation was developed that ecumenism did not mean to be undenominational,
but interdenominational, namely, it was made possible that loyal members from the different Churches could meet together without making any compromise to truth or to their convictions.[2] Thus contemporary ecumenical movement was prepared by the Voluntary Movements of the late 19th century, and the great leaders and pioneers of ecumenical movement were born in and brought up by the SCM, YMCA and YWCA.

The two World Wars and the sufferings, agonies, and catastrophies they inflicted upon humanity aroused in the minds of many Christians a longing for unity and a sense of responsibility that the Churches should function as a force of unity in a disintegrating and divided world. It is often said that the contemporary ecumenical movement was born in the prison cells and in the concentration camps where Christians from different Churches experienced a deeper fellowship and thus discovered that they had much more in common than they had thought and that they should express their unity in a visible way.

The experience of a deeper unity among the Christians was supported and nurtured by the great theological movements of the 1940's and 1950's, like, Biblical Theology, Liturgical Movement, and the scientific study of the history of the Church and its divisions, all of which cut across denominational divisions. Although the Bible was accepted as the Word of God by all the denominations, the biblical interpretation had been for centuries the bone of contention among them. But modern scientific, historical, and critical tools and methods for studying the Bible provided a common basis for all Christians, and the biblical exegetes and theologians, irrespective of denominational differences reached the same conclusions. Thus contemporary biblical theology became the meeting-point of all the Churches and a force of unity. Similarly, the contemporary liturgical movement united all the Churches by means of an authentic liturgical reform in all the Churches, Catholic and Protestant. The Catholics rediscovered the importance of the Word of God and the Protestants the value of the sacraments. The scientific study of history which challenged and transcended all denominational readings and interpretations of history provided another strong basis or common meeting-place for all the Churches. It was admitted by all that denominational readings of history has been too subjective, partial, one-sided and often exaggerated. The Catholic historians began to admit the positive contributions of the Reformers, and the Protestant historians agreed that the Reformers, to a certain extent, distorted the authentic Christian tradition. The origin and growth of the contemporary ecumenical movement should be understood against the background of these strong theological foundations.

The contemporary ecumenical movement may be also seen as an alliance or union of the Churches to defend themselves against the onslaughts of a secularized world. As the world became more and more secular, the institutional religions began to lose their power and control over the society and became weaker and weaker in all respects. Their survival itself in the contemporary world became problematic. To face this situation, the Christian Churches of the same denomination formed themselves into World Denominational Fellowships, like the Lambeth Conference, the Lutheran World Federation, the Baptist World Alliance, and so on. This movement of the formation of the Confessional Families for mutual support and co-ordination was started in the last part of the 19th century and was completed in the beginning of the Twentieth century.[3] As a second phase of this movement, the Churches belonging to different denominations began to unite themselves forming ecumenical organizations with the same objective of strengthening themselves over against the world and its challenges. So there is some truth in the thesis of the American sociologist Peter Berger and others who see the contemporary ecumenical movement as a kind of "cartellization" or "common market" of the Churches.[4]

This brief sketch of the background of the contemporary ecumenical movement may not be complete if we do not take into consideration the increasing sense of unity and solidarity in mankind, and the worldwide movements for the unity of the nations and of mankind as a whole. The formation of the UNO, the peaceful coexistence of the nations of different ideologies, the dialogue between the rich and the poor nations, the worldwide movements for human rights, and similar international movements are clear expressions of mankind's search for unity and its increasing awareness of human solidarity and interdependence.

Finally, as Christian believers we are inclined to see behind the contemporary ecumenical movement the invisible hand of God, the movement of the Holy Spirit who will lead us into the fulness of truth and unity through our common search and prayer. We cannot see the contemporary ecumenical movement merely as a human or ecclesial attempt for unity, but as a divine initiative for the realization of Christ's prayer that "they all may be one in us as you are in me and I am in you, so that the world may believe it was you who sent me".[5]

Growth of the Ecumenical Movement

Although the contemporary ecumenical movement was inspired and shaped by several historical and theological forces, its immediate origin and rapid growth was due to the missionary movement. It was in the mission field that the problem, disadvantage and scandal of a divided Christianity, was acutely felt, and it was the missionaries who initiated denominational co-operation and joint action. Several attempts were made to undertake mission work on a non-denominational basis by forming non-denominational societies like the London Missionary Society (LMS) with the intention of converting people to Christianity as such, and not to any denomination. But it was found to be merely idealistic, impractical, and even dangerous as it contained seeds of new divisions or new denominations. Missionaries gradually realized that what is needed is mutual recognition and not rivalry or unnecessary competition or duplication of work in the same area. So the denominations and missionary societies began to co-ordinate their work with agreements of "comity" (agreement with regard to the geographical distribution of the mission work of different denominations in order to avoid scandal and unnecessary competition). They also co-operated in the areas of education, Bible translation, social work, and so on.

The ecumenical co-ordination and co-operation in the mission field was promoted by the regional, national, and international missionary conferences. The General Conference on Foreign Missions, London (1878), the Centenary Conference on Foreign Missions, London (1888), and the Ecumenical Missionary Conference, New York (1900) were some of the important international missionary conferences. But these missionary conferences were, first of all, mainly of the Evangelical or Protestant groups. The Catholic, Orthodox, and Anglican circles remained outside this movement on doctrinal grounds that such co-operation would involve compromise of convictions or truth and would imply the recognition of the other Churches. Secondly, these missionary conferences were not of the Churches as such, but meetings of interested individuals. The participants of these conferences were not official delegates of the Churches, and the Churches were not bound by their decisions. Thirdly, these conferences were organized and participated in mainly by the Western missionaries. The Christians from the Third World or the Mission Countries themselves were not involved in planning and shaping their destinies. Important decisions which affected them were made by others. Therefore, these missionary conferences of the Nineteenth century cannot be considered as ecumenical in the full sense.

The World Missionary Conference of Edinburgh (1910) may be said to be the first ecumenical conference on missions in the full sense, and is often said to be the birth-place of the contemporary ecumenical movement. This conference organized by John R. Mott, J. H. Oldham, and other pioneers of the ecumenical movement was attended by 1200 delegates from all over the world. The conference emphasized the need for co-operation and unity and called the Christians "to plant in each non-Christian nation One Undivided Church of Christ." The younger Churches of the mission countries declared that they were grateful to the Western Churches for their mission, but the problem of disunity in their countries would be settled by themselves independently of the views and wishes of their parent Churches. The conference did not directly deal with the doctrinal and theological differences between the Churches nor with the conditions for unity. But it was accepted by all that the mission of the Church and the question of the unity of the Church cannot be separated. This was, perhaps, the greatest contribution of Edinburgh; namely, the concerns of mission and unity were brought together once for all as in the prayer of Jesus, "that they all may be one . . . that the world may believe."

The Edinburgh Conference gave inspiration and initiative to three international ecumenical movements--the International Missionary Council (IMC), Faith and Order Movement (FO), and Life and Work Movement (LW). All these three were later merged in forming the World Council of Churches (WCC), which is today the official forum or body of the ecumenical movement. Edinburgh conference itself appointed a Continuation Committee to pursue the work of Edinburgh, and in 1921 this Continuation Committee was transformed into a permanent organization called the International Missionary Council (IMC). It was meant to be an ecumenical agency of the missionary movement "to stimulate thinking and investigation on questions related to the mission," to help co-ordinate the activities of the national missionary organizations and Christian councils of the different countries and bring out united action."[6] The IMC achieved to a great extent these objectives through the sustained activity of its efficient and dedicated staff and through a chain of international missionary conferences--Jerusalem (1928), Tambaram, Madras (1938), Whitby, Canada (1947), Willingen, Germany (1952), Ghana (1957) and others. In 1961 at the New Delhi meeting of the World Council of Churches, the IMC and the WCC were integrated and the IMC became the "Commission on World Mission and Evangelism" of the WCC. This union of the IMC and WCC was a blessing both to the missionary movement and to the ecumenical movement. It stimulated the missionary consciousness of the Churches and the ecclesial consciousness of Evangelism, and the concerns of unity and mission were seen inseparable as two sides of the same coin.

Faith and Order Movement has been another main stream of the ecumenical movement, and its objective was precisely the restoration of the visible unity of the Churches by means of doctrinal dialogue among the Churches and of reaching consensus in matters of faith and order in the Church. Faith and Order

Movement also got inspiration from the World Missionary Conference in Edinburgh. Edinburgh, in fact, did not discuss directly matters of faith and order which had divided the Churches, because many had feared that discussions on doctrines of faith and decisions or resolutions concerning them on the basis of majority opinion might demand compromise of convictions and might cause further divisions. But during the Edinburgh conference it was felt by many participants that while dealing with the mission of the Church the question of unity could not be left aside and that the Churches should be ready to enter into dialogue on matters of faith and order which had divided the Churches. Returning from Edinburgh in 1910, Bishop Charles Brent of the American Episcopal Church and others succeeded in persuading their Church to convene a World Conference to discuss matters of faith and order to which all Churches which confessed "Jesus Christ as God and Saviour" were invited. Almost all the Churches except the Roman Catholic Church, responded positively to this call and they came together at Geneva in 1920 for a preliminary meeting which prepared a plan for the World Conference. The first World Conference on Faith and Order was held at Lausanne in 1927, the second at Edinburgh in 1937, and the third at Lund in 1952. With the formation of the WCC in 1948, the Faith and Order Movement became a constituent part of the WCC, but it continued the discussion on matters of faith and order in the WCC Assemblies and in the meetings of the Faith and Order Standing Committees and Plenary Commissions.[7] In 1968 the Roman Catholic Church joined the Faith and Order Movement by permitting Catholic theologians to participate in the Faith and Order meetings as official members. After frank discussions and exchange for more than half a century, today the Churches in the Faith and Order Movement have learned from each other, reformed themselves, and are proposing now an act of mutual recognition on the basis of a common document on Baptism, Eucharist, and Ministry.[8]

Life and Work Movement was the third wing of the contemporary ecumenical movement which brought the Churches together not to discuss their internal disputes and differences, but to witness together as Christians in the world, to promote fellowship and peace among the nations torn apart by war and conflicts, and to establish justice and lawful order in society on the basis of the Christian principles of truth, justice and love. The watchword of the movement was "doctrine divides, service unites," which implied that the Churches will be reunited only by their common witness and action in the world. Although the movement had its antecedents in the World Alliance of the Churches for promoting International Friendship (Konstanz, 1914) and in the Conference on Christian Politics, Economics, and Citizenship (Birmingham, 1924), it was Nathan Soderblom, the Lutheran Archbishop of Uppsala who, on the eve of World War I, fully conscious of the Churches' role and task in an unjust and conflicting world, initiated and promoted the Life and Work Movement. The first World Conference of Life and Work was held at Stockholm in 1925 in which almost all the Churches except the Roman Catholic Church participated by sending official delegates. To carry on the work of the movement, a Continuation Committee was appointed by the Stockholm conference, and in 1930 this committee was reconstituted as a permanent body with the name, "The Universal Christian Council for Life and Work." The second World Conference of Life and Work was held at Oxford in 1937 and it passed the resolution to integrate it with the Faith and Order Movement in forming the World Conference of Churches. In the WCC, Life and Work Movement continued to function as the Department of Church and Society, which continuously remind the WCC and the ecumenical movement not to become introverted with the concerns of a narrow ecumenism, but to be involved in the world in the concrete problems of the wider humanity, for oikoumene means not merely the Church but the whole world.

The formation of the World Council of Churches heralded a new stage in the growth of the ecumenical movement. Inspired by the "League of Nations," a suggestion was made to form a "League of Churches" immediately after World War I. At the Faith and Order meeting of Lausanne (1927) it was proposed that a "Council of Churches" be evolved from the already existing ecumenical organizations. But some feared that it would endanger the independence and the particular objectives of the three movements--the Faith and Order, Life and Work, and International Missionary Council. But the leaders of the three movements were more or less the same persons, and the Churches actively involved in them were also the same that they increasingly realized that a lot of time, energy, and money was wasted by the independent existence and functioning of the three movements and that these movements should be co-ordinated and integrated. Besides, it also became clear that the concerns of these three movements are closely related that they can no more remain as separate: United service or joint action also required doctrinal and theological agreement that the dictum of "doctrine divides, service unites" had to be gradually abandoned. Faith and Order discussions also revealed that behind the doctrinal and theological disagreements lie deep the sociological, cultural, and political factors. Similarly, the mission of the Church was understood to be the unity of the whole mankind; mission and unity were found to be inseparable. These convictions paved the way to the formation of the World Council of Churches by the integration of the two movements--Faith and Order and Life and Work--in 1948 at Amsterdam₉ with the First Assembly of the World Council of Churches.[9] The Second Assembly of the WCC was held at Evanston (U.S.A.) in 1954, and the Third Assembly at New Delhi in 1961, where the International Missionary Council was also finally integrated to the WCC that it became fully the official organ of the contemporary ecumenical movement. The Fourth and Fifth Assemblies were held respectively at Uppsala (1968) and at Nairobi (1975), and the Sixth Assembly was recently held at Vancouver in 1983. Through these Assemblies of the WCC, which have become today world events, the ecumenical movement is undergoing significant changes. Thus, contemporary ecumenical movement is still in the process of growth and we cannot predict its future.

The WCC succeeded in co-ordinating all the ecumenical movements and organizations and in bringing the Churches together in a common forum for discussions, common witness, and joint action. Although the Churches are not bound by the decisions of the WCC, they can remain no more in isolation. The WCC today unites more than 300 member Churches representing about 400 million Christians. Although the Roman Catholic Church, which is the biggest Church, still does not have official membership in the WCC, there is official relationship between the two bodies in the form of a Joint Working Group to discuss common problems and concerns. The membership of the Roman Catholic Church in the WCC, although it involves tremendous psychological and administrative problems for the WCC, remains still an open question.

Stages in the Encounter between the Churches

The ecumenical movement is a movement of the Churches for the restoration of their visible unity which was lost due to the historical heresies, schisms, and divisions. The pioneers of the movement and the Churches themselves were fully aware that after centuries of separation unity could not be reestablished all on a sudden with one or two ecumenical conferences or joint statements, but it required continuous dialogue, sustained effort and patient awaiting. Ignorance and prejudice about the other Churches had to be shed off, and genuine mutual understanding had to be created. All Churches needed reform, renewal, and rediscovery of the wholeness of the Christian Gospel, as all of them without exception suffered from a certain fragmentation and disintegration of the Christian truth owing to the historical divisions and separations. The very concept of visible unity required revision.

Visible unity of the Churches should not be uniformity, but unity in faith and diversity in faith-expressions which would mean a "typology of Churches"[10] with mutual recognition, intercommunion, and a "conciliar fellowship." Thus the restoration of the visible unity of the Churches has entailed a long historical process, and, in fact, the encounter between the Churches has passed through different stages.

At the first stage of the encounter, the Churches in the ecumenical movement realized that it was premature to enter directly into any reunion negotiations, but certain first steps to unity were needed. Genuine mutual understanding was felt to be the necessary "first step" to unity. Centuries of isolated existence, inherited animosities, rivalries, prejudices, and mutual suspicion amounted to total ignorance and misunderstanding about the other Churches. The method used at this first stage for mutual understanding was the "comparative method." The pioneers of the ecumenical movement were convinced that "the beginnings of unity are to be found in the clear statement and full consideration of those things in which we differ as well as those things in which we are at one."[11] What they aimed at was "a candid but loving comparison of positive beliefs on the questions which need to be considered in promoting the unity for which the Saviour prayed."[12]

The comparative method practised at the first stage of the ecumenical movement was one of self-presentation and self-explanation by the representatives of the Churches, who were supposed to present the official views of their Churches, and not their person opinions. Nobody was expected to speak for others. The Churches patiently listened to each other. No discussion was held on who is right and who is wrong. No one was asked to give up anything or, for that matter, to accept anything. So, naturally, some of the Churches continued to claim absoluteness and exclusive possession of the fullness of the Christian truth and revelation, and argue that they alone are the true Church, whereas others accepted a kind of legitimate diversity acknowledging that the other Churches are also true and genuine. Once the different views and positions of the Churches on important doctrinal and theological questions were exposed clearly, it was natural and easy to compare them, to see the agreements and differences among them. Thus this stage of the encounter produced a lot of ecumenical documents stating the agreements and differences among the Churches on important doctrinal questions which were found to be crucial for the Churches' unity and disunity. To the surprise of all, the agreements among the Churches discovered that they were much closer to one another than they had thought. Thus the Churches realized that they had a fundamental unity which would provide a strong basis for visible unity.

Achievement of mutual understanding was the great asset of the first stage of the ecumenical movement. Listening directly to the representatives of the other Churches, encountering them in personal and private discussions, and stating clearly the agreements as well as differences among the Churches removed a number of misconceptions and prejudices and engendered better mutual understanding. Understanding and discovering others contributed to two other gains: First of all, listening to others and trying to understand their ideas, beliefs, and systems turned everybody back to himself, to understand, elaborate and interpret his own ideas, beliefs, and system and those of his own Church. Discovery of others led to the discovery of oneself. Secondly, the discovery of other Churches, their beliefs and practices meant a discovery of the fullness of the Christian Gospel and of the catholicity of the Church. The variety and richness of the many Churches provided a fuller and deeper understanding of the Christian truth and revelation and a new vision of Christian unity as the unity of a living organism with the diversity characteristic of the members of a healthy body.

But mutual understanding during the "comparative period" of the ecumenical movement was to a certain extent defective. Each one saw the other through the mirror of one's own Church, in one's own terms and categories. Real and genuine understanding of others required more strenuous work and more rigorous and scientific methods. Mutual discovery and understanding is rather a continuous task, an ongoing process, and at no point should it be stopped as if everything has been achieved, as if we have understood and discovered each other fully. Besides, mutual understanding among the participants of the ecumenical conferences did not mean by itself mutual understanding among the rank and file of the people and in the Churches as a whole.

The first encounter of the Churches and its comparative method had other setbacks too. Initial overenthusiasm in the ecumenical movement and the discovery of the fundamental unity among the Churches gave rise to a wrong tendency to avoid or minimize the real differences among the Churches. This tendency to gloss over the differences is clearly seen in the ecumenical statements of this period marked by a lot of ambiguous and vague formulas which have different meanings for different people. By voluntary ambiguity and calculated evasion of differences unity can never be achieved. Another defect of this stage of the ecumenical movement was a static conception of the views and positions of the

Churches as if they are fixed and unchangeable, and the defensive character of the comparative method which did not question any view or position with the consequence of a hardening of the differences and the revival of confessionalism. By confessionalism we mean the excessive consciousness of and concern for the particular doctrines and traditions of one's own denomination irrespective of the consideration of the question of truth and a tendency for absolutization and isolationism. Although the different Christian denominations or confessions are to be mutually recognized, confessionalism is something to be condemned. In confessionalism partial truths and insights are isolated and absolutized with the consequence of the refusal to examine seriously the claims of others of the possession of truth.

Discovery of the fundamental unity of all Christians was the great achievement of the first stage of the encounter between the Churches. But gradually the seriousness and stubbornness of the differences among the Churches began to be felt in the ecumenical movement. No way was found to tackle the fundamental differences among the Churches on the crucial question of the nature of the Church, its ministry, and sacraments. There appeared a definite cleavage among the Churches between the "authoritarian" and "personal" types of the Churches or between the "Catholic" and "Protestant" types of Churches. Thus the first stage of the encounter ended up in a cul de sac of diverse irreconcilable positions. And the major concern of the second stage of the encounter was how to deal with the differences among the Churches.[13]

The simple "comparative method" of the first stage could not deal with this question of the remaining differences. More critical methods were used to solve the problem of the differences among the Churches. Understanding others and their differences or disagreements became critical. The positions, views, practices, and life-styles of others were tested against the person of Jesus Christ and his teaching, against the Biblical witness and the Apostolic Tradition. Naturally, this critical norm was applied to one's own Church too. All Churches examined carefully how faithfully they preserved, interpreted, and handed down the Biblical message and the Apostolic Tradition, and whether they obscured, distorted, or fragmented it. It was a common study and search of all the Churches, demanded by their common life and fellowship in the ecumenical movement. The method they used at this second stage was the Christological Method. Namely, the positions, views, and practices of all the Churches were tested and questioned in the light of the teaching and example of Jesus

Christ as seen in the Biblical witness and in the Apostolic tradition. The Christological method, therefore, demanded common Biblical and historical studies. It challenged the historical positions, views, and practices in the light of the eschatological perspective which makes the historical traditions relative and provisional, inviting them to open up to the ever-coming inspirations of the Spirit of Christ who speaks through the "signs of the times."

The Christological method used at this stage of the encounter consisted of a twofold movement: First, it was a movement towards the center who is Jesus Christ. When we come closer to Christ, we become closer to one another; all the parts of a circle will be closer to each other when they come closer to the center. Unity is first and foremost not in relation to each other, but in relation to Christ. It was a call to all the Churches for self-criticism, for the reexamination of their positions, views, and practices, for renewal and reform by coming closer to Christ, and thus to be closer to one another. Secondly, it was a movement from the centre outwards to the different parts or points of the circle, a movement from Christ to the Church and to the Churches. Moving out from the centre on this Christological basis, it pushed the fundamental unity through the whole region of differences, until they are solved, or seen in a new light when related to the centre. By this process the fundamental unity of the Churches was seen in sharp relief, and many of the differences were pushed to a secondary place and seemed inclusive or less intractable. Focussing on the relation of Christ to the Church, its sacraments, and ministry made their sacramental nature (human and divine, visible and invisible) very clear as vehicles of God's grace. But, as human and visible, they were found to be in need of continuous reform. Thus at the second stage of the encounter the Churches made an attempt to overcome and transcend their differences by the Christological method and by the common study of the doctrinal issues, making use of the results of the contemporary Biblical and historical studies which were the meeting-point of all Churches. It made available to the Churches and the ecumenical movement a common language and a new experience of fellowship. Compared to the first stage and its comparative method, the Christological method was, indeed, a "Copernican change."[14] At the first stage each Church regarded the other Churches as planets rotating around it. But at the second stage all Churches perceived Christ as the sun, as the centre around whom all of them were rotating.

But the second stage and the Christological method did not succeed in achieving the visible unity of the Churches. The

Christological method had the presupposition that the common
Biblical and historical studies will at last lead the Churches
to the one true ecclesiology, to the one true Christology, to
the one true Pneumatology, to the one true sacramentology, and
to the one true doctrine of the ministry, and thus the differences
will be overcome. But this presupposition was challenged by
biblical scholars and historians who spoke of the existence of a
diversity of ecclesiologies, Christologies, Pneumatologies,
sacramentologies, and diverse concepts of ministry in the New
Testament.[15] Common biblical and historical studies in the
ecumenical movement confirmed this latter view, and thus once
again the ecumenical movement had to face squarely the differences
among the Churches. Many of the differences among the Churches
were found to be not only legitimate but also mutually enriching.
Thus, a new stage, a third stage, in the contemporary ecumenical
movement was begun with the discovery of the principle of "unity
in diversity."

Today we are at the third stage of the encounter between the
Churches where equal emphasis is given to unity and diversity.
Differences and diversities of the Churches are seen no more as an
obstacle to unity but as complementary and mutually enriching
factors, provided the Churches have communion in faith and
sacramental life. Pluralism has become today legitimate not only
because it is found in the Bible, but also because it is based on
contemporary man's experience. Pluralism is a contemporary fact
at all levels of human existence--cognitive, ethical and
existential--and it is accepted as legitimate, healthy, necessary,
and enriching. Pluralism in the Church or in theology or in
religion has a double source: First, the inexhaustible mystery
of God's being and of divine revelation cannot be contained in any
one of its expressions. Secondly, the diversity and the finiteness
of the modes of human existence and human perceptions which are
based on man's psycho-somatic, socio-economic, and cultural
differences automatically lead to the diversity of man's
understanding and creativity. In other words, pluralism in
theology means that theology is contextual. That is to say, as
many contexts are there, so many theologies are possible. So the
diversity and the differences among the Churches are understood
as arising from the inexhaustibility of the Gospel of Jesus Christ
and from the diversity of their particular contexts. Hence to
understand the differences of a Church means to understand its
specific context. To seek unity means to search for a dynamic
unity behind diversity.

At this stage of the ecumenical movement, the ecumenical
method seems to be "inter-contextual." The way to achieve unity

is not by "one common theology" or by "one common ecclesiology," but by means of a "Communion of Faith," maintained through and in spite of the diversity of the Churches and their diverse contexts and theologies. The communion of faith would require, or rather is expressed in, through and by an inter-contextual method, where the different Churches, their diverse theologies, or contexts are brought together and laid side by side with the task of emphasizing the special features of each Church and its context or the differences between the various contexts and at the same time comparing and relating them for mutual enrichment and correction for discovering their underlying unity and consequent convergence. The Churches have to recognize and accept not only the uniqueness of their differences but also their unity or their common center which is the person of Jesus Christ who gives all one and the same faith and hope. It means that the Churches have to continuously compare and relate themselves to discover their common centre or ground, but not without criticisms and corrections. The discovery of the common centre and the renewal and growth of all the Churches will gradually lead to the mutual recognition of the Churches.

The present stage of the ecumenical movement is, therefore, very promising as well as crucial. It has brought all the Churches together into a fellowship which seems to be irreversible. What unites them together is not only the concern for their visible unity, but the concern for the unity of the whole mankind. The unity of the Church is seen as a sign and sacrament of the unity of the whole mankind. Besides, visible unity of the Churches not only means the healing of all sorts of divisions in the Church, divisions in the name of race, class, sex, culture, language, etc. The success of the present stage of the ecumenical movement depends on the will and the courage of the Churches to live together, to grow together, and to accept each other as belonging to the One Church of Jesus Christ which is the sign and sacrament of the salvation of the whole mankind.

Future of the Ecumenical Movement

Ecumenical movement is the movement of the Churches for the restoration of their visible unity in plurality as a sign and sacrament of the unity of all humankind. The Church is the sacrament of the salvation of the whole world and the unity of the Church is the sign of the coming unity of mankind. The unity of the Church proclaims, points to, and anticipates the final unity of all humankind which is the ultimate goal of the ecumenical movement. Hence the goal of the ecumenical movement--the visible unity of the Churches--shall not be seen as an introverted,

ecclesio-centric and sectarian concern, and the Churches should
by all means, and without any fear or scruples, dedicate
themselves to the task of the restoration of the visible unity, of
course, always by making the sign character of the Church visible
and credible to the world through a common commitment to mission,
witness, and service and by keeping in mind the ultimate goal of
the unity of all humankind.

The ecumenical movement is advancing today at several
fronts. The Churches are seriously involved in the doctrinal
dialogue aimed at reaching certain doctrinal consensus as the
basis of visible unity. They are also committed to common
socio-political engagement and to the transformation of the society
fighting for the liberation, justice and peace for all, which should
be the basis of unity. Common proclamation of the Gospel to all
the nations is another wing of the ecumenical movement. "Spiritual
Ecumenism" advocates the need for fellowship and communion
between the members of the different Churches by means of
common prayer and worship. All these wings of the contemporary
ecumenical movement and all these concerns must be mutually
related, they must challenge each other, and they must learn
from each other for a healthy and balanced growth and
development of the ecumenical movement. Common proclamation of
the Gospel in today's world, common socio-political action, and
common prayer and worship will help the Churches build up and
experience a new fellowship and articulate their faith in new ways
so as to outdate many of the traditional doctrinal and theological
issues. The fact that all these movements are today held together
by the World Council of Churches where there are tremendous
opportunities for the interplay and interaction of these movements
gives us a sense of optimism.

The restoration of the visible unity of the Churches will not
be achieved at one stretch, but only through a long historical
process. After all, the final unity of the Church and the unity of
all mankind will be eschatological, and what we can aim at id only
certain penultimate goals. The future of the ecumenical movement
cannot be predicted as if it is something which simply happens to
us, but it is something which we have to work out by setting
concrete and tangible goals and by finding out the ways and means
to reach these goals.

The immediate goal of the ecumenical movement is the mutual
recognition of the Churches. The Churches in the WCC as well as
the Roman Catholic Church have recognized the "ecclesial elements"
in the other Churches. The time has now come to take the next
step of full mutual recognition of the other Churches as the

substantial embodiment of the basic and fundamental reality of the Church of Jesus Christ. In the ecumenical movement the Churches have grown together by mutual giving and taking and they have already recognized each other implicitly. All Churches that include the basic structures of the New Testament Christianity and claim to have followed the will of Christ according to the New Testament witness must be accepted as true, authentic, genuine, and legitimate. The Apostolic and primitive Christian Communities, all of them without exception, confessed and proclaimed the Lordship of Christ, believed that they were one fellowship in the Church as the one body of Christ, worshipped the God and Father of Jesus Christ, celebrated the mysteries of baptism and eucharist, continued the Apostolic ministry in one form or another, and they all possessed the Scriptures and the Apostolic witness as the common authoritative source and heritage. These elements and these alone seem to belong to the very esse of the church of the New Testament. Christian communities which manifest and cherish these elements in their life, practice, worship and proclamation as a whole, must recognize each other as true and legitimate Churches. In the light of the recent ecumenical consensus document on "Baptism, Eucharist and Ministry" (the Lima text of 1982), prepared by the representatives of all the churches, including the Roman Catholic Church, mutual recognition of the Churches, it seems, will become a reality in the near future.

Regular Intercommunion and Intercelebration would be the second tangible goal of the ecumenical movement. It may need further consensus concerning the order of the liturgy and the structure of the ordained ministry. Conciliar Fellowship and a New Ecumenical Council will be yet another distinctive goal of the ecumenical movement. It is mutual recognition which makes possible a "fellowship of Churches," and intercommunion which supplies the spiritual energy for sustaining the conciliar fellowship in the midst of tensions and conflicts. Conciliar fellowship is a fellowship of local Churches which are each within itself and all among themselves, fully united with the same Apostolic faith, the same Baptism and the same Eucharist, with the mutual recognition of the members and ministries, with a common commitment of witness on the world, and with a sustaining relationship in conciliar gatherings.[16]

Conciliar fellowship and a new ecumenical council participated by all the Churches will not be the end of the Churches' search for unity, but only a beginning. It will be the beginning of a new life together, a new way of being and living. For the Churches it will be the beginning of a new journey together with all other religions and the whole of mankind. In the encounter of the Churches with the other religions and ideologies, the lessons they have learned in their own encounter will be of great value and the stages and patterns of the new encounter could be more or less the same. Unity of the Church will be fully achieved only when the whole humanity will be fully united, when the <u>oikoumene</u> will actually include the whole world.

NOTES

[1] See William Richey Hogg, Ecumenical Foundation (New York: Harper and Brothers, 1952).

[2] Tissington Tatlow, The Story of the Student Christian Movement of Great Britain and Ireland (London: SCM, 1933), p. 138.

[3] Ruth Rouse and Stephen Neill, A History of the Ecumenical Movement 1857 - 1948, Vol. I (London: SPCK, 1954), pp. 263-268, 613-620.

[4] Peter L. Berger, The Sacred Canopy (New York: Doubleday, 1967).

[5] John 17: 21.

[6] From the Constitution of the IMC. See, David P. Gaines, The World Council of Churches: A Study of its Background and History (Petersborough: The Richard R. Smith Co. Inc., 1966), p. 23.

[7] For a brief outline of the History and the development of the methods in the Faith and Order Movement, See, Kuncheria Pathil, Models in Ecumenical Dialogue (Bangalore: Dharmaram Publications, 1981).

[8] Baptism, Eucharist and Ministry, Faith and Order Paper No. 111 (Geneva: WCC, 1982).

[9] See The Ten Formative Years 1938 - 1948: Report on the Activities of the World Council of Churches during its Period of Formation (Geneva: WCC, 1948).

[10] Jan Cardinal Willebrands, "Moving Towards a Typology of Churches", in The Catholic Mind, April 1970, pp. 40-42.

[11] Faith and Order Papers, Series I, No. 1 (1910), pp. 3-4.

[12] Ibid., No. 14 (1912), p. 4.

[13] K. Pathil, Models in Ecumenical Dialogue, pp. 276-285.

[14] Edmund Schlink, "The Unity and Diversity of the Church", in What Unity Implies (Geneva: WCC, 1969), pp. 35-36.

[15]E. Kasemann, "Unity and Diversity in New Testament Ecclesiology", and Raymond E. Brown, "The Unity and Diversity in the New Testament Ecclesiology", _Novum Testamentum_, 6 (1963), pp. 290-297, 298-308.

[16]_Faith and Order Papers No. 72_, pp. 113-114.

DIALOGUE AS MISSION: A PAPAL INITIATIVE

Frank Podgorski

Dialogue: A Recommendation of Pope Paul VI

It was to be a dramatic moment, indeed a moment of historic importance, and yet of all the thousands assembled in the impressive nave of St. Peter's Basilica in the Vatican on that day, only a few would hear clearly and even fewer appreciate fully the significance of four packed sentences climaxing a rich and classic Latin oration of almost two hours. Most had come to St. Peter's with the hope of finding answers to their own exact questions. Would this newly-elected Pope, Pope Paul VI, a rather severe and ascetical-looking professional, actually dare to continue the boldness of his beloved predecessor, the good Pope John XXIII? Would "aggiornamento," a search to discover how the vast Roman Catholic Church might serve better its members in the world, continue to characterize the discussions and debates of the many Patriarchs, Cardinals, Archbishops, Religious Superiors, and Experts gathered in the Vatican from all the four corners of the earth? Or would not, as many expressed it, brakes or at least old and well-tested directions now be reapplied to temper the enthusiasm and zeal still overflowing from the stimulating first session of the Second Vatican Council? One man, Pope Paul VI, clearly held the key answer to all these questions. The date was September 29th, 1963; the event the Inaugural Address of Pope Paul VI to the second session of the Second Vatican Council. As journals and newspapers in Rome and throughout Europe, the Americas, Africa, and Asia were trumpeting, this day was bound to be critical for the history of the Roman Catholic Church. Would the Church continue its Johannine thrust of opening humbly and candidly to a world very much in need, or would it once again retrench?

Well indeed did Pope Paul VI understand the significance of this moment; his answer had to be direct and crystal-clear. "Let this present address be a prelude not only to the Council but also to our Pontificate."[1] We must search for the positive, neither damning nor condemning, but simply looking for goodness, truth, beauty and holiness wherever they be found. "Develop the doctrine regarding the episcopate, its function and relationship with Peter,"[2] develop the principle of collegiality so that the Church may share in a mission which reaches to the very ends of the earth, the new Pope challenged. "Self-understanding, internal reform, unity in Christ, and genuine dialogue"[3] are four precise goals which the new Pope urged the Council to pursue. Yet perhaps even more important than any of these gracious words was a most striking and dramatic gesture. This newly-elected Pope had already indicated that he wished to communicate by the language of symbols; his gift of the ornate traditional triple tiara to benefit the poor had already alerted and even jolted some to reconsider the values of simplicity and poverty. Now just as Pope Paul VI approached the third major point of his address, his recommendation of the goal of unity, he

> turned around to his left, where the observer-delegates from other Christian communions were seated. He said that their presence at the Council stirred great hope in his heart, as well as a feeling of sadness at their separation. "If we are to blame in any way for that separation," he said to them, "we humbly beg God's forgiveness, and ask pardon, too of our brothers who feel themselves to have been injured by us."[4]

This unprecedented and historic utterance no doubt shocked some of the Council Fathers who had insisted that the Church is entirely without blemish, but to most of those in St. Peter's this must have been a great moment. By this very human and humble gesture of genuine sincerity, by this candid Papal apology, all questions were answered and many hearts melted. A Roman Catholic Pontiff in front of the most solemn assembly of the Church and before the eyes of the entire world sincerely asking forgiveness and pardon from his separated brothers for all past failings and wrongs: this was a confession of faith that could not but touch the hearts of others. The Council of Pope Paul VI would indeed be asked to incarnate and develop the outgoing, all-embracing creative spirit of beloved Pope John XXIII.

In the momentary awe before such magnanimity and graciousness, how could anyone be faulted for failing to hear clearly or grasp adequately the significance of Pope Paul's next few words, his fourth and critical final point, his announcement and heralding of genuine dialogue within a much broader frame? Yet, as many have observed, this recommendation of an entirely new attitude of humble search gave promise of stimulating and challenging the Church far more than any word or gesture previously uttered. The bell of a new age was beginning to toll for the Roman Catholic Church. Indeed, some have prophesied that this candid switch of posture from an attitude of defensive self-righteousness to an inviting and more humble quest for truth and service may very well stimulate the Church to a much greater and far more profound understanding of what it means to be called catholic. Pope Paul chose to introduce this lesson by his personal example. After pausing in admiration before the wondrous benefits and fruits of science, art, learning, and culture, the Pope then announced the new direction and the new path which he wished the Council and the Church to pursue, the path of humble and honest dialogue.

> The Catholic Church looks further into the distance . . . beyond the Christian horizon. For how can she put limits to her love if she should make her own the love of God and Father, who rains down His grace on all alike (Mt. 5:46), and who so loved the world as to give for it His only-begotten Son (Jn 3:16)? She looks, then, beyond her own domain and sees those other religions which maintain the concept of one God, creator, sustainer, sovereign, and transcendent, who worship God with sincere acts of piety, and whose beliefs and practice are the founding principles of their moral and social life. . . . She cannot help speaking to assure them of the esteem the Catholic Church has for all there is in them of truth, of goodness, and of the human.[5]

Awakening to, and indeed rejoicing in the profound human and spiritual values recognized in other religious traditions, Pope Paul sought to move the Church in the direction of appreciating and learning from other traditions while simultaneously offering her own spiritual treasures to them. A critical and decisive first step had been taken by the Pope himself. His four key sentences, generally overlooked in the initial reports of this extraordinary Inaugural Address, would become seeds or germs which would blossom quickly into the many conversations and dialogues which Christian, Hindu, and Buddhist scholars and monks would pursue in the next twenty years, a blossoming which is now extending itself into the Chinese, Islamic, and African spiritual worlds.[6] The Catholic Church has thus been officially challenged to expand its quest for religious values and truth far beyond traditional Christian boundaries. As the Pope himself had pointed out, no one ought dare to put limits on the love of God. Perhaps a Hindu or a Buddhist may help a Christian to intensify and deepen prayer and meditation and vice-versa; perhaps a Chinese may suggest ways of developing a more profound appreciation of the mystery of human society. And yet even while marvelling at this new doorway and path just beginning to open, it is helpful to recall

149

that Pope Paul VI is both echoing and clarifying an insight of Pope John XXIII who admired

> the countless masses of human beings not yet
> illuminated by the light of Christ, but who
> glory in an illustrious and ancient patrimony
> of civilization, inherited from their ancestors.
> Indeed they have nothing to fear from the light
> of the Gospel, which, as in past centuries, may
> contribute to cultivating and developing those
> very fruitful seeds of religiosity and culture
> which are proper to themselves. Our heart is
> turned in that direction.

Yet this first opening of the doorway of conversation with the positive values of non-Christian religious traditions ought most accurately be viewed as but an introduction. With warmth and graciousness, the Popes were suggesting that the Catholic Church extend her arms as widely as possible, announce with clarity her own name and mission, ponder, study, and admire the beauty and truth and special genius of the other, and thus begin a common search to see if a joining of hands and hearts might benefit all.

Yet this path to dialogue would need much encouragement and stimulation especially for a Church accustomed to identify principally with European values and standards. Once again, Pope Paul VI preferred to teach by actions rather than by words. During his Christmas pilgrimage to the Hold Land in 1963, Pope Paul VI had dramatically and warmly embraced Patriarch Athenagoras I, thereby promoting in a new and fresh way dialogue with the spiritually rich Orthodox traditions. In an even more dramatic moment during his journey to India in 1964, the Pope adopted the most famous prayer of the Hindu Upanishads while speaking of the spiritual treasures of India; this act touched the Hindu soul deeply and has already led to a series of conversations and meetings which promise to evolve into genuine and real dialogue. By such humble actions linked with an expressed testimony that the Roman Catholic has something extremely valuable to offer to all, the road to dialogue, a journey which promises to be immense, was announced by Pope Paul Vi. To foster such conversation and dialogue with the vast numbers of non-Christian believers, the Vatican Secretariat for Non-Christians was formally announced on Pentecost Day, 1964, and began its work shortly thereafter; initially this Secretariat was given the charge of welcoming all with warmth and hospitality and of reaching out to others with a "spirituality nourished by silence, prayer, love, and grace."[8] In the Decree of Institution, Pope Paul VI specified three goals for the Secretariat:

1. create a climate of warmth and cordiality between the Catholic Church and other religious traditions,

2. dispel and dissipate errors, misconceptions, and misinformation about other religions especially among Roman Catholics, and

3. establish and organize meetings and deeper discussions with representatives of different religious traditions.[9]

Pope Paul VI soon had additional words of direction for this newly-emerging path. On Easter Sunday of 1964, the Pope explained:

> Every religion contains sparks of light within itself which must neither be despised nor quenched, even though they are insufficient for giving clear vision. . . . Every religion raises us towards the Transcendent Being. . . . Every religion is a dawn of faith.[10]

Moreover, the new Pope's first encyclical letter, Ecclesiam Suam (August 24th, 1964), assumed responsibility for initiating and developing this new form of dialogue. "Clarity, meekness, trust, and genuine esteem for the other"[11] are prerequisites for authentic dialogue. Indeed, even "before speaking, it is necessary to listen, not only to a man's voice, but especially to his heart."[12] "Let us stress what we have in common rather than what divides us."[13] To genuinely listen to the aspirations of the human heart as each seeks to respond to the mystery of the Divine Call is the starting point of Pope Paul VI's recommendation for initiating authentic dialogue.

> We see another circle around us. This, too, is vast in its extent, yet it is not so far away from us. It is made up of those who adore the one, supreme God whom we adore.

> We mean the children, worthy of our affection and respect, of the Hebrew people, faithful to the religion that we call that of the Old Testament. Then, the adorers of God according to the concept of monotheism, especially the

religion of the Moslems which is deserving of
our admiration for all that is true and good in
their worship of God. And also the followers
of the great African and Asian religions.

Obviously we cannot share in these various
forms of religion nor can we remain indifferent
. . . . Indeed honesty compels us to declare
openly our conviction that there is but one
true religion, the religion of Christianity
. . . .

Yet we do, nevertheless, recognize and respect
the moral and spiritual values of the various
non-Christian religions, and we do desire to
join with them in promoting common ideals of
religious liberty, human brotherhood, good
culture, social welfare, and civic order.
For our part, we are ready to enter into
discussions on these common ideals, and will
not fail to take the initiative where our offer
of discussion in genuine, mutual respect would
be well-received.

Thus it now began to seem possible to formulate a principle for
dialogue with the non-Christian religious traditions.
Conversations, discussions, and authentic open dialogue concerning
moral and spiritual values, goals, and ideals, especially those
shared in common, are very much encouraged, provided clear and
candid testimony be given to one's Christian identity.
Furthermore, such recognized common ideals ought lead very
rapidly to specific social actions for the common good of all. A
step, feeble perhaps by some standards but yet very real, had
been taken: the recognition of common religious ideals and
aspirations had been acknowledged as good and desirable. A
positive appreciation of the human response to the mystery of the
Divine, regardless of its cultural and religious vesture, was
beginning to be articulated by Papal initiative and example.

An old Chinese proverb claims that acts and actions prove the
value of theories of the spirit: specific actions bring out
dimensions of reality which confirm intuitions of the spirit. As
Chu Hsi once phrased it, acts unveil and reveal knowledge and
wisdom. Pope Paul VI's journey to India in December of 1964
offered an opportunity to test an evolving Papal intuition. "We
must meet . . . as pilgrims who set out to find God. We must
come together with our hearts, in mutual understanding, esteem,

and love. . . . In this sacred communion, we must begin to work together to build the future."[15] According to the chroniclers, a visible change in appearance became noticeable in Pope Paul VI during his journey to India. As practice began to verify and confirm his instinctive intuition, his gestures, his words, and his outreach became warmer and more relaxed. "Paul VI's expressions became more penetrating, more positive, and bolder."[16] Addressing an assembly of non-Christians on December 8th, he was clearly moved and touched by the spirit and spirituality of India.

> Your land is a land of an ancient culture, the cradle of great religions, the home of a nation which has sought God with unceasing aspiration, in deep mediation and silence, and in hymns of fervent prayer. Rarely has this longing for God been expressed with words so full of the spirit of Advent as in the words written in your sacred books many centuries before Christ. "From the unreal, lead me to the Real; from darkness, lead me to Light; from death lead me to Immortality." This is a prayer which also belongs to our time. Today more than ever before it should spring forth from every human spirit.[17]

By embracing this ancient prayer of the Brihadaranayaka Upanishads, Pope Paul touched the very heart and soul of India. His choice of a Hindu sacred text could not have been more apt: for more than twenty-five hundred years, Hindus had prayed and meditated on these very words. "Lead me from the unreal to the Real" had undoubtedly been prayed earlier that morning by those very Hindus gathered before Pope Paul at that moment. It was indeed an historic moment; a Roman Catholic Pope had identified himself and his mission with the deepest aspirations of the Indian soul; a new form of Papal witness had come to India and Asia. The Christian understanding of mission could never be quite the same: openness to the other in spiritual search would have to become a characteristic of the genuine missionary.

And yet, for Pope Paul VI, such an understanding of mission was really very traditional. Indeed, it was but a deeper penetration of the meaning of catholicity.

> Catholicity indicated that ever extendable multiplicity of the human forms which can make up the one mystical body of Christ. . . .

153

We reflect upon this multiplicity which has to
be recognized, respected, and moreover, elevated
and invigorated. For that we need to have a
more adequate notion of the Church's catholicity,
a more comprehensive desire for human brotherhood
to educate and compel us. . . .

One obligation immediately appears, that of
getting to know better the peoples with whom
one comes into contact, because of the Gospel,
and to recognize all the good they possess,
not only in their history and civilization but
also in the heritage of moral and religious
values which they possess and conserve.

This imposes on the ministry of dialogue the
necessity of so much balance, so much wisdom,
and so much patience.[18]

With such strong Papal leadership setting the pace, the
practical work of evolving a "ministry of dialogue" began in
earnest. For the moment, let us pass over the extremely
important refinements and specifications of dialogue detailed by
the Second Vatican Council and the Bishops' Synod of 1974.
Although critical, the work of these assemblies must always be
viewed in light of the continuing leadership of the Papacy. Thus
practical details of initiating and developing this dialogue were
now delegated to the Secretariat for Non-Christians which soon
began gathering scholars and especially monks to develop the first
phases of dialogical contact and conversation. Following ten years
of such initial conversations, an explanation of the meaning of
dialogue was issued by the Secretariat in 1974.

Real dialogue must be established. Dialogue
presupposes that each side wishes to know the
other. It constitutes a particularly suitable
means of favoring a better mutual knowledge,
. . . of probing the depths of one's own
tradition. Dialogue demands respect for the
other as he is; above all, respect for his
faith and his religious convictions.[19]

Clearly, a variety of specialists especially those with a profound
spiritual orientation were needed for this new work. Seminars,
symposia, academic meetings, introductory conversations, and
candid exploratory sharings began to take place with frequency.
Bangkok (Thailand), 1968, Bangalore (India), 1973, Loppem

(Belgium), 1975, Petersham (U.S.A.), 1976, Vina (U.S.A.), 1977, Praglia (Italy), 1977-1979, 1982, and Holyoke (U.S.A.), 1980 are but a few of the sites which hosted these pioneering and, in the words of Pope John Paul II, even "epoch-making" encounters. Those familiar with contemplative spirituality seem especially suited for this work. To a group of participants returning from one of the first Praglia seminars, Pope Paul VI reflected:

> We are happy to know that, together with our Christian sons, you have presented to the world a united witness of the authentic spiritual values which are so very much needed in our time.[20]

This same warm and open embrace of non-Christians consistently characterized the entire Pontificate of Pope Paul VI. Indeed, just a few days before his death, the Pope addressed a group of Zen Buddhist monks with these tender words: "We ask the Lord that we may always be worthy to love you and to serve you."[21] Perhaps this beautiful challenge to "loving service" as the starting point for dialogue ought serve as Pope Paul VI's last testimony and legacy, his final explanation of the immense pathway and open doorway of the ministry of dialogue which has been bequeathed to future generations. Recalling the spirit of another Paul who opened a fledgling Church to a Hellenic world, Pope Paul VI's embrace of the entire "ecumene" marks him as another "apostle to the Gentiles."[22]

Missionary Witness: Pope John Paul II

With Pope John Paul II, a clearer awareness of the pastoral call for a ministry of dialogue as a response to the inspiration of the Holy Spirit has begun to emerge. Identifying dialogue as an eminently pastoral ministry, Pope John Paul II sees dialogue as a species and form of mission. Indeed, while respect and esteem for the sacredness of "the other" may awaken a Christian to a wondrous discovery of the richness of God in his unfathomable and unlimited depths, yet at the same time truth and sincerity demand that the Christian proclaim and articulate as clearly as possible his own identity and specific beliefs.[23] Nor may false irenicism ever blur the Christian imperative to proclaim the Gospel to the very ends of the earth. Indeed, only if a Christian identifies himself clearly and forthrightly can the stimulation of a dialogue ever hope to lead to the goals of deeper understanding and mutual respect. Perhaps Pope John Paul II's principle of dialogue may be expressed in this manner: a frank and precise declaration of one's own Christian identity, a clear testimony to one's own

155

faith and mission, will be enriched by a sincere esteem and respect for the values and followers of other religions; this very consciousness recognizes the Holy Spirit as being unlimited by any bonds whatsoever. Pope John Paul II thus consciously links sincere faith and genuine respect for "the other" as the two indispensable and interrelated foundations for a ministry of dialogue; his conversations and his encounters with non-Christians all illustrate this. Redemptor Hominis, his first encyclical letter, introduces this theme.

> We can together come close to the magnificent heritage of the human spirit that has been manifested to all religions. . . . We approach them with esteem, respect, and discernment that since the time of the Apostles has marked the missionary attitude, the very attitude of the missionary. Suffice it to mention Saint Paul and, for instance, his address in the Areopagus at Athens. (Acts 17:22-31). The missionary attitudes always begins with a feeling of deep esteem for "what is in man" (Jn 2:26), for what man has himself worked out in the depths of his spirit concerning these most profound and important problems. It is a question of respecting everything that has been brought about in him by the Spirit which "blows where it wills" (Jn 3: 8).[24]

From this missionary perspective, Pope John Paul II recommends "dialogue, contacts, prayer in common, investigations of the treasures of human spirituality."[25] Indeed, the Pope is fond of commenting that the obvious strong faith and noble moral and spiritual aspirations of many non-Christians ought serve as a splendid example of paradigm for Christians. "Does it not sometimes happen that the firm belief of the followers of non-Christian religions -- a belief that is also an effect of the Spirit of Truth operating outside the visible confines of the Mystical Body -- . . . can make Christians ashamed at being themselves so disposed to doubt concerning the truths revealed by God?[26]

At the First Plenary Meeting of the Secretariat for Non-Christians, Pope John Paul II began by repeating his double principle of faith and respect, his key to dialogue, and then chose to emphasize the creative influence of dynamic love.

It is essential for dialogue that there be full
respect and esteem "for the other," and this in
the very depths of the heart. There must be
added to this the discernment and sincere and
profound knowledge which cannot be gained
merely in books. They demand sympathy and
understanding. Long before the conditions for
dialogue were expressed in philosophical terms,
Saint Paul already spoke of his willingness "to be
all things to all." In dialogue, the word
cannot be efficacious without love.[27]

Thus Pope John Paul II sought to stimulate a pastoral ministry of
dialogue by emphasizing the dynamism of creative, outgoing warmth
and love. The example of his own personal ministry of dialogue,
his appeal and outreach to all others but especially to the
non-Christians of the Asian and African worlds, is grounded on
this three-fold understanding of the meaning of dialogue: to a
strong faith enriched by genuine esteem for "the others," there is
linked the motivating Gospel imperative of dynamic, creative love.

Pope John Paul II's journey to Asia both illustrates and
emphasizes this very pastoral application of a mission of a ministry
of dialogue. His Message to the Asian Peoples thus announced his
arrival as

the servant of Jesus Christ, following the
examples of Pope Paul VI and retracing the
footsteps of the great missionary apostles.
I have come to Asia in testimony to the
Spirit who works in the history of peoples
and nations, the Spirit who proceeds from
the Father and the Son. In the Holy Spirit,
every individual, because of the Cross and
Resurrection of Christ, has become a son of
God, shares in a Divine nature, and inherits
eternal life.[28]

Then this missionary Pope openly confesses esteem and respect for
the religious experiences of others.

The Catholic Church accepts the truth and
goodness found in these religions, and she
sees reflections there of the truth of
Christ, whom she proclaims as "the way,
the truth, and the life." She wishes to
do everything possible to cooperate with

other believers in preserving all that is good in their religions and cultures, stressing the things that are held in common, and helping all people to live as brothers and sisters. The Church of Jesus Christ in this age experiences a profound need to enter into contact and dialogue with all these religions. What seems to bring together and unite, in a particular way, Christians and believers of other religions is an acknowledgement of the need for prayer as an expression of spirituality directed toward the Absolute. Even when, for some, He is the Great Unknown, He nevertheless remains in reality the same living God. We trust that wherever the human spirit opens itself in prayer to this unknown God, an echo will be heard of the same Spirit who, knowing the limits and weakness of the human person, himself prays in us and on our behalf "expressing our plea in a way that could never be put into words." (Rom 8:26).

. . . Asia is the continent where the spiritual is held in high esteem and where the religious sense is deep and innate: the preservation of this precious heritage must be the common task of all.[29]

This approach of Pope John Paul II's "Message to Asia" may be characterized as that of an enlightened missionary: three guiding principles of dialogue emerge from his statement. Faith bids one announce frankly and clearly the central belief in Jesus Christ as "the way, the truth, and the life"; respect and esteem for the "other" inspires a solemn pledge to preserve all the "truth and goodness" observed in other religions, the preservation of this heritage being the common task of all; finally creative, dynamic, outgoing expressive love invites all to "unite" in prayer and profound spiritual search. This invitation to shared prayer, this acknowledgment "that wherever the human spirit opens itself in prayer, an echo will be heard of the same Spirit who, knowing the limits and weakness of the human person, himself prays in us and on our behalf" is a special contribution of Pope John Paul II to our understanding of the mission of dialogue.

By such sincerity in word and gestures while consistently witnessing to this three-fold principle of dialogue, Pope John Paul II deeply impressed the representatives of various non-Christian religious traditions. In Tokyo, an especially impressive moment occurred when the Pope appealed directly to the ancient and revered Wisdom tradition of Asia. Just as in Bombay seventeen years earlier, Pope Paul VI had touched the Hindu heart by invoking the Upanishads, so also in 1981 in Tokyo Pope John Paul II reached the Japanese heart by appealing to honored Shinto and Confucian values of conduct and morality and especially the esteemed teachings of Zen Master Saicho.

> I find in the virtues of kindness and goodness, discretion, gentleness and fortitude inculcated by your religious traditions the fruits of that Divine Spirit who according to our faith is "a friend to man, fills the whole world and holds all things together." (Wisdom 1:6-7). . . .
>
> What can this Pope who comes from Rome say to you on his first visit to this renowned country of the East? You are the heirs and custodians of a time-honored wisdom. That wisdom has inculcated in Japan and throughout the East high moral standards of life. It has taught you to venerate the pure, clear, and honest heart (akaku, kiyoku, naoki, kokoro). It has inspired you to see a divine presence in every creature, especially in every human being. It has instilled in you "selflessness and service of others as the summit of friendship and compassion," to use the words of your great teacher, Saicho.[30]

All of Pope John Paul II's exhortations to Asia, his messages and addresses to the people of Africa, as well as Catechesi Tradendae (October 16th, 1979), amplify, reinforce, and develop this theme of a pastoral mission of respectful dialogue to and with all. For Pope John Paul II, such a warm and enthusiastic and sincere outreach to "others" is the path and the direction that a contemporary ministry of dialogue ought articulate. Indeed, it is the "missionary witness" appropriate for our day. For a continent steeped in a revered spiritual heritage and still witnessing to rich varieties of profound spiritual search, Pope John Paul's hope and expressed prayer is that the treasure of the spiritual legacy of Jesus Christ be fittingly presented and appropriately introduced in this context. Moreover, the Holy Spirit appears to be opening the Church to this new awareness in our day.

Reflecting on the initiation and opening of a ministry of dialogue with non-Christian religious traditions, the personal leadership of the modern Papacy is dramatic and indeed very striking. Significantly, all of our modern Popes have adopted a custom initiated by Pope John XXIII, that of addressing their encyclicals to "all of good-will." This too is a sign of a horizon broadened beyond simply a Christian focus; it is outgoing and very impressive. As Pope Paul VI reminded the Fathers at the Second Vatican Council and constantly repeated in his encyclicals, the Church senses that it has something extremely valuable to offer to all who search. Gradually also, this Church is coming to a clearer understanding of its own role within a ministry of dialogue. Our modern Popes have helped to specify this role. From the initiating intuition of Pope John XXIII through the cautious first four sentences of Pope Paul VI's Inaugural Address at the Vatican Council to his touching adoption of the Hindu Upanishadic prayer in India to Pope John Paul II's enthusiastic appeal to the Zen Master Saicho in Japan, an incredible blossoming, expansion, and clarification of the pioneering Christian understanding of the ministry of dialogue has gradually taken place. Very appropriately, these Papal initiatives have always been accompanied by expansive, warm and compassionate gestures bearing witness to the central Christian virtue of love. For a Christian then, it is clear that a genuine ministry of dialogue must seek to combine graciously:

1. a sincere respect, esteem, and reverence for the values, traditions, and followers of other religious traditions,

2. a humble and open-hearted listening to the experience of others combined with a clear testimony to Christian beliefs in language sensitive to that experience,

3. a frank declaration and announcement of oneself as Christian, and

4. a creative dynamic open love leading to a mutual search through both common prayer and an investigation of the entire human legacy of spirituality.

The road from St. Peter's in the Vatican to Bombay and then to Tokyo has been and will continue to be long and arduous; certainly there are many, many miles waiting to be trod; yet the graciousness and humanness and enthusiasm and warmth and sincerity with which our modern Popes have spoken these initial words of dialogue have made these steps seem very natural and almost easy. To what enrichment and deeper understandings will this journey of religious conversation and dialogue lead? Although any response to such a critical question is bound to be immature, it at least seems clear that our modern Popes are pioneering the paths and directions to be trod.

NOTES

[1] Pope Paul VI, Inaugural Address to the Second Session of Vatican Council II (September 29th, 1963) in Acta Apostolicae Sedis 55 (1963) 843.

[2] AAS 55 (1963) 849.

[3] AAS 55 (1963) 847.

[4] Xavier Rynne, The Second Session (New York: Farrar, Strauss, and Company, 1963), p. 36.

[5] AAS 55 (1963) 857-858.

[6] Simon Tonini, L'Eglise, Les Non-Chrétiens, Les Moines (Vanves: Dialogue Interreligieux Monastique, 1982), pp. 57-102. See also: Thomas Aykara (ed.), Meeting of Religions: New Orientations and Perspectives (Bangalore: Dharmaram Publications, 1978).

[7] Pope John XXIII's Address at the Conclusion of the First Session of Vatican Council II (December 8th, 1962) in AAS 55 (1963) 35.

[8] Pope Paul VI's Pentecost Homily (May 17th, 1964) in AAS 56 (1964) 432-434.

[9] Ibid.

[10] Pope Paul VI's Easter Homily (March 29th, 1964) in AAS 56 (1964) 394.

[11] Pope Paul VI, Ecclesiam Suam (August 6th, 1964) translated in Paths of the Church (Washington: National Catholic Welfare Conference, 1964), # 81, p. 34.

[12] Ibid., # 87, p. 35.

[13] Ibid., # 109, p. 43.

[14] Ibid., # 107-108, pp. 42-43.

[15] Pope Paul VI's Address to the Non-Christian Communities (December 8th, 1964) in AAS 57 (1965) 132.

[16] Tonini, op. cit. p. 19.

[17] *Pope Paul VI's Address to the Non-Christian Communities* (December 8th, 1964) in AAS 57 (1965) 132.

[18] Pope Paul VI as cited in Tonini, op. cit. p. 21.

[19] "Guidelines on Religious Relations with the Jews" as found in Austin Flannery (ed.), *Vatican II: The Conciliar and Post-Conciliar Documents* (Northport, New York: Costello Publishing Company, 1975), p. 744.

[20] Tonini, op. cit. p. 72.

[21] Ibid.

[22] Two Gregorian University theses are currently developing various dimensions of this dimension of Pope Paul VI's dialogical thrust. Cf.: Crystian Gawron, *Dialogus ut Methodus Pastoralis in Magisterio Papae Pauli VI* (approbatur 1979); Basil Mendis-Arthadeva, *Evangelizatio secundum Doctrinam Paul VI* (1980).

[23] Cf.: René Latourelle, "Evangelisation et Temoignage" in M. Dhavamony (ed.), *Evangelisation* (Roma: Universita Gregoriana, 1975), Doc. Miss. # 9, pp. 77-110.

[24] Pope John Paul II, *Redemptor Hominis* (March 4th, 1979) translated as *Redeemer of Man* (Washington: United States Catholic Conference, 1979), p. 34. Cf. also AAS 71 (1979) 257 ff.

[25] Ibid., p. 17.

[26] Ibid., pp. 17-18.

[27] *Bulletin of the Secretariat of Non-Christians* (1979, # 41-42) as cited in Tonini, op. cit., p. 43.

[28] *Pope John Paul II's Message to Asia* (February 21st, 1981) as cited in Tonini, op. cit. # 1, p. 47.

[29] *Pope John Paul II's Message to Asia* (February 21st, 1981) as cited in Tonini, op. cit., # 3-4, pp. 49-51.

[30] *Pope John Paul II's Address to Representatives of Non-Christian Religions* (Tokyo: February 24th, 1981) as cited in Simon Tonini, *The Church, Non-Christians, Monks: Beginnings and Development of Dialogue* (St. Louis: U.S. National Center for A.I.M., 1982), pp. 43-44.

THE ROMAN CATHOLIC CHURCH
AND JUDAISM
SINCE THE SECOND VATICAN COUNCIL

Joseph P. Brennan

In its relationship with the world's great religions, Christianity is bound to Judaism in unique ways. Christians think of themselves as spiritual descendants of Abraham the Hebrew, as members of the new Israel, partakers in the new covenant, the true heirs of the ancient promises, and holders of the key to the interpretation of the Jewish Scriptures. Christian theology has from its very beginnings seen the church as the extension and fulfillment of the qahal, the ekklesia (congregation, gathering) which was first assembled by the God of Israel at the foot of Sinai. All of this, while making Christianity profoundly indebted to Judaism, has also put it on a level of competitiveness with Judaism for the past two millenia. And since it has been the sad fate of most Jews throughout this period to live as a tiny minority in the midst of a Christian majority, the relationship between the two communities has frequently been stormy and violent, with little possibility of true understanding on the one side or the other. An appreciation of the profound indebtedness of Christianity to Judaism, but also of the bitter legacy of suspicion and enmity between the two communities, is the first requirement for anyone wishing to understand the Jewish-Christian dialogue in our own times. The terrible events of the 1930's and 1940's in Hitler's Europe, followed by the emergence of a Jewish State of Israel have shaped contemporary Christian thinking about Judaism in profoundly new, if not always unambiguous, ways. For Catholics this new approach towards Judaism was given dramatic expression in the Second Vatican Council's Declaration on the Relationship of the Church to Non-Christian Religions.[1] This paper will attempt to outline some of the more significant aspects of that Declaration, and to recount some of the ways in which subsequent official Church statements have developed the thinking of the Council more fully.

Nostra Aetate and the Jews

On October 28, 1965 the Second Vatican Council promulgated its Declaration on the Relationship of the Church to Non-Christian Religions, usually referred to as Nostra Aetate, from the first words of the Latin text. While the briefest of the documents of the Council, it is surely one of the most revolutionary, in that it marks a radical break with traditional Roman Catholic attitudes, and sets Catholic thinking and practice on a dramatically new course. The first three sections set out a sympathetic and respectful approach to Hinduism, Buddhism, Islam and other world religions, while the fourth examines in somewhat greater detail Christianity's relationship with Judaism. A renewed understanding of and appreciation for the latter is seen to be part of the process in which the Church "searches into her own mystery" and is required by the "great patrimony common to Christians and Jews." This patrimony is summed up in an acknowledgement first of all that the Church has "received the revelation of the Old Testament through the people with whom God in His inexpressible mercy concluded the Ancient Covenant", and secondly that Jesus was himself a Jew, as were Mary, and "the Apostles, the Church's mainstay and pillars, as well as most of the early disciples who proclaimed Christ's Gospel to the world."

But in addition to a shared past, the Council also sees Christians and Jews as sharing a common future, for with them "the Church awaits the day, known to God alone, on which all peoples will address the Lord in a single voice and 'serve him shoulder to shoulder' (Zeph 3:9)."

Sharing as they do such a past and such a future, the Declaration expresses the hope that Christians and Jews will be able to approach each other at last with that "mutual understanding and respect which is the fruit, above all, of biblical and theological studies as well as of fraternal dialogues." The discussion of Judaism ends with a reminder to Christians that, while "the Church is the new people of God, the Jews should not be presented as rejected or accursed by God, as if this followed from the Holy Scriptures...The Church...decries hatred, persecutions, displays of anti-semitism, directed against the Jews at any time and by anyone." Catholics are warned not to "charge against all the Jews, without distinction, then alive, nor against the Jews of today" the guilt for the death of Christ, which was the work of "the Jewish authorities and those who followed their lead." The cross of Christ ought to be proclaimed "as the sign of God's all-embracing love and as the fountain from which every grace flows" rather than as an incitement to hatred and contempt for the Jews.

From these brief but seminal statements of the Second Vatican Council, modest and cautious though they seemed at the time, many encouraging developments have emerged.

Guidelines and Suggestions for Implementing
the Conciliar Declaration Nostra Aetate

Shortly after the conclusion of the Council, the Vatican set up a special Office for Catholic-Jewish Relations, which on 22 October 1974 became the Commission for Religious Relations with the Jews. In January 1975 this Commission celebrated the tenth anniversary of Nostra Aetate by issuing a set of Guidelines and Suggestions for Implementing the Conciliar Declaration Nostra Aetate.[2] These Guidelines, while reaffirming most of the points made in the earlier Conciliar Declaration, do introduce some major new developments, and translate the general principles of the Declaration into more concrete terms. It is to the new developments that we now turn our attention.

The first advance of the Guidelines over the Declaration is in the guarded admission that "the gap dividing Christianity and Judaism" may well be the fault of Christians as well as of Jews. The possibility of Christian guilt is already hinted at in the opening paragraphs of the Guidelines, which set the Declaration in the historical context of "the persecution and massacre of Jews which took place in Europe just before and during the Second World War." But a much clearer admission comes later, in the section on Dialogue, where Christians are reminded that "while it is true that a widespread air of suspicion, inspired by an unfortunate past, is still dominant in this particular area, Christians for their past will be able to see to what extent the responsibility is theirs and deduce practical conclusions for the future." A rather roundabout and half-hearted statement of guilt and amendment of life, perhaps, but certainly a step in the right direction.

The second advance is in the extensive development of the idea of "dialogue"--a theme which various documents of the Council, the Declaration among them, frequently evoke, without ever analyzing it in depth.[3] The Guidelines however make it clear that the "monologue" which has been the norm between Christians and Jews until now must be replaced by a genuine dialogue in which "each side wishes to know the other, and wishes to increase and deepen its knowledge of the other...Dialogue demands respect for the other as he is; above all respect for his faith and his religious convictions." It also "constitutes a particularly suitable means... of probing the riches of one's own tradition."

It is worth noting that the Working Document which served as a base for the discussions leading to these Guidelines had spelled out specifically at this point that in true dialogue "all intent of

proselytizing and conversion is excluded."[4]   And indeed, the
Guidelines for Catholic Jewish Relations issued by the National
Conference of Catholic Bishops of the United States in 1967 did
state that "Proselytizing is to be carefully avoided in the
dialogue."[5]   It might seem that the Vatican Guidelines reflect a
less forthright approach in dealing with proselytism, but it is not
inappropriate to read them against the background of the Conciliar
Declaration on Religious Liberty, promulgated on 7 December 1965,
which had stated that "in spreading religious belief and in
introducing religious practices everybody must at all times avoid
any action which seems to suggest coercion or dishonesty or
unworthy persuasion, especially when dealing with the uneducated
or the poor. Such a manner of acting must be considered an
abuse of one's own right and an infringement of the rights of
others."[6]   Hence, even though the Guidelines do not tackle the
question of proselytism or even of Christian missionary activity
among Jews, in a direct manner, they do at least make it clear
that Christians have a duty above all to "learn by what essential
traits the Jews define themselves in the light of their own religious
experience" and to approach them "with better mutual
understanding and renewed mutual esteem."

The third significant advance of the 1975 Guidelines over
Nostra Aetate is to be found in the attempt to come to grips with
the anti-Jewish coloring of many passages in the Catholic liturgy.
There had already by 1975 been an extensive reform of the
liturgical rites and texts of the Church, resulting, among other
things, in a more positive attitude towards Judaism. This was
most evident in the revision of the Good Friday rites, though by
no means confined to them. It must be admitted, however, that it
is much easier to revise liturgical texts than it is to deal with the
words of the New Testament itself. The Guidelines recommended
that homilies based on liturgical readings "not distort their
meaning, especially when it is a question of passages which seem
to show the Jewish people as such in an unfavorable light." And
efforts were urged "so to instruct the Christian people that they
will understand the true interpretation of all the texts and their
meaning for the contemporary believer." Specific mention is made
of two problem areas: first, the tendency in the Gospel of John
to group all the various adversaries of Jesus under the heading of
"the Jews"--thus blurring the synoptic distinction between people
and leaders, and giving rise to countless Good Friday programs
down through the centuries; second, the pejorative interpretation
of Pharisaism and the Pharisses which has become normative in
Christianity as a result of the New Testament presentation of the
Pharisaic movement.

The Guidelines imply that efforts to get at the "true interpretation of all the texts" and to "express better the thought of the Evangelist" will reduce, or even eliminate the danger of Christian anti-Jewish prejudice. More and more New Testament scholars, however, are coming to the conclusion that the problem is deeper than this, an that a "true interpretation of all the texts" will only reveal that most of the New Testament books were written in an atmosphere of intense anti-Jewish polemic. The tendency to present official Judaism and its adherents as radically opposed to God, and ultimately rejected by him is, according to these scholars, most evident in John and Paul, but it is to be found throughout the New Testament, and it lies at the root of 2000 years of Christian anti-semitism and anti-Judaism.[7] Hence it will require more than new translations and efforts to "express better the thought of the Evangelist" if the roots of Christian anti-semitism are to be eliminated. Still, it is heartening to see an official Church document acknowledging this problem, and attempting to reach a solution for it, even though both the statement of the problem and the solution proposed may strike us as inadequate.

The fourth, and final significant advance of the 1975 Guidelines over Nostra Aetate is in the recognition that "respecting the Jew as he is" means looking at Judaism not simply as a prelude to Christianity, or as a means of "probing the riches of one's own tradition", but on its own terms. Both Judaism and Christianity have evolved considerably during the past two millenia, and Christians must learn to look at Judaism not primarily as it is represented in the pages of the Old and New Testaments, but as it has developed down to the present day. Nostra Aetate looks at Judaism through Christian eyes, whereas the Guidelines remind Christians that "the history of Judaism did not end with the destruction of Jerusalem, but rather went on to develop a religious tradition. And, although we believe that the importance and meaning of that tradition were deeply affected by the coming of Christ, it is nonetheless rich in religious values." Dialogue with contemporary Judaism requires that Christians recognize that both Jews and Christians are the beneficiaries of immensely rich post-biblical traditions, and that these two great traditions have developed along quite different lines.

The 1975 Guidelines, with their tentative admission of Christian guilt, their call for genuine dialogue, their acknowledgement of anti-Jewish tendencies on the New Testament writings, and their recognition that Judaism is not just a biblical phenomenon or a historical curiosity, but a living, dynamic religious system, do indeed move beyond the Conciliar Declaration, albeit circumspectly. But they in their turn have opened the way for further developments, and it is to these that we now turn.

Official Statements of Some National Hierarchies

The 1975 Guidelines had reaffirmed Nostra Aetate's opening theme by stating that "the problem of Jewish-Christian relations concerns the Church as such, since it is when 'pondering her own mystery' that she encounters the mystery of Israel." For this reason, even where no Jewish communities exist, Christians are urged to give thought to the relationship between Christianity and Judaism. Nevertheless, it has been chiefly in those parts of the world where Jews have been most numerous that the possibilities for dialogue at both the theological and the popular level have been most available. Hence, it is not surprising to find the national hierarchies of countries like France, Germany, Holland, and the United States, issuing official statements and guidelines of their own. In many of these national documents the themes referred to above are given a more expanded, and sometimes more forthright expression.

Thus, for example, the complicity of Christians in the terrible persecutions of the Jews is clearly acknowledged by the Bishops of the Federal Republic of Germany in their 1975 statement:

> Our country's recent political history is darkened by the systematic attempt to wipe out the Jewish people. Apart from some admirable efforts by individuals and groups, most of us during the time of National Socialism formed a church community preoccupied with the threat to our own institutions. We turned our backs to this persecuted Jewish people, and were silent about the crimes perpetrated on Jews and Judaism. Many became guilty from sheer fear for their lives. We feel particularly distressed about the fact that Christians even took active part in these persecutions. The honesty of our intention to renew ourselves depends on the admission of this guilt, incurred by our country and our church...On our church falls the special obligation of improving the tainted relationship between the Church as a whole and the Jewish people and its religion.[8]

The pastoral Council of the Catholic Church in the Netherlands, in 1970, after recalling "the destruction of most of the Jewish communities in the Netherlands in the horrifying persecution during the years of occupation--1940-1945", refers to the fact that "many Christians failed in their duty as a consequence of centuries of Christian anti-semitism,"[9] while the United States Bishops, in their 1967 Guidelines, call for a "frank and honest treatment of the history of Christian anti-semitism" in Roman Catholic history books, courses, and curricula.[10]

The extent to which the call for dialogue in the 1975 Guidelines affects Christian proselytism or missionary activity among Jews is also dealt with by some of the national hierarchies. Thus, the United States Bishops in 1967 stated that "it is understood that proselytizing is to be carefully avoided in the dialogue",[11] while the Dutch Pastoral Council in 1970 rejects "any intention or design for proselytism...as contrary to human dignity and Christian conviction...the position of the Jewish people with regard to the universal message of Christ cannot be equated with the position of those professing other non-Christian religions."[12] The French Bishops' Committees for Relations with Jews speaks in very similar terms in its 1973 statement, concluding its discussion of the implications of dialogue with the reminder that "far from envisaging the disappearance of the Jewish community, the Church is in search of living bonds with it."[13]

It is worth noting in this connection that Pope John Paul II, in a widely misquoted speech given 6 March 1982, spoke in similar terms:

> Christians are on the right path, that of justice and brotherhood, when they seek, with respect and perseverance, to gather with their Semitic brethren around the common heritage which is a wealth to us all. Is there any need to point out, above all to those who remain sceptical or even hostile, that such a rapprochement should not be confused with a certain religious relativism, still less with a loss of identity?...May God grant that Christians and Jews may hold more in-depth exchanges based on their own identities, without ever allowing the one side or the other to be obscured, but always seeking the will of the God who revealed himself.[14]

In the matter of revising liturgical readings, and in coming to terms with Judaism as a contemporary phenomenon, the statements of the various hierarchies do not significantly progress beyond the 1975 Guidelines, but in their 1975 Statement on Catholic-Jewish Relations, the United States Bishops point to what must surely be the greatest challenge now facing Christian theologians engaged in the dialogue with Judaism, namely the need for a Christian theology of Judaism:

171

Much of the alienation between Christian and Jew found its origins in a certain anti-Judaism theology which over the centuries has led not only to social friction with Jews but often to their oppression. One of the most hopeful developments in our time...has been the decline of the old anti-Judaism and the reformation of Christian theological expositions of Judaism along more constructive lines...There is here a task incumbent on theologians, as yet hardly begun, to explore the continuing relationship of the Jewish people with God and their spiritual bonds with the New Covenant and the fulfillment of God's plan for both Church and Synagogue.[15]

Surely an integral part of such a "theology of Judaism" would be a study of the central role played by the Land of Israel in Jewish thought and piety. Since many, indeed most, Jews would include the relationship between the People of Israel and the Land of Israel as "one of the essential traits (by which) the Jews define themselves in the light of their own religious experience," [16] Christian theology will need to probe this bond more seriously. This in fact is already being done, and the statements of some of the national hierarchies reflect that fact, even though neither Nostra Aetate nor the 1975 Guidelines dealt with the matter.[17]

The Future

In a paper of this scope it is impossible to do more than suggest some of the ground that has been covered since the Second Vatican Council. A survey of official church documents tells little of the arduous work of countless theologians, Jewish and Christian, who, like the diggers in Hezekiah's tunnel, are striving to establish Christian Commissions which have been operating at the local, national, and international levels. Perhaps, more importantly, it says nothing of the growing "mutual knowledge and respect" which ordinary Jews and Christians increasingly have for each other's "faith and religious convictions".[18] While barriers and divisions that have stood for nineteen hundred years are at last being broken down, the work is far from completed. If anything, we are only at the beginnings. Wounds that have festered for so long will not heal overnight, and misunderstandings so deeply rooted will not immediately give way to mutual sympathy and comprehension. What matters now is that a beginning has been made, at every level of the Church. If we are to continue advancing along the road pointed out to us in the official documents quoted in this paper, we shall have to reflect seriously in the years ahead upon the four major questions already referred to:

1) How can Christians bear witness to the message of the New Testament in ways which do not deny validity to the Jewish religious experience and create an atmosphere in which both Judaism and the Jewish people lose any legitimate grounds for existence?

2) Can a place be found within Christian theology for the phenomenon of a living, dynamic contemporary Judaism?

3) To what extent is Christian missionary activity compatible with the Jewish-Christian dialogue?

4) What attitude is the Christian to take to the contemporary phenomenon of the restoration of the bond between "the people" and "the land" in the Jewish State of Israel?

These questions will not admit easy answers. But gratitude for the patrimony we share with the Jewish people, respect for them, a longing for the day when we shall all together "address the Lord in a single voice and 'serve him shoulder to shoulder'"[19] - and above all a passionate love of the truth, will not let us rest until we have faced them squarely. May he who has begun this work bring it to a happy conclusion!

NOTES

[1] For the complete English text of the Declaration of the Church to Non-Christian Religions, see Vatican Council II, the Conciliar and Post-Conciliar Documents, edited by Austin Flannery, O.P. (Leominster: Fowler Wright Book Ltd, 1975), pp. 378-342. For the section of the Declaration pertaining to Catholic-Jewish relations, see also Stepping-Stones to Further Jewish-Christian Relations, an Unabridged Collection of Christian Documents, compiled by Helga Croner (Stimulus Books: London/New York, 1977), pp. 1-2. All quotations from official documents in this article, unless otherwise noted, are taken from the latter collection. The two compilations will henceforth be referred to as "Flannery" and "Croner" respectively.

[2] Flannery, pp. 743-749; Croner, pp. 11-16.

[3] The closest that Nostra Aetate comes to defining dialogue is in the concluding paragraph of the section on Hinduism and Buddhism, where Christians are urged, "while witnessing to their own faith and way of life, (to) acknowledge, preserve, and encourage the spiritual and moral truths found among non-Christians, also their social life and culture." Flannery, p. 739.

[4] Croner, p. 7.

[5] Croner, p. 18.

[6] Flannery, p. 803.

[7] A good survey of current literature on this problem can be found in John T. Pawlikowski, What are they Saying about Christian-Jewish Relations? (Paulist Press: New York, 1980).

[8] Croner, p. 66.

[9] Croner, p. 48. It should be noted that the quotations from the Dutch Pastoral Council in this paragraph and the next were a part of the document presented by the Sub-Commission on "The Church and Israel" but were not voted on as part of the official "Pastoral Recommendations."

[10] Croner, p. 20.

[11] Croner, p. 18.

[12]Croner, p. 51.

[13]Croner, p. 64.

[14]The English text of the Pope's address to the delegates of the various Bishops' Conferences on relations with Judaism can be found in Origins, 11:41 (25 March 1982). p. 660.

[15]Croner, pp. 31-33.

[16]The words quoted are from the Vatican Guidelines. Croner, p. 12.

[17]There is a brief survey of "Christian Theology and the Jewish Land Tradition" in Pawlikowski, pp. 109-128. Statements of the United States Bishops, and of the French Bishops, will be found in Croner, pp. 34 and 63-64 respectively.

[18]The words quoted are taken from the Guidelines. Croner, p. 12.

[19]The words quoted are taken from the Guidelines, which take them from Nostra Aetate. Croner, pp. 14 and 1 respectively.

ASIAN SPIRITUALITY: ITS IMPORTANCE IN AMERICA

Thomas Berry

America is no longer religiously composed simply of Catholics, Protestants, and Jews. All the major religions of the world are here. Most of them in a thriving condition, their ancient spiritual disciplines are attracting large numbers of followers. Some are setting up centers in which the interior life is cultivated with an intensity not often found among Christians.

Spiritualities Rather Than A Spirituality

While California is outstanding in the riches of its spiritual-religious foundations with such places as Mount Baldy, Tassajara, the Blue Mountain Meditation Center and the Nyingma Buddhist Institute, there are many places in the East, places like the Tibetan Tail of the Tiger Monastery in Vermont and the Sivananda Conservatory of Yoga in the Poconos. But more immdediately present in New York are the Integral Yoga Institute presided over by Swami Satchidananda, the Zendo directed by Eido Roshi, and the Aurobindo Center, and oldest of them all, the Vedanta Center founded by Swami Vivekananda during the last decade of the nineteenth century. More recently there is the Krishna Consciousness Movement founded by Swami Bhaktivedanta. There are also the influences of the Chinese Confucian and Taoist traditions which are having extensive influence mainly through the courses being given in colleges and through reading and consultation of the I Ching. Finally, there is the influence of the mystical Sufi tradition of Islam.

Obviously, these constitute an extensive complex of spiritualities rather than a single Asian spirituality -- which is the first thing to be noted by anyone interested in the meeting of Christianity with other spiritual traditions which presently is taking place in New York. Several of these, especially Buddhism, Yoga, and Islam, are, individually, as massive or nearly as massive in their impact on the world as is Christian spirituality. In this country India and Japan can be considered the dominant influences at the present time. Because this presentation must be rather brief, we will concern ourselves with the Yoga tradition, Zen, and the intuitive-devotional aspects of the Hindu tradition.

Yoga

The Yogic meditation discipline is so important in the spiritual life of mankind that it might be referred to as man's basic meditation tradition. Originating in primordial India, Yoga has influenced the whole of Asia and now has extended its influence to most of the world. This is due primarily to its depth of insight into the science and practice of interiority. Yoga has concerned itself with the entire psychosomatic process and has established, through interior observation and long centuries of experience, just how a person best enters into the subjective depths of his own being where experience of divine reality takes place.

There are, in the Yogic discipline, eight basic steps toward complete indwelling of the personal consciousness within itself. The first two of these guide the person to a moral rectification of life and to fulfillment of his religious duties. The next three stages indicate just how a person should position the body in the meditation process by sitting in an upright posture with the legs crossed and with a feeling of absolute firmness throughout a person's being. The emotions are then quieted and the first steps toward interior recollection are established by quiet, rhythmic breathing. After this the discipline is trained in the manner in which exterior distraction of the senses is eliminated. The last three stages of Yogic practice include fixation of consciousness on a single point (preferably upon Ishwara, God), the sustaining of this attention, and finally the complete withdrawal of the mind into a state that is known as kaivalya or complete liberation from the temporal mode of being, a state in which the divine reality emerges into a state of pure consciousness.

Zen

The second of the Asian spiritual traditions to be considered here is that of Zen Buddhism. From its beginnings in the sixth century B.C. Buddhism has insisted even more forcefully than Yoga on the insubstantial character of the phenomenal world. The primary experience of Buddhism is Dukha, sorrow. The final experience is Nirvana, bliss. Transformation from sorrow to bliss is achieved by a threefold process beginning with Sila, moral rectification of life, and continuing through Samadhi, intensive development of interior consciousness, until a culminating experience is reached in Nirvana. At this moment a person attains a transcendent mode of being in which all earthly things are seen as transient and ultimately as devoid of reality, as Sunyata. But this moment which is the experience of emptiness is also the experience of fullness, of bliss. Thus Buddhism, which begins in the most absolute sense of an all-pervading pain that is inherent and coextensive with phenomenal existence, ends in absolute bliss.

178

Buddhist tradition developed through many stages and expressed itself in high intellectual achievements in India, and then in the early centuries of our era it moved into China where, in the sixth century A.D., the Zen phase of Buddhism came into existence. Characteristic of Zen is its emphasis on "sudden enlightenment" attained principally by meditation but also by the total life discipline and life experience of a person. The Zen mode of bringing about the transition from pain to bliss is to thwart the reasoning processes on the rational plane and thus to force the mind to break through the basic paradoxes of reality by a sudden illumination in which the mind comes to itself in a moment of pure awareness. This state of absolute simplicity reflects the absolute simplicity of the primordial reality of things. Because of this simplicity Zen fosters a radical spontaneity, a spontaneity, however, which is not that of naivete but of total sophistication.

The attraction of Zen is precisely in this experiential aspect of its teaching, in awakening the depths of the subjective personality, in its ability to evoke creativity, in its sense of identity with the total order of things. Zen sees things as they are and as they are not, for in this state of total awareness a coincidence of opposites takes place. The fixation of things is lost. The upsidedownness of things is seen, as well as the rightsideupness. There is a new appreciation of the rough rather than the pretty, of the natural rather than the artificial, the immediate rather than the derived, the simple rather than the complex, the absolute beyond all relativity.

Hinduism

A third spiritual tradition that is having a significant but less organized influence in America is the mystical-devotional tradition of Hinduism. The doctrine of God in Hinduism is one of the most profound and richest of all the traditions. It begins with the Upanishadic writings. These indicate that the only way of indicating God is to say of him that "He is," or by Svabhava, a word that translates into the Latin Esse Sui Ipsius, or Esse Subsistens, Pure Being. Otherwise the divine is completely ineffable: "There the eye cannot go, nor speech, nor the mind. We neither know nor can we understand how anyone can attain it. It is other than the known and other than the unknown." This sense of the divine is further expressed: "There the sun shines not, nor moon, nor stars. From his radiance everything shines. This whole world is ablaze with his light. It is within everything, it is outside everything." Both transcendence and immanence of the divine are expressed in this passage: "He who dwells in the earth, yet is other than the earth, whom the earth does not know,

179

of whom the earth is the body; He who rules the earth from
within, He is your very Self, the ruler within, the Immortal One."
When we come to liberation from the sorrows of the human
condition we are instructed: "By knowing God, man is freed from
all bonds. His form cannot be seen, no one beholds him with the
eye. He is attained by the heart, by thought, by the mind.
Those who know this become immortal." The need for grace is
indicated: "This Reality is not to be attained by teaching, nor by
intellect, nor by extensive learning. He is attained only by that
one whom he chooses; to him the Supreme Reality reveals his own
form."

In a special manner this sense of the divine is found in the
beautiful prayer of Jnanadeva, an Indian saint of the Marathi
region of India in the twelfth century A.D. He wrote this prayer
of thanksgiving at the end of his commentary on the Bhagavadgita:

> And now may God, Soul of the Universe,
> Be pleased with this my offering of words.
> And being pleased may He give me
> This favor in return.
> That the crookedness of evil men may cease,
> And that the love of goodness may grow in them.
> May all beings experience from one another
> Friendship of heart.
> May the darkness of sin disappear.
> May the universe see the rising of the Sun of
>   Righteousness.
> Whatever is desired, may it be received
> By every living being.
> And may the Supreme Being be worshipped
> For ever and ever.

In all three of these traditions there is a strong sense
1) that pain is coextensive with the human condition, 2) that the
remedy for the human condition is found in a transformation of life
so absolute that it requires a total change in modes of human
awareness and affection, 3) that this change is brought about
within the depths of the subject by a systematic spiritual
discipline known as a Sadhana, 4) in the subjective depths of
man's own being (the Urgrund) he discovers the true, the
numinous, the divine reality and in some manner participates in
this numinous mode of being.

The Christian Response

The proper Christian response to these traditions must include, first of all, a recognition of the spiritual wisdom that they contain and a recognition that divine reality communicates himself abundantly through these traditions, not only to many persons, but to whole societies of mankind. While the Vatican Council indicated only that "a ray of divine light" is evident in these traditions, it might be said more properly that floods of light pour over the earth from these traditions. It is especially important that these traditions not be set aside and opposed simply as "pantheistic" or as "monistic" since, alongside statements of intimate divine presence in things, there is a corresponding emphasis on a total difference between the divine and the human.

The second response must be to indicate that these spiritual practices are not inherently opposed to Christian revelation. They can and must work together that the redemptive transformation of man might take place on a comprehensive global scale as well as on a local or regional or cultural scale. That Christianity has a unique and universal mission in the world does not imply that these other traditions do not also have universal and unique missions. The universalization of one does not imply the extinction of the others. As with the Hellenistic influences on Saint Clement of Alexandria, as with the neo-Platonic influences on Augustine, as with the Aristotelian influences on Aquinas, these influences from Asian spiritual traditions will henceforth be a part of the Christian process itself.

A third response to these traditions must be a realization that the terms "Eastern" and "Western" as used in the spiritual and religious and intellectual orders are no longer simply geographical designations. They refer rather to certain tendencies of the mind and emotions. Thus New York is no longer simply "Western" in a religious-spiritual sense. It is also "Eastern." Once the importance of this has been grasped it will be seen that much more attention should be given to this "Eastern" component of contemporary spirituality in America. This "Eastern" component implies a new emphasis on the subjective, the contemplative, and the natural over the objective, the rational, the technological and the institutional. In a special way it implies a profound sense of the ephemeral character of the entire temporal order of things. While these designations are by no means exclusive to the Eastern or to the Western, there are identifiable differences that can be noted. For India especially the "objective" world that Western man so frequently experiences as "true" reality is experienced by India as so ephemeral that it can almost be called illusory.

A fourth response or effect of contact with these Eastern spiritualities should be the renewal of the mystical traditions of the West. The West is not deficient in this mystical quality of life. The mystical traditions of the Victorines, Saint Bonaventure, Eckhart, Tauler, Ruysbruck, John of the Cross and Teresa have not, however, been dominant influences in the spirituality of Christians in recent centuries. A renewal of these traditions would go far toward enabling Christians to enter into the discussions now taking place concerning the mystical modes of man's religious life. The dogmatic, the moral, and the sacramental need their fulfillment in the immediate experience of the divine. We have been so concerned with means that we may be deficient in our capacity for and understanding of the ecstatic union itself toward which these means are ordained.

While there is not space here to develop any full explanation of the influence of these other spiritual traditions on Christianity, it should be obvious that we are entering a new religious and spiritual "climate." The three basic components of religious teaching -- belief, morality, and worship -- are all being subordinated to that high mode of life formation and spiritual fruition that is generally designated as "spirituality." Without diminishing the importance of belief, morality and worship, these can no longer be the exclusive concern of Christian leaders, whether as theologians, as ecclesiastical authorities, or as pastors. The challenge now is not precisely here but in the personal life-transformation and the modes of interior experience that are achieved within this context. Mankind is starved for the divine, especially our youth of college age. For many reasons, however valid or invalid, large numbers of people have become convinced that this immediacy with the divine is not really available within the existing Christian order of life. The challenge we face is to demonstrate that this experience is available, and abundantly available, within the Christian life context and that it is the normal fulfillment of Christian belief, of Christian life discipline, and the Christian sacraments.

BEING A HINDU IN AMERICA:

A VIEW OF HINDUISM FROM AMERICA BY A HINDU TRANSCENDENTALIST

Satya Pachori

Sarvepalli Radhakrishnan wrote a few years ago: "Though Asia and Europe are different, they are not so completely different as to disallow an interchange of goods, material and spiritual. This interchange has occurred throughout the centuries and points to the underlying unity of the human mind." Likewise, Hinduism and Christianity--though different in creed, metaphysics, character, and observance--have gone through a process of mutual interchange in the past decades. Christian missionaries have been spreading their message in the East since the eighteenth century, as the Hindu swamis have been enlightening the Westerners, especially Americans, since 1893 when Swami Vivekananda delivered his speeches on Hinduism at the World's Parliament of Religions in Chicago and other places during his prolonged stay in the United States. Today many such sages and saints are sharing their Hindu thoughts with their Christian counterparts and general folks in this land.

But beyond their mutual interaction, there is an interesting aspect of glimpsing a view of Hinduism from the largest Christian country in the world. Having lived in America for over two decades now and observed multifarious phases of its lifestyle and thinking, I will venture to examine my own faith in the best possible manner in this short study. It is likely that in this process I may tend to raise some speculative questions and perspectives which, I hope, would be interpreted objectively by the reader, since my own point of view is accountable for the remarks. Besides my long stay here, my teaching obligations to offer courses in Literature of the East, Literature and Religion, Mysticism: East and West, and the like, have aided me to gain a unique insight into the strengths and weaknesses of Hinduism and its devoted followers. Possibly, I would have been deprived of this impetus had I been living in India all these years. Familiar surroundings, as we know, fail to arouse inquisitiveness and indepth probing in one's own faith. Everything then bears to have a Popean deistic overtone of "Whatever is, is right." Geographical distance, on the one hand, reduces intellectual and spiritual distance, and on the other enhances emotional perception of one's religious and cultural heritage. An enlightened view of Hinduism--its strengths and weaknesses alike--could really be possible for me only from the distance of about ten thousand miles, while living and earning my bread in this society of fast moving technology and scientific view of life.

A prevalent Western view about Hinduism seems to be that it concedes no reality to life, that it despises vital aims and materialistic satisfaction, and that it imparts no inspiring motive to human effort. Contrary to the popular impression, Hinduism does not repudiate the world, negate social values, forbid the enjoyment of legitimate pleasures. It points the way to enduring happiness both here and hereafter. Ancient Indian history vouches for this premise in that when the country was spiritually great it was also materially prosperous and culturally creative. Also, if spirit and life are unrelated, spiritual freedom and its constant search would become an unattainable goal, a remote passion of only a few visionaries. The Hindu teachings, as enunciated in the Bhagavad-Gita, Upanishads, and the epics of the Ramayana, and Mahabharata, clearly emphasize that man must pass through the normal life conscientiously, enjoying the fruits of worldly knowledge and values and that he must not be opposed to rational thinking. A Hindu does not ignore the social aspects of man's life. He always thinks of himself as belonging to a family, a varna, or a community.

Moreover, with respect to an average Hindu in the United States, if we examine closely, he does not emphasize the obligation to improve the social groups to which he belongs. After he has paid his membership dues and nominally participated in their social activities, he thinks he has fulfilled his responsibility. That is the reason that most of the Hindus in America socialize so little with their American counterparts that it generates a feeling of provincialism and narrow-minded perception of the West. However, a broader view of universal brotherhood that a typical Hindu tends to nourish while living in the Western society should primarily be oriented to the cultural activities of the community and the subdivision he lives in. The Dharma view of human life, according to the fundemental tenets of Hinduism, is the view of social relationships and obligations which the Hindus ought to be implementing in their lifestyles in America.

One of the major reasons, however, for the Hindus in this country to remain confined to their native cultural groups and their activities is to preserve and uphold their religious values in the midst of alien environment, which is not as much permeated with Christian values as the very life of India is centered in religion. It is inherent in customs regarding marriage, vocation, dining, social and religious festivities and occasions, and other activities of primary group relationships. A Hindu, like his

184

Christian friend, does not make a decision about his involvement in such cultural activities, but feels innately a part of these. An average Hindu in America, as my perceptions may have convinced me, takes no cognizance of religion as an independent phenomenon as is done by his colleagues or neighbors. In the West there seems to be an obvious conflict between religion and science, Church and State, faith and reason. I trust that my fellow-Indians would continue keeping their faith inseparable from communal and social life, and thus also convince their American friends about the value of religion in day-to-day life.

Hinduism, unlike Christianity, is a way of life unseparated from politics, economics, and to a degree from sciences. Today, it is quite fashionable and popular to harp the songs of secularism toward the development of science and technology. However, a fundamental premise remains that the physical sciences, like religion, are governed by universal laws, and if they are animated by certain spiritual ideals they could bring about an ideal world. Religions, too, if oriented to the scientific spirit of reasoning and experimentation, can remove dogmatism and parochialism from their creeds. Without the help of technology, it should be asserted here, many of the cherished ideals of universal brotherhood would remain mere abstract theories when the world is suffering from overpopulation, malnutrition, unknown diseases, hunger, and poverty. May I suggest that the separation of science and religion in the name of secularism has been a major tragedy for mankind in the twentieth century. The relationship of science and religion can "be likened to that of body and soul: the body without a soul is a mere corpse, and the soul without a body, a mere phantom."[2]

Another practical dilemma that an average Hindu encounters in the United States is the glaring want of temples and other facilities for collective and individual worship with the exception of large cities like New York, Chicago, Los Angeles, Pittsburgh, Houston, and Toronto, where the largest number of Hindu population is centered. Popular worship in India is generally pervaded by a spirit of joyousness and merriment. The atmosphere of a Hindu temple reverberates with songs, hymns, mirth, and bliss, procreated by the presence of the deity, incenses and fragrant flowers. Devotees in times of grief and sorrow get relief and solace by assuming that their prayers are being accepted by their deity, hence deliverance is on hand.

The lack of proper worship-centers for the Hindus in America is somehow countered by family worship at home. Most of the devout Hindus keep images and pictures of their favorite deities in a sacred corner at their homes, which is a convenient substitute

for a formal temple. These images and pictures of humanized
manifestation of the Godhead--Vishnu, Shiva, Rama, Krsna--serve
as symbols of certain powers and attributes of the Supreme, thus
helping devotees to establish a definite relationship with Him.
Performance of certain rituals is considered a necessary part of
Hindu worship, because rituals are conducive to deeper
concentration, hence leading to immediate spiritual values. The
highest tangible result of ritual with meditation is an intuitive
feeling of bliss, an exalted form of phenomenal bliss. By means of
ritual with mediation, that is upasana, a sincere devotee can
gradually sublimate his desires for crude materialistic objects.
The reason most of the Hindus perform and believe in certain
rituals is that rituals also help create a religious environment,
which may lead to the devotee's exuberance of sentiments at a
particular festival or occasion.

Transcending the ritual worship, Hinduism also stresses the
mental or spiritual worship, something which an average Hindu in
this country is likely to practice. He or she can do so anywhere
without a formal consecrated atmosphere. This is possible on the
way to the office in the car, or in the office chair during the
lunch or coffee breaks. During the course of the mental worship,
the devotee can regard the heart as the seat of the deity whom he
conceives as having a luminous body. All the articles of worship,
such as flowers, light, incense, food, and water, can be formed
into mental images. This kind of mental worship as opposed to
physical worship is a more spiritual and a practically convenient
way of offering one's prayers in a society where the hectic pace of
life tends to make time so precious. A related method of both
mental and physical worship can be observing fasts. What else
does fasting provide other that inner purity? That is what a
Hindu in the West finds convenient for him to observe and thus
seek perfect religious illumination for his own individual self.

Another spark of the ancient heritage that the Hindus
perpetuate in this country is their "intense individualism of the
Indo-Aryans," which has led us "to attach little importance to the
social aspect of man, of man's duty to society,"[3] as I have
referred to earlier. This exclusive individualism has imprisoned
the mind of our people even in the fold of the Hindu caste system.
Fortunately, along with the growth of the rigidity in the caste
system in India, the Hindus here have undermined the caste
consideration and prejudice in their social fellowship, but have
kept the barrier alive to a large degree in the marital relationship
of their sons and daughters. The fanaticism of casteism, however,
which has hurt India incalculably in the past, has been replaced
by provincialism and linguistic prejudices. In every major

cosmopolitan city, one can find independent cultural organizations of various provincial affiliations like those of the Gujaratis, Marathis, Bengalis, Panjabis, Tamilians, Biharis, and others. Their pretext might be the preservation of their social customs and linguistic affinities that possibly might beguile the universal character of Hinduism. By all means, this ultimately leads to narrow parochialism and social and political conflicts among themselves. This further generates uncivil snobbery, envy, and superiority-inferiority complexes, bringing shame and disgrace to one of the ancient religions in the world.

What is so stunning about this lasting and perpetual evil of Hinduism is that it would likely affect even the younger generation of American Hinduism. What we have not been able to learn from our Christian neighbors, friends, and colleagues is that the ties of regionalism and linguistic fanaticism ought to be overcome at least in a society that is equal to any other society on this planet. A Christian from Texas will not suffer from the Southern heritage when socializing with a Northerner from Maine. I really expected that the Hindus in America, so highly educated and professionally advanced, would have learned a valuable lesson from their Christian friends about the social futility and the cancerous character of casteism and provincialism. Unfortunately, we have not done so and our personal ideologies are pretty much formulated by our shallow bonds, which hurt us enormously in our perception of Western values and pragmatism. Our inability to appreciate the true character of American individualism born of Franklinian Protestant Ethic or the work ethic of hard work and integrity-- which in essence seems to be a blend of Hindu Dharma and Karma--has kept us less than utilitarian and pragmatic in our ways, manners, and values, despite our preachings of the so-called Oriental idealism.

A thought-provoking but somewhat controversial question arises here: Does an average Hindu in America desire to learn and practice the basic ingredients of Americanism? My straightforward answer is in the negative. The obstacles for him are his provincial attitudes, self-serving ends, self-seeking motives, and the lack of individual morality and ethical standards. Oddly enough, what he enjoys learning most is a blind imitation of Western values without rhyme and reason, which ironically tempts him to lose his self-respect and dignity. His unthoughtful approach to the terrors and temptations of Western society by adopting, for example, the dating system, sexual promiscuity, exotic fashionable clothes, food, and perfumes, makes him a willing victim of his self-imposed degradation. What is worse and sickening is that he lays no restraints of discipline upon his teenage children who are rather encouraged to feel a sense of pride in imitating the behavior of their American counterparts.

About two years ago, while reading an article, "When the Twain Does Meet," by one Gitanjali in <u>Femina</u> (May 8-22, 1981), my wife pointed out to me the trends of young Indian women, aged 16 to 23, for becoming more Americanized than their American girlfriends. They were interviewed by the author at the Indian pavilion of Man and His World, Montreal, Canada. Their complete rejection of the Hindu arranged-marriage system, subservence to a man (husband or father), unthinking obedience to parents, and outdated concept of modesty and grace, was just too appalling to comprehend. On the other hand, their slavish acceptance of dating and qualified acceptance of pre-marital sex and living-together with male friends sounded very much like a clarion call for the death of innate Hinduism--its distinct self-discipline of virginity and control of senses--in the West. Their overwhelming support for divorce in the name of incompatibility between married couples bore the imprint of the darker side of Americanism. Likewise their concept of Western freedom was centered on the physical as opposed to the intellectual freedom:

> What do they like about the West? 'The freedom, beginning with freedom for the body...We don't have to worry about what we wear, what's covered up and what's not. When the mercury rises, the clothes drop.'... Their sense of physical freedom is just the outward expression of an inner freedom they find here in the West--honesty, frankness, and something they'd like to have more of--freedom from guilt (p. 17)

Even a mature Hindu mother, embodying the best qualities of South Indian womanhood--warm, cultured, well-educated, strong, feminine, and expressive--told Gitanjali: "Being brought up in India doesn't equip one for life in the West. Bringing up my sons was easy, but my daughter, well, it is difficult. Everyday I'm learning. I know I have to give her freedom" (p. 17). Lots of luck to the psuedo-liberal and spurious ultra-modern Hindu mother who misconstrued the meaning of freedom as much as her daughter! In all earnestness, they both failed to appreciate the social but sensual character of Western dating. For them, kissing, touching, embracing, much less sex, outside marriage was an indispensable part of Western socializing for a balanced growth of one's personality. I can surmise that the mother may not have approved of her dear daughter's demand for such physical freedom as long as the deep imprint of Hinduism remained ingrained in her value-system which should have at one time consisted of control, discipline, inner strength, and modesty. But with the passage of her stay in the heat of the passionate West, all this evaporated fast.

Ironically, the dear mother did not realize for a minute that her daughter's friends--boys and girls alike--remained uninfluenced from her Indian association and the impact of her native culture. How many Americans have ever adopted any moral values of the Hindus despite their decades-old social relationship with them? How many divorced American couples have accepted the strengthening bonds of the Hindu marriage system? None whatsoever in my recollection, and no one will ever do, for the assaults of senses are hard to overcome in an industrialized society. Had the freedom-loving girls interviewed by Gitanjali raised the issues of Eastern dowry vs. Western divorce along with the problems of peer pressure and professional competition that they encountered during their schooling and vocation, a different perspective about their thinking personality would have emerged. They then could have strengthened their reasoning for adopting Western behavior to a certain extent. This was not to be so.

At times we just happen to wonder about the unethical impact of the separation of religion from day-to-day life, so glaringly present in the entire West. I hate to question the fragile practice of Christianity and its virtues by its followers in practical life. My repeated study and teaching of the Bible--both the New Testament and the Old Testament--have fully convinced me that the spiritual message in the pages of these scriptures is as didactic and viable as in any major scriptures of other faiths. Why are the basic ennobling teachings of Jesus Christ being unhelpful to ameliorate the decaying morality of the West, especially in the field of marital relationship which is inundated with broken marriages, divorces, and motherless or fatherless children? Evidently, in my view, Christianity has not yet become a way of life as is Hinduism in India, where divorce is as much a rarity as parental control in America.

There are ways when life and religion take different routes for the sake of their convenience, so that one does not conflict with the other. The day may not be far off when the Hindus in the West, like Gitanjali's mother, would gladly accept their designation as Anglo-Hindus--Christian in physical freedom and Hindu in family's security. Such Hindus will be happy to live with two kinds of discipline: domestic discipline at home when their children may not be disrespectful to their elders, even though they may not accept their norms of life; and professional discipline in the outside world in order to gain better advancement in their vocations. There is, however, a noticeable dichotomy between domestic and professional discipline in the American society. One can find an independent relationship between an American father and a son, a mother and a daughter--something not normally seen in an Indian household--, but they are at their best on their jobs. The domestic fragility is replaced by the strength of professional discipline, an important phenomenon in reverse in India where professional discipline has virtually gone out of sight and has been replaced by corruption, nepotism, bribery, casteism, and provincialism. The Hindus in America, either by compulsion, peer pressure, or the fear of job security, have effectively inculcated professional discipline in their personal system, even though they may be getting weaker in domestic discipline (unlike their folks in India) out of sheer imitation of the society in which they live and move about. The Western principle of activity, even if with a deep involvement in materialistic activity, has been fully accepted instead of the Hindu <u>Karma</u> as an affirmation of life.

Regardless of Eastern and Western differences of value-systems and their heterogeneous lifestyles, I would consider both Hinduism and Christianity steeped in the best liberal tradition of tolerance and understanding. The religious philosophies of these two faiths, notwithstanding their ages and longevity of following, are among the most open-minded philosophies that I have ever studied. Christ and Krsna, Moses and Manu, St. Augustine and Buddha have been accepted as manifestations of the divine power. Consequently, an average Hindu can adjust himself (herself) well in this largest Christian nation in the world and does well professionally as well as morally as long as he preserved his own heritage and respects the ethical system as given in his sacred scriptures. A Hindu does not reject anything that he can possibly absorb, nor does he declare to be false that which might have a modicum of truth. Intellectual tolerance is also an expression of the Hindu way of thinking. A typical manner of Hindu thought is an exploration of possibilities rather than the reaching of conclusions. An average Hindu in America ought to specialize in hypothesis formation of heterogeneous factors of human values and ought not to push a single hypothesis into the role of the solution of a set of problems. That is why I shall refrain from suggesting any concrete solutions to the varied problems faced by the Hindu parents in raising their teenage children and seeking social adjustment in this society. I am somewhat leery lest in doing so my own values should conflict with theirs. Let their experience be their own guide.

The Christian spirit of catholicity matches well with the Hindu spirit of universal brotherhood or "Vasudeva Kutumbakam." The catholicity of Hinduism is best understood and felt as a transcendental Hindu looks at it from the United States. Then only its integrative personality and culture scintillate. A Westerner will have difficulty in understanding this unique aspect of Hindu culture because, whereas in the West the national state and politics are the chief agents of integration, in the East the people are united by myth, metaphysics, and art.

The Hindus living in America ought to be aware of the fundamental teachings of their faith and learn the most sublime truth of Dharma and Karma through the work ethic of American pragmatism. They should be reminded of what Swami Vivekananda told a reporter of the Daily Tribune in Bay City, Michigan, March 12, 1894, regarding his impressions of this country: "This is a great land, but I wouldn't like to live here. Americans think too much of money. They give it preference over everything else. Your people have much to learn. When your nation is as old as ours you will be wiser."[4]

NOTES

[1] Eastern Religions and Western Thought (Oxford, 1967), p. 115.

[2] Swami Nikhilananda, Hinduism: Its Meaning for the Liberation of the Spirit (Madras, 1968), p. 15.

[3] Jawaharlal Nehru, The Discovery of India (New York, 1960), pp. 60-61.

[4] The Complete Works of Swami Vivekananda (Calcutta, 1976), p. 479.

THE MUSIC OF THE EARTH:
THE EPISTEMOLOGY OF MORAL CULTURES

Antonio T. de Nicolas

> Not from me but from my mother
> comes the tale how Earth and Sky
> were once together, but being rent asunder
> brought forth all things, . . .
> (Euripides, Fragment 484)
>
> The Earth is my mother;
> I am the son of the Earth.
> (Atharva Veda 12, 12.)

Introduction

The greatest enemy of history is chronology, and the greatest ally of chronology is nominalism. Through semantic transpositions the world is made linguistically uniform; possibilities are obliterated; univocal meanings are universalised; chronology blankets the world and history; the actual history of Man is full of empty spaces.

This essay is an effort at reviving an old theme, an idea as old as humanity itself: the return to the power of the Earth. We shall develop this theme by touching on the Earth as present need, as opening the empty spaces of history, as forgotten epistemology, as the breath of Man breathing himself and his gods. This is an effort to release Man from the present controls of a technological epistemology which has momentarily obliterated Man's memory of Man's human body and reduced him to wander the circles of this controlling epistemology.

We presuppose that the reader is familiar with the major texts of Eastern cultures and religions, especially Vedic and Hindu, and to a certain degree with our own work about these cultures.

Destitute Times

These are destitute times, as Heidegger and Nietzsche remind us. These are destitute times for all, the men and women in the street as well as those in academic circles, for those who pray and for those who interpret:

It is the time of the gods that have fled
and of the god that is coming. It is the
time of need, because it lies under a
double lack and a double Not: the No-more
of the gods that have fled and the Not-yet
of the god that is coming.[1]

Man has been abandoned by the sun and the light, the same
sun and the same light he enthroned in the sky.

The time of the world's night is the
destitute time, because it becomes ever
more destitute. It has already grown so
destitute, it can no longer discern the
default of God as a default.[2]

There are no centers any longer for Man; no stars in the
sky. The things of the worlds of Man are tumbling in the dark
and heading for the Abyss.

The default of God means that no god
any longer gathers men and things unto
himself, visibly and unequivocally, and
by such gathering disposes the world's
history and man's sojourn in it.[3]

It is the time of ideologies, of opinions, of knowledge and trivia
without understanding. It is the time when the last children--
things and ideas--of an epistemology in the throngs of death is
procreating in an already overpopulated world.

These destitute times are, according to Nietzsche, the result
of a universal lapse in memory. We have forgotten the Earth of
which we were born and have stubbornly followed the path of the
sun--a particular theoretical path--of which we are the victims:

What did we do when we unchained this earth
from its sun? Whither is it moving now?
Whither are we moving now? Away from all suns?
Are we not plunging continually? Backward,
sideward, forward, in all directions? Is
there any up or down left? Are we not
straying as through an infinite nothing?
Do we feel the breath of empty space? Has
it not become colder? Is not night and more
night coming on all the while?[4]

Both Heidegger and Nietzsche strove through philosophy to recapture the origins of Man's memory by returning to an absolute origin of Man himself. They wanted to save Man from his circling path. Unfortunately, for them and for those who followed them, their origins were completely unoriginal. By a sleight of the hand they place Man's origins and Man's ability to recover his memories by returning to Greece. Thus, the Earth, with all its history and its possibilities, was reduced to a particular world of a few men and their limited memories. But the Earth is not the world; the Earth, rather, is the womb of all the worlds, many worlds, the womb of all flesh, the womb of all memories of which Greece is but an instance.

Man's origins are as elusive as his future; but, unless he recovers them, he will forever be a child of alien powers with a predetermined destiny. Western philosophers returning to Greece searching for origins did not only invent those origins, but they also had to invent "Greece." Our memories, as Western Men's, are already culturally distorted.

The "return to Greece" was started in Greece itself by the Greeks with their superior way of handling barbarians.[5] Greece was culturally self-possessed, while the barbarian was an "outsider." But Oedipus already pointed out: "I was evil from birth"--a remark which has escaped those who have found absolute integrity in Greece to be the worthwhile reason to return to it again and again. Rome, the Fathers of the Church, the Italian Renaissance, Romanticism, all turned to Greece for a justification of their present glory; but in doing so, they established Greece as the exclusive "origin" of our own culture. The preponderance of Greek studies, as opposed to the scarcity of other cultural studies, the exuberance of praise lavished on the Greek metaphor easily clouded the fact that Greece was overcoming and submerging all other cultures. "No other mythology known to us--developed or primitive, ancient or modern--is marked by quite the same complexity and systematic quality as the Greek."[6] Although such a typical Western cliche rings with comforting appeal, it is not true; for all other mythologies and cultures must be measured by their own criteria, not the metaphorical "Greek" criterion. Indeed the "Greece" we speak of is as mythological as its myths. It includes all periods from Minoan to Hellenistic, all localities from Asia Minor to Sicily, and a multitude of other cultures from the Far and Near East. In fact, ". . . until the age of Romanticism, Greece was no more than a museum inhabited by people beyond contempt."[7] And had it not been that we needed to go somewhere else--the past--in order to patch up the present, we certainly would have left the dead buried.

Augustine went to Greece to rationalize the universal image
of man he already believed in; St. Thomas Aquinas followed suit.
Petrarch, who could not read Greek, did more in the fourteenth
century than anyone else to revive the literature of Greece; he
strove to discover a way of acting which, by being identified as
Greek, would be termed more human. Winkelmann, who fathered
the idolatry of Greece in the eighteenth century, never actually
set foot in Athens, nor did Racine, nor Goethe, Holderlin, Hegel,
Heine, Keats, nor even Nietzsche. Yet for all these people, as
well as for Stravinsky, Picasso, Heidegger, Joyce, Freud, and
Jung, the return to Greece was essential for aesthetic,
philosophical and psychological motivations. Yet this Greece we
are told to return to is an "emotion-charged image of Greece."[8]
By focusing on that metaphorical image, we reinforce our present
condition of disintegration which fathered the idealization of
Greece in the first place. But by closing ourselves into a
pre-established image of our past, we turn away from our current
opportunity of rediscovering the primordial ground of our flesh,
and of our human culture. Neither memory nor imagination may
liberate us from our present predicament--from the predicament of
the present--in fact, they seem to bury us more deeply there. We
need to discover not theories, but the activity in which both
theories and communication about theories were originally rooted.
Our alternative is to remain mired in chronology, thus circling
the same theoretical wagons. The wings of our memories and
imagination are ensnared by the string of a method that makes a
liberating flight impossible.

Psychology as well as philosophy has been unable to discover
our origins. Psychology has only taught the individual to revert
to his childhood through memory (Freud) or to return to Greece in
search of original archetypes through the use of imagination
(Jung). The rest of psychology has become caught in a semantical
game; the only invariant for the individual in search of therapy
is the theoretical demand that sickness and health both be reduced
to fleshless names: radical nominalism and cultural lobotomy.
Thus, the individual seems condemned to end up where he always
is: in the same place where he started his past; memory then
becomes a reinforcement of the same idea of individuality which
led him to the psychiatric couch. Or he is again sent, through
imagination to Greece in search of origins: and in place of
origins, he discovers a multiplicity of archetypes or personalities
with which he can do a number of things--but he can never
embody them. These archetypes are not the radical origins of
man; they are only images of a more radical man, who was or is
yet to be. But by returning to Greece as the origin of Western

man, what Western man does is to draw an imaginary line between himself and the rest of humanity. By acting thus, all he does is reinforce the controls of his present cultural isolation and sickness. "The whole of Western philosophy" Whitehead said, "is just a footnote to Plato." But what hardly anyone has bothered to find out is how Plato himself is a footnote to previous cultures, for neither Plato nor Greece are absolute beings.[9] Underlying them there is still Man, the maker of ideas and cultures of Man.

No human therapy is possible unless memory, imagination, and names are released from the controls of their methods and stretched as far as what Ortega y Gasset called "lived memories." Man must not only face his images and theories about himself--which are easily verifiable--but he must confront his radical capacity to falsify the theories and images of Man; it is only at this level that man can execute his right to freedom and continuity through the surrounding controls by inhabiting the epistemological skin facing him in the form of the other.

Man, thus understood, bespeaks the possibilities of Man as realized by Man, and in this realization Man exercises his right to innovation and continuity. Our human path cannot be saved by a leap of faith away from Man, or a leap into the superhuman future or Super-Man. As Nietzsche says, quoting Holderlin's poem "Mnemosyne":

> . . . The heavenly powers
> Cannot do all things. It is the mortals
> Who reach sooner into the Abyss. So the turn is
> With these.[10]

Our human path is the Earth. But how can we uncover the Earth without splitting it open again? The uncovering of the Earth is, of course, not a solution; it is rather a journey into the history of the Earth. It is a jump into a historical epistemological Abyss, a jump which needs execution every time Man faces Man, or Man finds himself destitute, caught or frozen into a repetitious path.

The Epistemology of the Earth

It will not be possible for us to release the memories of the Earth unless we gain some distance from the present epistemology ruling the Earth. As Heidegger remarks:

> Even this, that man becomes the subject
> and the world the object, is a consequence
> of technology's nature establishing itself,

and not the other way around.[11]

Contemporary Man is moved around by the hidden forces of technology's epistemology. By this epistemology the Earth and the world are objects twisted around human beings. To paraphrase Heidegger, against this world as object, Man stations himself and sets himself up as the one who deliberately exhausts all productivity from artifacts to interpretations of others. The confusion that has been produced in modern languages by the pair of Greek words dynamis and energeia is not simply chance. In Greek dynamis is opposed to energeia in the way "potentiality" is opposed to "actuality." Possibility and capacity belong to the first, while actual things, reality, belong to the second. For contemporary Man, however, "power" and "possibilities" (dynamis) have become identified with "energy" (energeia), which in Greek would not exhaust the possibilities. Possibilities are thereby destroyed, and yet empty scholarship continues.

We have, therefore, no other alternative but to be daring and attempt an epistemological jump away from our contemporary conditioning into the multiple presuppositions, criteria, and beliefs which form the epistemological field of other cultures and thus suggest the source of our suppressed memories.

We must dialogue with those cultures, those worlds which took sound and its criteria as the model of language--action, theory, communication--and which for thousands of years made the men and women of the oral cultures of India, Sumer, Babylon, Egypt, China, Palestine, what they were. They also belong to our memories stored within each human despite formidable cultural controls.

Epistemological Fields

From the simple analysis of speaking and listening, we know that a word spoken in a sentence does not simply gain meaning from the relationship of words within a sentence. The sentence is not the source from which the inanimate, individual word receives its life; rather a linguistic field, common and present to the speaker and hearer, form the silent background out of which the sentence emerges, and within which certain individual words gain meaning. If an individual word is to be understood, it will speak only in accord with the norms of the entire linguistic field. Thus some words and sentences may break this inaudible and silent background, create an audible style, movement, and foreground, but only on the basis of the total linguistic background. The meaning of a word is only in the total linguistic field and only yields its meaning in terms of that specific field.

Words and linguistic fields need to appear simultaneously for any word to have meaning; simple succession of words or sentences is meaningless unless the entire linguistic field or language appears simultaneously. This means that an interpretation of a particular historical text cannot be accomplished by etymology alone; in fact, etymology may imply certain universal affinities among words which have no radical relationship in their historical linguistic fields; or, because of the etymological relationships, designating meaning though etymology may erase any and all historical sources of meaning.

The silent and historical field, the background, the linguistic whole is vibrated and broken by the spoken word without its being erased or cancelled. Thus, philosophy's task is to return the act of creation to the history of language by retrieving, with each historical verbal gesture, the historical linguistic field, or consciousness it counts on in order to emerge. It is in such terms that we may understand the meaning of a particular word from different historical periods or even from one historical period.

No later than the third millenium B.C. and probably more than a thousand years earlier, man discovered that the intervals between tones could be defined by the ratios of the lengths of pipes and strings which sounded them. It was the ear that made ratios invariant; by its vivid memory of the simpler intervals, the ear made the development of science of pure relations possible within the theory of numbers, the tone-field being isomorphic with the number field. From this musicalized number theory, which we know as "ratio theory," but which the ancients simply called "music," man began his model building. The ratios of the first six integers defined the primary building blocks: the octave 1:2, the fifth 2:3, the fourth 3:4, the major third 4:5, and the minor third 5:6. From these first six integers, functioning as multiples and submultiples of any reference unit ("1") of length or frequency, a numerological cosmology was developed throughout the Near and Far East. The ultimate source of this "Pythagorean" development is unknown. The hymns of the Rg Veda, the Gita, and Buddhism resound with evidence that their authors were fully aware of or conditioned by it and alive to the variety of models it could provide.

Tones recur cyclically at every doubling or halving of frequency or wave-length, and they are reciprocal: Vrtra-Agni; Prakrti-Purusa; Arjuna-Krsna; Samsar-Nirvana; thus the "basic miracle of music." From this acoustical phenomenon, the number 2 acquires a "female" status; it defines invariantly the octave matrix within which all tones come to birth. Here, in this initial identification of the octave with the ratio 1:2, is the root of all the problems which haunt the acoustical theorist, problems which the ancient theorist conceived as symbolizing the imperfection and disorder of the universe and also its renewal through new tones, new births, new songs, and new gods. The octave refuses to be subdivided into subordinate cycles by the only language ancient man knew -- the language of natural number, or integers, and the rational numbers derived from them. It is a blunt arithmetical fact that the higher powers of 3 and 5 which define subordinate intervals of music never agree with higher powers of 2 which define octave cycles. Thus man's yearning for this impossible agreement introduced a hierarchy of values into the number field. For our ancestors, the essence of the world and of the numbers which interpreted that world was sound, not substance, and that world was rife with disagreement among an endless number of possible structures, possible worlds. The epistemological field of sound remained invariant.

Therefore, from a linguistic and cultural perspective, we have to be aware that we are dealing with languages where tonal and arithmetical relations establish the epistemological invariances. Invariance was not physical, but epistemological; ratio theory was a science of pure relations; its fixed elements came from the recognition of the octave, fifth, and derivative tonal relations which made ratio concrete. The divorce of music from mathematics came later. Language grounded in music is grounded thereby on context dependency; any tone can have any possible relation to other tones, and the shift from one tone to another, which alone makes melody possible, is a shift in perspective which the singer himself embodies. Any perspective (tone) must be "sacrificed" for a new one to come into being; the song is a radical activity which requires innovation while maintaining continuity, and the "world" is the creation of the singer, who shares its dimensions with the song. The octave remained the epistemological invariant, "Mother-Earth," of which all these worlds are the offspring.

In ancient times, the infinite possibilities of the number field were considered isomorphic with the infinite possibilities of tone. Pythagorean tuning theory set no theoretical limit to the divisions of an octave; it knew many alternative definitions of the scale, and allowed for extensive modal permutation of that material. Today in the West, we use number to constrict all possibility to an economically convenient limit; the international pitch standard of

A = 44 Hertz and the limitation to 12 equal semi-tones within the octave seem antithetical to the spirit and needs of music. Ancient, oral man, like his Greek counterparts, knew himself to be the organizer of the scale, and thus cherished the multitude of possibilities open to him too much to freeze himself into a single dogmatic posture. His language kept alive an openness to alternatives, and still avoided entrapment in anarchy. It also resolved the fixity of theory by setting the body of man historically moving through the freedom of musical spaces, viewpoint transpositions, reciprocals, pluralism, and finally, an absolute radical sacrifice of all theory as fixed invariant. The Earth was alive and procreating.

Thus, a vibrating string of any reference length, the "Norm" of which grounded all early civilizations in mathematical acoustics, could be halved to sound the octave higher or doubled to sound the octave lower. Since all tones recur cyclically at the octave, any octave can serve as the model for all possible octaves, at least for the general purposes of tuning theory. The cyclic structure of the octave is the invariant ground common to all systems of tuning, and the explicit references to circles in the Ṛg Veda, as in Plato, suggest that the tones were actually graphed in a "tone-circle," which functioned as a cyclic matrix or "mother" within which derivative tones came to birth, or were generated. Unless one has the experience of actually tuning an instrument, behaving as "midwife" to successive tones, the activity of generation may have little meaning. This may be the reason why Plato's genetic theory, with its sexual metaphors, has never been fully understood.

Indeed Plato reminds us of the traditions we are now recalling. Musical criteria introduce a hierarchy into the field of number; even numbers define the octave matrix as "female"; odd numbers fill that matrix with "tone-children" and are defined as "males"; the smaller numbers define intervals of greater importance, and poetic metaphor (or an allusion to sound criteria) differentiate number ages before our specialized mathematical vocabulary was developed. The part of the continuum of real number which lies beyond rational number belongs to non-Existence (Asat) and the Dragon (Vṛtra). Though to a mathematician all numbers may be holy, to a musician some are far more valuable than others: the "divinity" of 3, the "humanity" of 5, and the "sexual roles" of even and odd reflect their tonal functions. The number 2 is "female," Mother, Earth—in the sense that it creates the matrix—the octave—in which all other tones are born. However, by itself it can only create, as in Socrates' phrase, "cycles of barrenness," for multiplication and division by 2 can never introduce new tones into the tone-mandala. It is a theme of ancient cultures, and of the Ṛg Veda in particular, that the Original Unity is hermaphrodite, producing a daughter, "2," by a process of division without benefit of a mother. God is "1," but he cannot procreate except via his daughter, "2," the female principle and mother of all:

> Not from me but from my mother
> comes the tale how earth and sky
> were once together, but being rent asunder
> brought forth all things, . . .

as Euripides reminds us in Fragment 484, echoing a cultural theme as early as the Ṛg Veda.

Ancient hymns of the Ṛg Veda, for example, describe numbers poetically by distinguishing "sets" or "quanta" by classes of gods and dragons and heroes, and also by portraying tonal and arithmetical relations with graphic sexual and musical metaphors. The continuum of the circle (Vṛtra) is dismembered repeatedly by Indra, for it embraces all possible differentiations. The conflict between Indra and Vṛta never ends; it is the conflict between the field of rational numbers and the continuum of real number. Integers which introduce new "cuts" in the tone-mandala demonstrate "Indra power" over Vṛtra; Vṛtra (Puruṣa--Man--for that matter) is "cut to pieces"--"dismembered"--in every battle with the gods, for his death is their own. Without the Asat, or its equivalent, Vrtra--the Dragon--there would be no Indra, nor even the gods; for he is their container.

The Earth is Mother, embracing all possibilities, defining all cycles, creating continuously, but determining nothing within things, cycles or creations. It is sheer possibility.

The Way of the Earth: Language on the Model of Sound.

Since I and others have already verified these points elsewhere,[12] I would like at this point to draw some inevitable conclusions in as plain a language as possible.

The Spanish philosopher, Miguel de Unanumo, in one of his most inspired moments wrote: "Yo no naci'; me nacieron," which means: "I wasn't born; they bore me." Epistemology is primary as is its movement.

Harmonical analysis or the correlation between tone and number stands in ancient cultures as the epistemological ground of apparently plural ontologies. One of the earliest physical facts recognized by man was that nature presents itself as restless and impermanent and that nothing physical is unchanging.

Philosophers in India, Sumer, Babylon, Egypt, Palestine, and China established the first epistemological invariant: the musical octave of the ratio 1:2, which functions as a matrix for all smaller intervals and provides the metric basis for a tonal algebra. Though today we know that octave invariance is modified in extreme ranges of pitch, this first myth of invariance gave us some of the most enlightened cultures on this planet while creating also the basis for abstract numbers theory and geometrical algebra. This simple explanation of the myth of invariance will account not only for the cultures known as Buddhism and Hinduism, but also for the subcultures or counter-cultures which from monasteries or the forests tried to challenge this original myth of octave invariance by trying to reach the extreme ranges of pitch.

Tuning theory establishes for us certain epistemological criteria which we need bear in mind if any meaning is to be derived from any culture which takes tone as the ground of language: a) it is not the case that numbers or ratios control movement, but it is the case that movement may be ordered according to certain ratios; we are not watching the movement of certain sounds, but rather we are watching how movement becomes certain sounds; b) tones may be generated by numbers; this generation does not give us isolated elements, but rather constellations of elements in which each tone is context-and structure-dependent; c) within the matrix of the octave any tonal pattern may rise or fall, hence opposite or reciprocal possibilities are equally relevant, both in the sense of time (order) and space (rising-falling); d) any perspective remains just one out of a group of equally valid perspectives, and the variety of possible perspectives from which to view any set of tones is apparently inexhaustible; any realization (i.e., any song) excludes all other possibilities while it is sounding, but no song has so universal an appeal that it terminates the invention of new ones; e) linguistic statements remain structure-and context-dependent, and the function of any language is to make clear its own dependence on and reference to other linguistic systems; a model based on the primacy of sound is not based on the reality of substance. Whereas the eye fastens on what is fixed, the ear is open to the world of movement in which "Existence" (Sat) and "Non-Existence" (Asat) are locked in an eternal and present absence/presence.

G. Spencer Brown in his Laws of Form writes:

A universe comes into being when a space is severed
or taken apart. The skin of a living organism cuts
off an outside from an inside. So does the
circumference of a circle in a plane. By tracing
the way we represent such a severance, we can
begin to reconstruct, with an accuracy and
coverage that appear almost uncanny, the basic
forms underlying linguistic, mathematical, physical
and biological science, and begin to see how the
familiar laws of our own experience follow
inexorably from the initial act of severance.
The act itself is always remembered, even if
unconsciously, as our first attempt to
distinguish things in a world where, in the
first place, the boundaries can be drawn anywhere
we please. At this stage the universe cannot be
distinguished from how we act upon it and the world
may seem like shifting sand beneath our feet.

Although all forms and thus all universes are
possible, and any particular form is mutable, it
becomes evident that the laws relating such forms
are the same in any universe.[13]

Our most basic pattern, then, is simply a distinction, a
severance, a dismemberment, an inside and an outside or a sound
carved into the sphere of silent potentiality. It is some form by
which to distinguish and relate other forms by. Having made the
initial severance, further subdivisions are inevitable, and various
universes--languages--evolve.

The act of subdivision implies some sort of numerical
groupings or patterns and it follows that the next group of
elementary patterns-equations must deal with the simplest ways of
grouping the subdivisions in a field. As it so happens, one of the
most common pattern characteristics in many disciplines is the
distinction between events occurring in groups of twos or multiples
thereof and events occurring in groups of threes. Most familiar
geometric shapes can be constructed by sticking together groups
of triangles (threes) and groups of quadrilaterals (22). In music,
the simplest rhythmic distinctions deal with grouping pulses in
"duple meters" or "triple meters" and then combinations thereof.
As one continues subdividing, and adding and multiplying
asymmetrical groups of twos and threes, notions of proportion and
interrelations of forms arise. Later corollaries to the process of
division are notions of aesthetics, of tension and repose

(tonality!) based on the relationships of proportions within a language. Thus, although equating specifics in one field to specifics in another may prove difficult, it becomes possible to say that things in one field are related to each other in ways which are similar to the way things in another field are related to each other. Perspectives and relationships are inherent in any universe.

Unfortunately, perhaps, our perception of forms and languages cannot follow such a simple, chronological evolutionary pattern as the one just sketched. We are never given the occasion to see a field evolve in building block fashion, but rather are confronted with the whole of a field in all of its facets simultaneously. From this whole we may try to extract parts to see how they add up, but it is rarely the case that a whole is equal simply to the linear sum of its parts. Remote components tend to somehow influence the being or motion of other parts of the whole. As we sit back and begin to understand some system, we often note that various parts seem to evolve simultaneously and almost spontaneously. Intuitively, we can no longer separate them into building block units--they function quite differently on a global scale than they might appear to do locally. Take, for instance, any simple harmonic progression. The result of playing the notes of the chord simultaneously has an entirely different effect than simply playing the notes individually. The components of simultaneities react to and upon each other in ways which would be totally unpredictable by looking at the notes separately. Music is a field of sound-and-pattern interaction apart from the universe. It is a complete body existing as one aspect of a universe which is reflected in any facet of itself.

Music is a field of aural dimensions where the only substance is its own structure and the dynamic movement which carves it out from the reverberant sphere of silent potentiality. There are no lasting invariants--the form of the construction and the "rules of the game" last only as long as the duration of the piece. Each tone is subject to redefinition and shifts in perspective. Unlike an architectural--spatial--construction, which once completed remains static with its elements forever locked into a set pattern, a musical piece comes and goes, is called and recalled into existence any number of times, during which it exists as concretely as any visual or tactile construction. Each time a piece is played, it is carved anew out of an infinite resource of sound-possibility, and each subsequent playing is an act of creation--as Spencer Brown states in his first axiom to Laws of Form, "For any name, to recall is to call." Or as the Rg Veda chanted:

"Let us now with skill proclaim the origin of the gods so that in a later age someone may see them (origins) when these hymns are being changed." (Ṛg Veda 10.72.1)

Each act of creation, though physically/aurally separate, is connected to each and every other act of creation by a continuous path of memory and movement, lending as much "concreteness" to a musical world as notions of metric distance lend to a visual/tactile world.

It is precisely its transience which gives a sound-universe its dimensions. By its continual motion and the possibility of superimposing perspectives--literally or through memory--music functions within a field which transcends the three-dimensional static space. Each note springs forth rather from a sort of infinite-dimensional musical manifold--an unbounded space of shifting tonal possibilities.

A form, or song as it were, born of this space becomes one possibility manifest--one possibility existing at the temporary sacrifice of all other possibilities. A choice must be made for existence to be. A song can be sung in only one key at a time to be recognizable as a coherent form/song; and, for this choice of key, tuning system, and interpretation, to be made, one must sacrifice all other possibilities for the duration of the piece's performance. But since a musical creation can be called and recalled into being any number of times, the "sacrifice" is not a dogmatic invariant. For at each playing any potential perspective/interpretation can be made manifest and superimposed in time upon the original creation. Without a choice of frameworks--intentional or otherwise--a song cannot manifest itself; but once a choice has been made, only that one possibility can come into being for as long as the choice is retained.

Yet no choice is an absolute in the field of time, for perspectives can change, either after a piece is completed or within its own structure, in the form of modulation to another gravitational center. But modulation is not a random jump--there is always the linking factor of memory. Modulation has no meaning without the memory of where the song came from and where it is going. Each movement is glued together by a memory which flows in a continuous omni-directional path. Direction and intent in music are based on a memory preceding events but also on an image of the construction in its entirety. It is this continuity of memory which determines the forward motion of the piece and the meaning of each tone when it is recalled in subsequent playings--the tones have no choice but to slide along the path already charted by memory.

On a microcosmic note-for-note level, we find that there are as many ways of interpreting or playing a note as there are notes which precede, follow, or occur simultaneously with that tone. Harmony, linear or horizontal, is the perspective where the tone is an independent variable. Thus, every note which is preceded or followed by another contains both itself and a sense of perspective based on the memory of what has happened before, an instantaneous awareness of the "now" and the intent or motion of that tone towards the next set of tones. In fact, any tone carries with it some degree of perspective and memory, simply by sounding not only the fundamental pitch but also all of the overtones which constitute that tone. Harmony is not something imposed on unique and independent tones--it is an intrinsic and inseparable part of each note. Preferences for certain interval combinations are not matters of some sort of "free aesthetic will," for they are inherent in the subtle interaction of tones and overtones in the second continuum.

While certain preferences for intervals and compositional forms may prevail at various times, there can never by any one system which gains sovereignty over all others since the grounds upon which musical possibility stands is an infinite array of subtle interaction where all permutations of possibility can never exist simultaneously. In fact, if any one ideal system ever could be devised, there would no longer be such a thing as music, for music functions as a dynamic system of continuous and infinite variety, telescoping and defining the "all" into ever-changing patterns and perspectives.

Had we not removed music from the curriculum we might not have so much difficulty in understanding oral cultures, and therefore in recovering our own memories. For this reason any construction of these cultures is simultaneously a deconstruction. We are forced to cross a sound barrier which we did not know existed and which originally was taken for granted or was slowly being forgotten. Sound gave birth to symbol, but we cannot exalt the offspring without killing the mother. Thus, it is obvious that statements from oral cultures will remain unintelligible as long as they are not read against the background model which gave them birth: the Earth as language.

The Earth as language is that Earth which started as the sound-string for oral cultures. The generalization of the musical model into a language disguises the radical musicality in the thought and writings of the oral cultures. By recovering the Earth as language, possibilities of new worlds are thus opened, where all the doors seem to be closed.

On this model of sound, language gains a new vital authenticity. Where twos appear we have inevitable reciprocity; threes chart the path of the gods; fives that of Man.

The essence of the world is not substance, but sound--a grouping of relations arising simultaneously.

Perspective is a shift of key, a modulation--the ability to move with the present sounding movement. What is true in one perspective is not true in another, even if the names remain the same.

Movement is primary and its manifestation is through the flesh appearing in front of our eyes. To move with the movement, man has to leave behind the continuity of ideas and agents and leap, innocent and detached, into the new movement facing him. Plato was aware of this when after every logical order of argumentation he would break the order with myths, stories, music or simply by bringing in the clowns.

If this miracle of life--or the model of music--is not realized, oral cultures will remain dead forever; contemporary man will remain the victim of present controls; and the Earth as Mother will forever be killed by her own progeny.

Contemporary man and contemporary science, especially psychology, must ponder this sin; for, unless memory and imagination are freed from the theoretical constraints limiting their movement, man and woman cannot recover their body completely. Not allowed to reach the beginnings of the human body we will carry with us, the present crisis of contemporary man and woman is not only the verification of this ancient insight but also the falsification of any substitute theory of creation imposed on our contemporary world. Sadly we have praised many saviors, but we have lost our own act of creation and the power to revive it. We have forgotten the Dragon, the Snake, the Silence, and the Flesh that want to be music. We have forgotten the Power of the Earth.

NOTES

[1] Martin Heidegger, "Hölderlin and the Essence of Poetry," in Existence and Being. Tran. Douglas Scott. (Chicago: Henry Regnery, 1949. Gateway edition, 1968), p. 289.

[2] Martin Heidegger, "What are Poets For?" in Poetry, Language, Thought. Tran. Albert Holstadter. (New York: Harper and Row, 1971), p. 91.

[3] Ibid.

[4] Friedrich Nietzsche, The Gay Science, in The Portable Nietzsche. Translated and edited by Walter Kaufman. (New York: Harper Colophon, 1972), p. 95.

[5] Walter J. Ong, The Barbarian Within. (New York: The McMillan Company, 1954).

[6] G. S. Kirk, Myth: Its Meaning and Function in Ancient and Other Cultures. (Cambridge, Eng. and Berkely, Calif.: The Univ. Press and Univ. of California Press, 1970), p. 205.

[7] Roberto Weiss, The Renaissance Discovery of Classical Antiquity. (Oxford: Blackwell, 1969), p. 140.

[8] J. M. Osborn. "Travel Literature and the Rise of Neo-Hellenism in England," Bull. N.Y. Public Library 67 (1963): 300.

[9] Ernest McClain, "Plato's Musical Cosmology," Main Currents in Modern Thought. 30, 1 (Sept.-Oct. 1973), pp. 34-42; Ernest McClain, The Myth of Invariance: The Origin of the Gods, Mathematics and Music from the Rg Veda to Plato. (New York: Nicolas Hays, 1976); Ernest McClain, The Pythagorean Plato: Prelude to the Song Itself. (New York: Nicolas Hays, 1977); Robert S. Brumbaugh. Plato's Mathematical Imagination. (Bloomington: Indiana University Publications, 1954 and New York: The MacMillan Company, 1954).

[10] Friedrich Nietzsche, The Gay Science, in The Portable Nietzsche. Translated and edited by Walter Kaufman. (New York: Viking Press, 1954), p. 95.

[11] Martin Heidegger, "What Are Poets For?" in Poetry, Language, Thought. Tran. Albert Holstadter. (New York: Harper and Row, 1971), p. 111.

[12] Antonio T. De Nicolas, Avatāra: The Humanization of Philosophy Through the Bhagavad Gita. (New York: Nicolas Hays, 1976); Antonio T. de Nicolas. Meditations Through the Rg Veda: Four Dimensional Man. (New York: Nicolas Hays, 1976). Earnest McClain, The Pythagorean Plato: Prelude to the Song Itself. (New York: Nicolas Hays, 1977); Ernest McClain, The Myth of Invarience: The Origin of the Gods, Mathematics and Music From the Rg Veda to Plato. (New York: Nicolas Hays, 1977).

[13] Spencer Brown, Laws of Form. (New York: Bantam Books, 1972), p. v.

ĀTMAN AS ABIDING LOGOS

V. Francis Vineeth

Ātman and Logos are two key words which have captured and considerably controlled the thinking of the East and the West respectively. Ātman, as the abiding presence of the ultimate in everything, was very central in the development of Indian religious thinking. Logos as the ground and goal of all creative process was the fulcrum on which Western thought, especially Christian thinking evolved. A deep study of Ātman and Logos, as it takes us to two different worlds of philosophical genius, may also point to the possibility of or synthesis between the East and the West and their patterns of thought. Hence this study on Ātman and Logos. Since the word Ātman is ambivalent, a study of Ātman should take us to the basic as well as the interpretative meanings of the word Ātman. Accordingly, in this article we deal with the notion of Atman in the Upaniṣads as developed by two main schools of Vedānta, Advaita and Viśiṣtadvaita. We would also analyse the Johannine Logos through whom and for whom everything was created and in whose abiding presence Christians believe.

1. Ātman in the Upanisads.

Ātman is the keyword the Upaniṣads offers to solve the problem of the polarity between God and man, the universal and the particular. Ātman can be understood as the all-pervading universal self and also as the individual self. Later on the universal self came to be known as the paramātman and the individual self, the jīvātman.[1] The jīvātman, together with the psychosomatic organism it is attached to, is what we call man. The word Ātman is found in the earliest Upaniṣads.

In the beginning this (world) was only the self (Ātman), in the shape of a person,[2] says the Bṛhadāraṇyaka Upaniṣad, one of the earliest Upaniṣads. Ātman was the ultimate reality. But it was in the form of a person (puruṣa). Hence it was also called puruṣa. After eight verses the same Upaniṣad says: "Brahman, indeed, was this in the beginning."[3] Ātman who is puruṣa is also Brahman. With slight variations we find the same idea in the Chāndogya Upaniṣad. Instructing his son on the nature of the ultimate reality, Uddhalaka Aruni, a great teacher in the Chāndogya Upaniṣad, says: "In the beginning, my dear, this was being alone."[4] Ātman, who is puruṣa, and Brahman are pure Being, the substratum and foundation of everything. The ultimate reality is, therefore, pure Being, which is designated as Brahman,

Ātman and Puruṣa. The Upaniṣads use these words indiscriminately. But one could say that the reality considered in itself as pure and transcendent being is Brahman, the same as immanent in everything is Ātman and in its personal aspect is Puruṣa. The transcendent Ātman is Brahman and the immanent Brahman is Ātman. Both refer to the puruṣa of the Ṛgveda,[5] the cosmic man from whose sacrifice the Universe arose. As the sacrificed puruṣa forms the foundation and the vital principle of the Universe, so is Brahman its creative ground and Ātman its inner spirit. The upaniṣadic Self is, therefore, a triad of Brahman, Puruṣa and Ātman.

The Universe has its origin from the Ātman which was also Brahman, because, "differentiated by name and form,"[6] it "became all."[7] Everything is, therefore, the modification of Brahman and in knowing Brahman (Ātman) we know everything.[8] The underlying reality of all is the same, though referred to as Brahman who manifests and Ātman who indwells.

This dual nature of reality as Brahman and Ātman, and its allusion to puruṣa which adds a personal color to it, poses the problem of Brahman's separation from and identity with the individual self. Obviously the word Ātman in the Upaniṣads does not always refer to the individual self. But there are cases in which it is referred to the individual self, the sense of which is very ambiguous, and leaves room for different interpretations. Thus in the Chāndogya Upaniṣad the great teacher Uddalaka Aruni concludes his teaching on Being as follows: "That which is the most minute, the whole world has it for its Self (Ātman); that is the self, that art thou."[9] Sankara finds here the perfect identity of the individual self with the Universal Self or Brahman[10] whereas Ramanuja sees an identity only in the sense that the individual self is grounded on Brahman and forms its body.[11] The ambiguity remains. One thing is true: the nature of the Self is not easily understood and it is best sought in one's own self. The discovery of the universal Self in one's own self does not necessarily mean absolute monism, though it certainly rules out an absolute dualism. The presence of the Self, "the bodiless among the bodies, the stable among the unstable, the great, the all-pervading,"[12] transcends all other forms of presence we are acquainted with.

This element of ambiguity found in the word Ātman belonged to the very essence of the Vedāntic tradition, and to a large extent, the interpretation of it determined the destiny of its different schools. The Vedānta has developed two basic trends which could rightly be designated as monistic and theistic. Monism

is best represented by Sankara and theism by Ramanuja, to mention
only one of the most influential of the theistic systems within
the school of the Vedānta. Both claim that their doctrines are
founded on the Upaniṣads, the Bhagavadgītā and the
Vedāntasūtras. The nature of Ātman and its divine
characteristics are to be seen from the standpoint of each school.
Hence the different concepts of Ātman in the systems of Sankara
and Ramanuja.

2. Ātman in the Advaitavēdānta of Śankara.

Advaita unconditionally asserts the oneness of reality.
Reality is one and undivided.[13] It is beyond all possible
distinctions. It is existence in its purity and by its very
nature absolutely transcendent. This reality is Brahman. Its
true nature is beyond our grasp and surpasses all attempts of
human understanding.[14] We cannot attribute to it any qualities
of beings we see here, because all of them involve distinction.
The reality, on the other hand, is the "wholly other" and is to
be designated as "not this." Hence it is called nirguṇa
(unqualified).[15] This negative designation does not mean that
Brahman is a mere blank devoid of all perfections. In fact what
is denied is the negations involved in all finite perfections.
Brahman is the Supreme Being and all perfections belonging to the
Supreme Being belong to it; we cannot attribute anything to it,
because our notions are derived from things that are different
from Brahman. As the supreme existence, it is the most real
(paramārthikasatya), by nature self-luminous
(svayamprakāśatvam), and therefore subsisting consciousness
(cit) and bliss (ānanda).[16] It is beyond all change and its
nature is always the same.[17] But this Absolute is beyond all
human grasp. The moment we think about it, it becomes a part of
the world of our experience.

Though Brahman is absolutely transcendent, it is also
profoundly immanent in the heart of every being.[18] In fact, it is
the Ātman, the ultimate Self of every being,[19] and the individual
self, in whom the eternal consciousness of Brahman reflects, is
bound to discover this truth of its identity with Brahman. But
jīva on account of the physical adjuncts with which it is united,
thinks itself to be something different from Brahman or the Self.
This is avidya or ignorance. "The difference between the
individual self and the highest Lord is due to wrong knowledge
only."[20] Just as in a dream, the place, time, and objects are
false, so also this world of waking state, being a product of one's
own ajñāna is unreal or false.[21] This false sense of the

213

distinction of the self from the Absolute must be removed by true knowledge. Then the individual self will experience itself to be the Self, Brahman.

3. Atman in the Visistadvaita of Ramanuja

Ramanuja, the great philosopher of the Vaisnavite movement, attacks Sankara's absolute monism and in his commentary of the Vedāntasūtras. Ramanuja presents Sankara's view as that of the adversary against whom he has to defend his thesis. The thesis defended, however, is not non-dualism itself, but a different sort of non-dualism. Reality is one for Ramanuja; but this one reality is not without distinctions. It is a complex reality. Reality includes God, the individual selves (jīva), and matter (acit).[22] They are, however, inseparably united to form one absolute which is Brahman. The individual selves and matter, though part of reality, entirely depend on God for their existence. They are the attributes or qualifications (viśeṣaṇa) of God and God is the qualifiable (viśeṣya). Reality is the complex whole which is, therefore, qualified (viśiṣṭa). Hence the name qualified non-dualism (viśiṣṭādvaita).

In Ramanuja's system of Viśiṣṭadvaita Brahman, the Absolute is identified with the personal God, Krishṇa, the Lord of the Bhagavadgītā. As Ātman and Antaryāmin the same Brahman who is the Lord Krishna, resides in all creation, especially in man, which altogether forms the body or attribute of Brahman. The individual self (jīvātman) is a spiritual attribute of God. Though by nature finite and dependent on God, the individual self is of the very nature of God. It is a particle of pure consciousness. Its true nature is unlimited knowledge.[23] This essential nature of knowledge is common to all selves.[24] As such the self is "eternal, indestructible and unfathomable."[25] But for the time being it is in a state of ignorance and is under the influence of the beginningless chain of works.[26] Here, too, ignorance is the misapprehension of the self about itself. But the nature of the misapprehension is different from what Sankara understands by the word ignorance. Instead of considering its true nature as a spark of God and unlimited knowledge, the self, deluded by the senses of the body thinks itself to be the body. Consequently, it engages itself in activities pleasing to the body and gets immersed in samsāra (the circle of birth and rebirth). This ignorance is to be removed by true knowledge and especially by loving devotion to God who, according to Ramanuja, is a personal God.

214

4.   The Existential Tragedy of the Individual Self (jivatman).

The true nature of the individual self is really divine.
According to Sankara, it is identical with Brahman; according to
Ramanuja, it is very similar to God. As the Gita says, "Never is
it born nor dies; never did it come to be nor will it ever come to
be again: unborn, eternal, everlasting is the self."[27] But this
lofty position of the individual self is lost when it expresses
itself as an individual existence in man. Its knowledge becomes
limited and it falls under the spell of ignorance. It confuses
itself with its egoity, its body, and the material universe to which
it is attached through the body. To be human means to miss its
own abode of bliss and unlimited knowledge or to lose the
consciousness of identity with Brahman. This is the tragedy of
human existence. This tragedy occurs, because in realizing itself
in man, the self assumes human body, and, by assuming a human
body, the self allows itself to be bound by it. The body keeps
the self in bondage.

The present consciousness of man is, therefore, not the
authentic consciousness of the individual self. The authentic
consciousness is divine in nature, be it of identity or of
similarity. Man, existentially realized as he is, is essentially
unauthentic until the true light of wisdom will dawn upon him and
thus he realizes his real and true self. The existential man,
groping in the darkness of ignorance, should try to expel his
ignorance by true knowledge. Avidya is to be expelled by vidya.
As avidya blurs, vidya enlightens. Avidya with its associate
karma (work) binds man. Karma binds, because it is originated
from and leads to desire. Desire, on the other hand, is the result
of the misapprehension of the self about itself. Because the self
thinks it to be the Ego and the body, it works for the satisfaction
of the body and thus becomes addicted to matter. Thus through
false desires its true consciousness gets vitiated. In the last
analysis, it is not action that binds, but desire. And desire
binds because of ignorance, which is false consciousness. The
state of false consciousness is, therefore, the state of bondage.
The revival of the true consciousness of man and thus the
discovery of his authentic self is the goal of everyman. This
is the purpose of yoga.

5.   Yoga and the Discovery of the Authentic Self of Man.

The discovery of the authentic self of man is worked out by
way of concentration. Yoga is defined by Patanjali as
concentration (samadhi)[28]; but this concentration is so profound
that it implies "the cessation of all discursive thought."[29] This

concentration is directed to what is divine in man and as the divine shines forth, the non-divine or the material is expected to recede. Focusing his attention on the divine in him, yoga reintegrates man in his spirit, which man, the self is bondage, so badly needs. Yogic integration is, therefore, at the same time the revival of divine consciousness in man or the discovery of the authentic self of man. Because spirit integrates and whereas matter disintegrates, the yogic integration tends to dissociate spirit from matter or sublimate matter to the level of the spirit.

Yoga is said to be threefold: they are karmayoga, jñānayoga, and bhaktiyoga.

Karma is the cause of bondage which leaves the self in the sea of saṃsāra. If karma was the cause of bondage, karma can also be the cause of release. In order for karma to become the cause of release, one has to perform karma with a new disposition of mind. This is the spirit of renunciation. The yogin who is intent on developing the divine consciousness in him should act dispassionately. Action as such is indifferent. It is desire and attachment to the result of action that matters. Action or work is not something wrong. Performed selflessly, it can even become salvific, a means for final release. But desire is binding. Action binds through desire. Action binds by attaching the self to the results of the action. Action binds when it is done in ignorance of the real self, mistaking the body or egohood as the real self. Action binds again by making the self believe it is the real agent of the action which in reality it is not. And from the very outset of history man finds himself action-bound (karmabandhah).

In order to revive the divine consciousness of man and thus to discover his authentic self, the Karmayogin has to reverse the process. If action (karma) with attachment caused the bondage of the self, it has to strive for its release by performing action with detachment.[30] Detached activity becomes the threshold of salvation. This is what makes karma a karmayoga. Karma is binding whereas karmayoga is releasing. Karmayoga is, thus, no renunciation of action, but renunciation in action. This spirit of renunciation gives him greater balance of mind, leads him to right evaluation of things and thus deepens his own self-knowledge. Thus Karmayoga paves way for jñānayoga (the yoga of knowledge).

Sankara considers jñānayoga as the most important of all the yogas, whereas Ramanuja, for whom God is personal, thinks bhaktiyoga of greater importance. In the school of advaita (nondualism) jñāna means the knowledge of the oneness of the self and jñānayoga is the supreme yoga meant for the acquisition of this truth. "Pure self-knowledge alone is the means for the highest bliss."[31] This knowledge of the self culminates in the complete isolation of the self (kaivalya)[32] by which the self realizes itself to be Brahman. Since in the system of advaita no finite self exists apart from the Supreme Self, the question of self-realization does not arise apart from that of Brahma-realization. Self-realization itself is brahmanization. The revival of authentic consciousness of man is, therefore, the realization of man's God-consciousness, a consciousness of perfect identity with Brahman. The paths of karma and bhakti are proposed in this system as the means for obtaining cittasuddhi and cittaikagrya, purification and concentration of mind and jñānayoga for atmaikyajñāna (knowledge of the identity of the self).

This is not so in the school of viśiṣṭadvaita where bhaktiyoga is superior to the other two yogas. The ātmāvalōkana (the vision of the self), on the other hand, is the vision of the self as it is in itself. And it sees itself similar to other selves all of whom have the same form of wisdom. Devoid of material nature, the self is of the form of pure knowledge. In this respect one self is similar to the other. It is material nature that veils the vision of this similarity. The integrated man, since he is free from the confusion caused by the material nature, can see deep into the true nature of the self and thereby realize the basic similarity the selves devoid of material nature bear to one another. Though not in the same way as the advaitin, he too "sees his self in all beings and all beings (selves) in his self."[33]

This kind of self-knowledge often expresses itself in samādhi[34] which is "that type of introverted mystical experience in which there is experience of nothing except an unchanging, purely static oneness."[35] For the advaitin this nirvāṇa-type ecstasy ends up in kaivalya (isolation) which is the final liberation. But for Ramanuja, this state of brahmahood or the vision of the self as it is in itself is only a intermediary step on man's way to a personal God. For, the Lord of the Gita has already revealed himself even above brahmanirvāṇa[36] as the Supreme person who is Wisdom's highest goal.[37] This personal God is to be worshipped by Bhaktiyoga and that is a more efficient way of transcending matter and obtaining the knowledge of the self. And only when one pays homage to God in this manner does he attain the real self as it is, for God is the base supporting the self and the individual self is only its attribute. Hence here the ātmāvalōkana of the self ceases to be pure seeing of the self in itself and orientates itself to the seeing of the self in God. Thus the enstasy (remaining in oneself) of the kevalin turns out to be the ecstasy (remaining outside oneself) of the devotee. The supreme path of liberation is neither the performance of sacrificial rites nor the pure knowledge of one's own self-identity with Brahman. It is rather one's loyal devotion to the Supreme Brahman, who is the Highest Person. And the devotee is expected to foster it by continued remembrance of the Supreme God.

> (There) let him sit, (his) self all stilled, his fear all gone, firm in his vow of chastity, his mind controlled, his thought on Me, integrated (yet) intent on Me.[38]

The authentic self (Ātman) of man is divine here; but it is divine not by way of identity-experience, but by way of an intense communion with a personal God. To foster the awareness of this communion, Ramanuja recommends meditation. Thus bhaktiyoga becomes the yoga of meditation on God who for Ramanuja is the Lord Krisna of the Bhagavadgīta.

> Meditation is the steady remembrance, i.e. the continuity of the steady remembrance, uninterrupted like the flow of the oil . . . Such remembrance is of the same character of intuition.[39]

Bhakti is the uninterrupted fixation of one's mind on God by way of steady remembrance. Thus the mind of the devotee is always with God and, in being with God, the individual self finds its authentic existence, which is only a part of God, an attribute of the Supreme Brahman.

Thus Yoga helps man discover his true identity and revive his authentic consciousness. His authentic consciousness has divine characteristics. It is God's own consciousness in the system of Advaita whereas, in the system of Viśiṣṭadvaita, it is the consciousness of an intimate divine communion. The divine consciousness of man, is, therefore, the consciousness of identity or of unity with divine existence. In either case it is actually the consciousness of the individual self and needs awakening. Once awake, the individual self shines forth with the luster of the divine. Thus, in the final analysis the inner content of the individual self is to be understood as divine. The individual self, in spite of its distinction from Brahman, as in the system of Viśiṣṭadvaita, has to resemble Brahman, has to reawaken Brahman in itself, has to be charged with the divine splendor, and is ultimately to be moved and guided by the Supreme Self who is the inner controller of all selves.

6. The Centrality of the Logos in Christian Thinking

In the Christian understanding of man and his Universe the Logos plays a central role. The Logos who is supremely transcendent in His divine character is at the same time the foundation of all creative process. By becoming flesh He became the divine indweller of all human nature. Human nature too contains the Logos within itself. The Logos, in spite of His transcendence and consubstantiality with the Father, is also immanent in human nature as its ultimate content and unalterable foundation. It is not in the human nature alone the presence of the Logos is to be seen, but in the whole creation, which proceeds from Him, evolves in Him, and returns to Him. This centrality of the Logos in all creative process is presented by the evangelist St. John as follows:

> In the beginning was the Word.
> The Word was with God,
> and the Word was God.
> He was with God in the beginning.
> Through him all things came to be,
> not one thing had its being but through him...
> The Word was made flesh.
> He lived among us...[40]

God's self-communication was through the medium of the Word. And Christ was the fulness of this divine self-communication. Christ is the very self-expression of the Word. The Word was made flesh, says the Christian faith. That is to say: God became man. Christianity does not believe in a God who refuses all possibility of self-becoming. The Christian God became man. And that is Christ.[41] The idea of becoming something is, therefore, not incompatible with the Christian concept of God. Perhaps no religion in the world stresses God's becoming man so much as Christianity or least certain branches of the Christian faith, Roman Catholics, for example. It is not necessary that that which becomes something change entirely in order to become what it becomes. It can remain unchanged in one respect and still become what it wants to be. This is what happened in Incarnation. God remaining Himself unchanged in his existence which is common to all the three terms of the divine dynamism (that is, the three persons in traditional terminology), becomes man by his Word, the second term or person of the divine Trinity. There was no change in the divine existence; but there was change in the Word of God, because it became flesh. Christ was in the mind of God as the possibility of His (God's) self-expression. Hence the thought of God which was of "becoming flesh" precontained in itself human nature in its totality as its inner content, as the very constitutive element of the Word, the Logos.[42] The Upaniṣads speak of the thought of God of "becoming many." Christianity speaks of the "thought of God" of "becoming flesh." They both are very closely inter-related. Without a world of many the Word-made-flesh is incomplete and meaningless. The thought of God (the Word) which was the thought of becoming flesh really meant what it thought and did become flesh in Christ, who was the primal man who had been thought of from the beginning. In becoming Christ the divine Word assumed human dimensions into it. But this was not assumed from outside, rather was produced from inside, because it is the self-same Word that became man. In this sense the Word of God underwent transformation which can be termed in sanskrit as vivarta or pariṇāma.[43] This does not mean that the entire divinity was subject to change. The Word alone was subject to transformation; but only insofar as it is the Word of God. That is to say, in the ground of its own existence, which is common to all the three persons, it is simple, undivided, unchangeable and infinite existence. This existence does not change, but gives substratum for the Word as well as to its becoming, which is realized in Christ. This is the mystery of the hypostatic union where the uncreated divine existence actuate the created being of Christ.

According to St. John, the Word, the Logos, the principle of divine self-manifestation, became flesh (man); it was through that Word the whole universe came to be earlier. According to Ramanuja, that part of Brahman modified by prakṛti underwent transformation and gave rise to the Universe. The part modified by prakṛti is Brahman considered in the aspect of containing the Universe in Himself. Ramanuja does not call it the Word of God. But the Christian concept of the Word of God contains in itself the human nature as the possibility of the Word's own self-expression and consequently the entire Universe. As the Word becomes flesh remaining unchanged in its eternal existence, so does Ramanuja's Brahman assume the world-body, remaining unchanged in his eternal existence which is the substratum also of the part that transforms into the world-body. God remains immutable in spite of the Word's becoming flesh. Brahman remains immutable in spite of his transformation into the world-body.

One striking difference here is that, while Christianity speaks of God's becoming man, Ramanuja speaks of Brahman becoming the Universe. Though this difference is to be reckoned with, it is clear that the "becoming flesh" or assuming the human nature, in fact, contains the entire Universe within it.

7.   The Divine Kenosis and the Origin of Matter

One of the ancient poems of the Hindu scriptures speaks of the sacrifice of a Primal Man from which the universe arose.[44] The idea of the Primal Man draws our attention to the first man in the mind of God, who was the Word to be made flesh. In the preceding section we saw that the Word became flesh and, in becoming flesh, it emptied out its own inner content. The self-emptying of the Word into the form of human nature is the core of the doctrine if Incarnation. This Self-emptying of the Word of God is known as the divine Kenosis. How does the divine Kenosis relate itself to the cause of the Universe? Like the Rg-Vedic sacrifice, was a divine Kenosis necessary for the origin of the universe? These questions, if asked a priori, will take us nowhere. Seen from the Christian faith, what we know for certain is that there was a divine Kenosis. Here we are only trying to understand the meaning of this Kenosis and to see whether this idea of Kenosis will help us with a better understanding of the origin of the Universe as in Indian thinking. this study, therefore, has à posteriori character, as any question dealing with Incarnation is bound to have. What we really aim at in this study is to understand what has been handed down to us by revelation from an Indian stand-point. Let us begin it with an analysis of the Kenosis. What is the divine Kenosis? St. Paul gives the answer. Speaking of Christ, the Word-made-flesh, he writes:

> His state was divine, yet he did not cling to his equality
> with God, but emptied himself to assume the condition of a
> slave, and became as men are...[45]

The one who emptied himself is the Word of God, the eternal Son of the Father. But by emptying himself he did not lose his divinity. He remains God even after Incarnation. By remaining God, the Word unites himself with matter; this is the core of Kenosis. The union with matter is in fact His own self-expression in matter. The Christian understanding of creation allows no medium except that of the Word. It is said to create out of nothing. Precisely because creation is out of nothing it is from God Himself. This means the matter in which He expressed Himself in becoming flesh was somehow existing in him already before. It was already in Him in the very idea of Christ, the human nature the Word was to assume. This is not posting any imperfection in God. Every effect virtually pre-exists in its efficient cause, and, as St. Thomas puts it, "to pre-exist virtually in an efficient cause is to pre-exist not in a more imperfect, but in a perfect way."[46] In this eminent mode of pre-existence the effect is in the mind of God and is actually identical with the

being of God, because God is for St. Thomas pure being or
actus purus. However, the pre-existing thing externalized itself
in the form of gross matter in the person of Jesus Christ. The
gross matter and the human nature attached to it is a far lower
form of existence than the form of the existence of all perfections,
God. Hence it was divine Kenosis, both in the sense of "emptying
out" and of sacrifice. All the same, it was the realization of the
ineffable perfections that are in God in time
and space. In emptying itself out in a form that is not God, that
is not the identity of all perfections, the Word finds its own utter
Kenosis; but it is at the same time the basis for the origin of
everything that is not God, the human nature of Christ, man and
his Universe. Through His own Kenosis the Word gave origin to
all. He gave origin to all by His own self-emptying. The Word
also resides in everything. He becomes the real inner controller
of all.

8.   Ātman as abiding Logos:

According to Indian thinking, Brahman who is absolutely
transcendent is Ātman by the power of his immanence. Ātman is
Brahman himself residing within. The individual self reflects and
realizes this Supreme self within itself. This dynamics of
God-realization in the Indian way of thinking can be usefully
referred to the christian understanding of the Logos in man and
the possibility of its realization in our human nature.

As already mentioned above, man was originally conceived as
the expression of the Logos. The Logos is his inner content.
Man, in his final state of existence, is supposed to be divinely
transparent. The reflection of God that man bears is more
fundamentally imprinted in the spirit of man, and it is by
concentrating on the spirit that the divine dimension of man is to
be illumined. Christ is the typical example of this divine
illumination. In Him matter is transparent because the divine
shines forth through the material. This is what, at least
analogically, every man is supposed to be like. The entire being
of man needs transformation, and when transformed, he will be
Christ-like. He will be relieved of the existential estrangement
he is in and will be sharing the essential manhood of Christ, which
has overcome all separation from God.

The divine reflection that is in man is the abiding Logos,
the very spirit of God that is within man. Created in the image of
God, man carries this divine reflection as a constitutive element
of his being. Conceived in and through the Logos and brought to
existence by Him, man cannot think of any form of existence

222

separate from the Logos. The Logos is an abiding presence in man. In the words Yajnavalkya:

> He is the Seer who is not seen,
> He is the Hearer who is not heard,
> The Thinker who is not thought of,
> And the Knower who is not yet known.
> There is no other Seer but He,
> There is no other Hearer but He,
> There is no other Thinker but He,
> There is no other Knower but He.
> He is your self (atman),
> The Inner Controller,
> The Immortal[47]

To sum up: The word Ātman is understood in diverse ways in Indian traditions. It can denote identity with or similarity to Brahman. Even in similarity it is not an external configuration that is understood. Man is jīvātman because man bears the divine nature within him. And with regard to this 'minimum' of divine in man, almost all schools of Indian thought agree. Both Man and God are Ātman, Spirit, Self. Man is self (Ātman) in the process of realization (hence, jīvātman), whereas God is the Absolute Ātman (hence, paramātman). But man is man only because he carries the spark of God within him. Basically, he belongs to the family of God.

The Christian vision of the origin of man from the Kenosis of the Logos takes us to an understanding of man which is strikingly parallel. The Logos is the Supreme Self. Human nature is the expression of the Logos. As every expression carries the expressed, every man carries the Logos as his inner content. The Logos is the abiding Ātman in everyman. Deep in our consciousness there is a hearer of the Word of God, there is a Seer of the divine vision, there is a Knower of God's eternal being, there is a thinker of God's own thought. But we are not conscious of this presence as it really is. But it resurges, time and again, to the upper layers of our consciousness, bids us do what is right, and leave undone what is wrong. Sometimes we call it conscience, sometimes light, sometimes grace. Whatever be the name we give it, it essentially belongs to what we are and forms the very base of our being. The being of man has a divine nucleus, and the nucleus is the image of God. This image of God is, therefore, nothing exterior to him. It is his very being. Man is the expression of the thought of God, the expression of what has been conceived in Christ. Since he is conceived in Christ, he is also to be interpreted in terms of Christ. And Christ is the Logos made flesh. Therefore, man also must be understood in terms of the Logos abiding in him.

This divine nucleus, which is the Logos abiding in everyman, has been obscured by man's imprisonment in matter. Hence, by a process of discrimination, and that is what yoga means, he has to rediscover this divine center which is the nucleus around which the being of man has been formed. Yoga, with its threefold emphasis on detachment, self-knowledge and devotion, effects this liberation. In fact, it is one and the same Self, the Word of God expressing itself in Christ. The Word is the ultimate and unchanging substratum of the humanity of Christ, of the mankind in general, and of the whole Universe.

Fundamentally, salvation consists in the re-discovery of this divine nucleus in man, as it is in himself and as it is in itself. This means man's knowledge of God as immanent and as transcendent. Because his own self bears the impression of the Universal Self, and is the image of the Transcendent Self, this discovery of the self leads him to God who is both immanent and transcendent. In this process of salvific self-discovery, Christ is always before him as his model and goal, as his power and motivating force. His self-discovery is always the discovery of Christ in whom he was originally conceived and through and for whom he was brought into expression. So also his discovery of Christ is always the discovery of his own self, because it is in Christ he finds his own nature spotlessly expressed and divinely illumined. As the Logos made flesh, Christ is the perfect transparency of the Divine in human flesh. The ultimate Self (Ātman) in Christ is the Logos. Conceived in Christ and brought to existence in the humanity of Christ, every man carries within him the same Logos. In the depth of our own self the Logos abides as the foundation of our being and as the light of our consciousness. The Logos is the abiding Ātman in every one of us.

Abide in me and I will abide in you...
I am the vine and you are the branches.
Whoever abides in me and I in him will bear much fruit;
for you can do nothing without me.[49]

NOTES

[1] It is called jīva or jivatman, because it is a life-monad. It is also called śarīrin (prakrtyapēksya śarīri, Yadīndramatadīpika, VIII, 9) and dehin (dehe vartamānasya dehināh, Ramanuja's Gītabhāṣya, 2.13) because it abides in the body (śarīra or deha) and works as its inner principle.

[2] Brh. Up. I.4.1.: ātmaivedam agra āsīt puruṣavidha.

[3] Ibid. I.4.10: brahma vā idam agra āsīt.

[4] Ch. Up. VI.2.1: sadeva, saumya, idam agra āsīt.

[5] RgVeda X.90.1-16.

[6] Brh.Up. I.4.7.

[7] Ibid. I.4.10.

[8] Ibid. IV.5.6.

[9] Ch. Up. VI.9.4.

[10] See Śankara's commentary of the Chandógya Upaniṣad.

[11] Cf. Śribhāṣya, I.1.1. Eng. Trans. George Thibaut, The Vedāntasūtras with the Commentary of Ramanuja, The Sacred Books of the East, Vol. XLVIII (Oxford: Clarendon Press, 1904), pp. 130 ff. Hereafter SB for Sribhasya.

[12] Kata Up. I.2.22.

[13] Sankarabhāsya on the Vedāntasūtra, I.4.22; Eng. trans. George Thibaut, The Vedāntasūtras with the Commentary by Śankarácārya, SBE, Vols. XXXIV and XXXVIII (Oxford: Clarendon Press, 1890, 1896). Hereafter Śankarabhāṣya.

[14] Sankarabhāṣya, III.2.23.

[15] Sankarabhāṣya, I.1.11.

[16] Sankarabhāṣya, I.1.4.

[17] Sankarabhāṣya, I.3.1.

[18] Sankarabhāṣya, I.2.8.

[19]Sankarabhāṣya, I.3.19.

[20]Sankarabhāṣya, I.3.19.

[21]Vivēkacūḍāmaṇi, 254; cf. also Māṇḍukya Up. 7.12.

[22]SB, I.1.1: Vedārthasamgraha, critically ed. and trans. by Van Buitinen (Poona: Deccan College, Research Institute, 1956), par. 18, 19. Hereafter, VS.

[23]SB, I.2.12; VS, par. 5.

[24]Plurality of selves is an accepted doctrine in the viśiṣṭadvaita of Ramanuja. It is also seen in the Samkhya school of philosophy. (The Samkhya-kārika, XVIII). Cf. also the Bhagavadgīta, 5.16; Ramanuja's Gitabhasya, 5.16; Yadindramatadipika, VIII.10.

[25]The Bhagavadgīta, 2.18.

[26]SB, I.2.12.

[27]The Bhagavadgīta, 2.20.

[28]Yogasūtra, I.1.

[29]Yogasūtra, I.2: cittavṛtti-nirodha.

[30]The Bhagavadgīta, 5.11.

[31]Sankara, The Gītabhāṣya, 18.66.

[32]Ibid.

[33]GB, 6.19.

[34]The Bhagavadgīta, 2.53.

[35]R. C. Zaehner, The Bhagavadgīta, p. 143.

[36]The Bhagavadgīta, 6.15.

[37]Ibid, 11.18.

[38]Ibid. 6.14.

[39]SB, I.1.1, Thibaut, pp. 14-15.

[41] . . . unum eumdemque confiteri Filium Dominum Nostrum Jesum Christum consonanter omnes docemus, eumdem perfectum in deitate, eumdem perfectum in humanitate, Deum Vere et hominem vere, eumdem ex anima rationali et corpore, consubstantialem patri secundum deitatem et consubstantialem nobis eumdem secundum humanitatem, 'per omina nobis similem absque peccato' . . . (Actio V, 22.Oct.451: Symbolum Chalcedonense, quoted in: Enchiridion Symbolorum etc. by Denzinger and Schönmetzer, no. 300.

[42] Cf. Karl Rahner, The Trinity (New York: Herder and Herder, 1970), p. 33.

[43] The transformation of Brahman into the phenomenal universe is explained by Sankara as Vivarta (unrolling or displaying) and by Ramanuja as pariṇāma (evolution, modification). Both of these terms can be understood rightly in our context, though not exactly in the sense in which they have been used by these authors. The term vivarta should not necessarily be linked with the "all-encompassing ignorance" as it is in the system of The Samkhyan contention of the underlying pradhāna (primal substance of evolution) as in Ramanuja. Neither Sankara nor Ramanuja lays special emphasis on the cit-character of Brahman in the unfolding of the divine into the phenomenal world, as the Evangelist and consequently Christianity does. The Logos unrolls itself (vivartatē) emptying out its own inner content which is of human nature and the universe related to it. In emptying out its own inner content, it evolves (pariṇāmayati) into what has been seminally contained in itself, namely, the human nature and the universe related to it.

[44] Ṛg-Veda X.90.1-16.

[45] Phil. 2:6-7.

[46] Summa, I.q.4.a.2. When St. Thomas says "it is impossible that matter should exist in God" (Summa, I.q.3.a.2) he means the gross matter as it is experienced here.

[47] Brhadāranyaka Upaniṣad, III.7.23.

[48] For a detailed analysis of yoga as an aid to the self-discovery of man cf. V. F. Vineeth, "Yoga and the Reversal of the Fall" in Jeevadhara, No. 36 (Nov.-Dec., 1976), pp. 537-551.

[49] John. 15,4-5.

EAST AND WEST MEET: BEYOND IDEOLOGIES?

Inter-Religious Dialogue - A Pilgrimage in Tension

Albert Nambiaparambil

"I had been listening to a Hindu Swami in disguise" was the very first comment that I heard from one of the participants in a consultation seminar organized by the Vatican Secretariat for non-Christian Religions, in October 1972, on a paper that I presented on the 'Hindu self-understanding'."[1] This statement came as a surprise to me. The paper that I presented there took off from an experience with which I grew up: the sight of my Hindu friends and neighbors making their pilgrimage, after 41 days of fasting and penance, with the offerings on their head, with the cry of śaranam--of deep trust--on their lips, to the hilltop-temple of Lord Ayyappa. The main thrust of the paper was that, in the Hindu self-understanding, life is a pilgrimage in quest for the union with the Absolute. For one used to a very valid, fruitful, analytic approach in religious studies, the tenor of that paper was perhaps a little too liberal. Looking back on that comment from a scholar on Hinduism, I am now surprised at my own surprise. My answer then was more or less to this tune: It is not fair to analyze any religion by fossilizing it; just as you cannot approve of a stand taken by a Hindu who says "this is christianity" after giving a scholarly analysis of a chapter of Summa Theologica, we cannot say "this is Hinduism"--after giving an analytical study of any text of the Hindu Dharma.

A New Exodus

The plea was for an exodus from an impersonal dialogue on religion to enter into inter-religious dialogue as a communion of persons with different religious experiences. Now, almost ten years after that consultation, looking back on these years committed to the cause of inter-religious dialogue, the whole story can be seen as an arduous path or an exodus away from dialogues "on" religion. This criticism, of course, bears on the Indian scene. However, I am not passing a negative judgement on efforts in religious dialogues held in India. The tension referred to above is the tension between two perceptions: I can either see myself as belonging to the fellowship of an open community in dialogue with other fellowships or I can perceive persons of other communities as potential converts to my faith community. Such a tension exists in many of us engaged in inter-religious dialogue. This tension, though altogether avoidable, is nonetheless religiously healthy.

The post-Vatican Council period was for the Church in India one of rather serious commitment in the field of inter-religious dialogue. This doesn't mean that nothing was done prior to the Vatican Council, nor that dialogue had top priority in this period. We saw many concerted, organized efforts from the side of the institutional Church at an examination of her attitude towards other religions.[2] Many a center group, with this inter-religious dialogue as the goal, started functioning in different parts of the country. These centers were the first visible signs of an exodus for many faithful from a closed society to open communities.

Tourists and Pilgrims

An easy attitude towards religion from one's own fortress of isolation is that of a tourist. He needs a few pictures of that religion. The need may spring from a so-called "missionary" approach. The tourist-missionary is analytic, detached, cool, and objectifying. He takes these pictures without in any way changing or calling into question his own pictures about his own religion. He loves to give lectures on other religions with the help of these tidy, casual portraits. But the moment the Christian communities turned to other religions in open communion, this touristic attitude was found hollow and empty.

Back in 1964 Pope Paul VI made a plea to the followers of other religious traditions who met him in Bombay to "meet not as tourists, but as pilgrims set out to find God."[3] How easy it is to meet as tourists! How difficult it is to meet as pilgrims! Almost all the recent religious dialogues that took place in India tell the story of an exodus from the tourist's attitude to that of a pilgrim and, paradoxically, of an unfortunate return from the pilgrim attitude to that of a tourist. This last statement may offend a few, but I have to announce it: The tourist attitude is back in fashion among many specialists on religion.

Let me add a note of caution here. A theoretical, analytic study of religion is of great help in arriving at an understanding conducive to dialogue. But there is this inherent danger in dialogues on religion; many students of foreign religions tend to dissect religious phenomena and in the process murder religion; they are good at analysis, but bad in synthesis. In this effort they overlook the functional aspect of religious language and cult; they see trees, but not the forest.

While moving around the country I had answered a few repeated questions: What have you achieved in and through all these years of dialogue? Are you sincere to your religion when you "sincerely" hold dialogues with other religions? You know that you have the "full" truth; what then do you hope to gain from these dialogues? Are you not compromising on your faith-commitment on the uniqueness of Christ and on the uniqueness of Christianity? Back in 1971, at the Asian theological Consultation on Evangelization, Dialogue and Development held at Nagpur a tension surfaced: Is dialogue a means to the mission of evangelization or can dialogue be separated from proselytizing? There is another unresolved question that is raised in many multi-religious gatherings, consultations, and courses or dialogues held in India: Is it our "religious duty" or Christian duty to provide religious education to those of other faiths in the Christian institutions as a preparation for dialogue? Although the Patna Consultation of Evangelization (1974) stated clearly that dialogue, far from being a hindrance to the mission work, makes the same more meaningful, the obvious fact is that for many ordinary Christians dialogue is a block to the commitment to missionary work. For many, the salvation in and through the Christian economy set side by side with the salutary work of God in other religious traditions raises afresh the problem: are they saved in and through or in spite of and outside of the Christian fellowship?

Dialogue as as Communion of Hope

Dialogue was not that difficult for me as long as I remained in the field of discussions of shared reflections on religion. Let me give an example: the sessions of Kerala philosophical Congress, with the annual symposia running into two days, involving believers of different traditions and non-believers, was not that difficult. The participants would remain in the luxury of a kind of isolation and detachment and return home from the encounter by saying that "we agreed to disagree". But in the dialogues that were really inter-religious and inter-religious, the partners had to enter somehow a no-man's land. Or rather, it was an attempt to discover the everyman's land. This effort necessarily—and does almost in every dialogue worth the name "religious"—involves a tension.

The following is an open confession and expression of this tension: "We are aware that we do not have a common religious language among ourselves. Although we have tried to express ourselves in the most general terms, still much of what many of us shared together was colored with meanings and connotations which may not be fully acceptable to persons of all religious traditions. Theistic words like "God", for instance, "creator" or "divine" are unacceptable to Buddhists and Jains and others of the atheistic religious traditions. We want to state, however, that it is always our intention in this declaration to include all genuinely religious experience even if our limitations of language sometimes prevent us from doing this with sufficient clarity and accuracy."[4]

The participants in the World Conference of Religions, Cochin, would recall the sense of release that was there in that general session which voted upon the final declaration of the conference after the impasse created by a section of the participants. This new additional clause proposed by Raimundo Panikkar, far form resolving the tension, points to the existing tension.

Going through the workshop sessions, we get a feel of very tense situations that existed among the partners when they brought the religious concern around issues as conversion, religion and politics, and exploitation within the very religious communities. In the group-sharing on the dialogue experienced at a religious level, one of the participants had this to say: "I have a dialogue within myself through which my own attitudes to God, religion, nature, and mankind, are changing." His Christian attitude and his human attitude to nature had been changing after his reading of the Buddhist and Hindu Scriptures. He had come to realize that, instead of harnessing nature, he himself and nature are there as part of something whole.

Conversion--The Issue

Dialogue is a pilgrimage in tension not only for the Christians but also for the partners from other religious traditions. If dialogue is related to mission, conversion is a bone of contention and tension not only for the Christians in dialogue but also for the Hindu and Muslim participants. In a live-together organized by the Dialogue Commission in Hyderabad, India, a Hindu teacher--he took part in the dialogue only because of his personal relationship with the manager of a school who in turn was involved in the organization of that dialogue--expressed on the second day his candid view that his fellow teachers and he himself has suspected that there might be at the meeting the hidden trap of conversion; but the first day's experience showed him that this fear was unfounded; he was taking part in the sharing-sessions of the second day along with the very fellow teachers who objected to his participation! How is this conversion-tension of the Hindu friends related to the conversion-dialogue of the Christian fellowship? Have he and his friends resolved the tension of conversion-dialogue?

A Hindu partner of the live-together sessions of Trivandrum pondering over the theme of sharing for the next day, glanced through a copy of the Illustrated Weekly of India. He read: "What does my religious experience mean to me?" As he admitted the next day, that was the first time that he raised the question seriously. He saw the picture of Mother Theresa holding the crucifix and pouring out christian love on a dying black child. He said that tears dropped from his eyes and that he understood then and there what his religious experience should mean to him. Was this a conversation? Was this a Hindu experience or a Christian experience? He may have gone home from that encounter of the experience more confirmed in his sense of belonging in the Hindu fellowship. In this very process he may also have gone closer and nearer to Christ and to the Christian fellowship!

"Conversion based on personal conviction and not by unfair inducements should be considered normal."[5] This sentence from the declaration of the World Conference of Religions is so innocent that anyone reading the declaration might not even notice this sentence. But behind and within that assertion, we see the unresolved tension of the Hindus, Muslims, Buddhists, Christians, Jains, and Sikhs coming together face to face with their own fears that are historical, cultural, and political, often resulting from a kind of "religio-social" exploitation and at times taking them back to the days of colonialism. Many participants from outside India failed to understand why this issue of conversion produced so much of the heat in that fellowship of Cochin. This Conference was held at the time when the mass-conversion of a village in Tamilnadu from Hinduism to Islam was making headlines in the dailies and news magazines of India. The workshop reports spoke loudly of the tension that was there in those intimate sharing sessions; we saw a fellowship emerging with two statements in the first draft to the effect that individual conversions, not resulting from unfair inducements, should be considered normal and that there should be no more mass-conversions.

An explosive situation was brewing in the auditorium when the draft came up for discussion. The suggestions supporting and blocking the right to conversion were raised; the draft was sent back to the drafting committee made up of the representatives of all religious denominations taking part in the conference. Was this a conversion? Yes. The participants went through a conversion to reach the vision of the complex situation and background within which each community raises the very issue of conversion. The report from one of the workshops draws in colors the vivid picture of this pilgrimage of conversion in tension:

"The cultural issue, as related to conversion, causes concern among the Hindu majority as regards Islam and Christianity. The Hindu sees Islam and Christianity as highly organized while Hinduism in not and feels at a disadvantage. Also, these two religions are seen by many Hindus to pose a cultural threat to the traditional Indian values.

This raises the historical perspective of concern about conversion. India has been subjected to several invasions... and Indians have also done their share of invasion. These invasions have brought a forced imposition of new religion and culture.

India thus is sensitive to the concept of conversion. Closer discussion, however, revealed that the major cultural threat today was not from Christianity or Islam but from modernization such as forced family planning or a compulsory common code of conduct.

Indian Christians and Indian Muslims do understand the concern of Hindus about the different cultural values. Indian Christians are particularly making efforts to acculturize and indigenize Christianity. There was concern expressed by Hindus about possible separationist attitude on behalf of Indian Muslims. The Muslims understand the Hindu concern and wish to deal with it with both sides looking at themselves self-critically."[6]

How easy it is to discuss religion, especially the other religions, in an objective way! The great temptation in many dialogues is that the partners take a stance of speaking "on" religion, without a self-critical attitude, without taking into account the concern of other religions when they face an issue such as conversion. There was a surprise in store for the visitors from the West to the East: The environmental issues did not elicit much interest and any enthusiasm from the Hindu and Muslim participants. Why, they asked. For the majority of the Christian, Hindu, and Muslim participants this has not yet become the overriding issue as it has in the West. Technology has not yet become a destructive and disruptive force in India.

Confusion of Language:

To take dialogue between religions seriously is to enter the other religions seriously, not merely in theory but on the practical level of encounter of persons and the flow of religious experience.

This dialogic exposure brings with it for the partners the risk of being misunderstood. An outsider, looking at dialogue with a theoretical interest, may call it "syncretism" or an effort at compromising with one's own faith commitment. Two of the partners in the Cochin Conference, a Hindu and a Christian, created an impression on the public of disowning their Christian and Hindu labels. Of course, they were not denying or calling into doubt their faith commitments. They were rather challenging the narrow, isolationist ghetto-approach to their own religious affiliations.

Recently the writer took part in two spiritual fellowships in prayer, hymns, and meditations. In one a Swamiji, a well known spiritual leader, was the guru. In the other the guide was a Sufi mystic. In both of them the majority of participants were Christians. An outsider might label them as "crazy" people. After meeting individually a few of these Christians, it became later clear to me that they came to these groups in quest for real spiritual experiences. Indeed, the Christians made great sacrifices to join these prayer groups. They sang songs, bhajans, and verses drawn from the Hindu and Muslim scriptures. Were they thereby renouncing their faiths? The answer is far from a simple straightforward "no". They would be branded as rebels and apostates if they said, "yes". They "religiously" experienced something new. They felt the need of a new "language", religiously meaningful to the new experiences. They have entered on a quest; they are pilgrims.

Exodus from Self-Sufficiency:

While in consultation with the directors of dialogue centers and groups held in the Sivanandashram, Rishikesh (1980), linking this with shared reflections and meditation sessions with the inmates of the Sivanandashram as dialogue partners, I have encountered an incident that points to something that kills the dialogue initiative at the very onset. One of the participants, a "good" Christian lay person, in all sincerity and good faith, left the place on the very first evening. The reason was he could not reconcile himself to the use of the word om in the songs sung by the participants. It was a salutation of the divinity different from that to which he was accustomed to in the Christian Community. This person is not an exception; he represents the majority of the good Christians of India, if not the vast majority. So far the Indian Christians have found their own self-identity and self-consciousness as distinct from that of other religions, linking this with a particular way of praying, with a particular religious language, with a particular set of symbols, and with a consequent self-sufficiency. However, now that dialogue in India is becoming more and more prayer-meditation-bhajan experience, even those sessions wherein the participants express their views on any topic of common concern often begins and ends with prayer-services. New symbols are often being used to bring home to the partners the experience of the new fellowship and communion such as the act of lighting from the same lights, lighting different wicks of the same lamp and offering flowers. All these are being tried to get the partners on the way to an exodus from the self-sufficiency of religious language.

In some Christian churches we see pictures which put the symbols of various religions on an equal basis or in circles or around the same center to produce the desired effect. The functions of these symbols are different in different religions. It was as part of a search for a new symbol that expresses the felt need for another kind of religious fellowship at the same time pointing to the role of the different fellowships in this very pilgrimage of hope that at Cochin we selected the atomic structure of mutually inclusive movements with a burning oil-lamp at the center. Does this entail any kind of unfaithfulness to one's own religious identity?

Identity and openness:

At the Rishikesh consultation referred to above, Monsignor P. Rossano, Secretary of the Secretariate for Non-Christian Religions, in his sharing said that there would always exist a creative tension between identity and openness, between faithfulness to one's own heritage and dynamic openness to those of the other faiths. Swami Chidananda, President of the Sivanandashram, observed that, while identity is a keynote in inter-religious dialogue, what draws immediate response from the Hindus and others to the Christians is their openness. Can Christians remain open to their faiths without renouncing their commitment to missionary work?

Perhaps in this very process of dialogic communion we can discover a new open identity. Perhaps this dialogic search will lead us to a dialogic language in prayer, in the techniques of prayer, in the selection of hymns, and in the new prayer-services that emerge in these multi-religious fellowships. There will be, and there are, moments in dialogue-pilgrimage when I as a Christian and he or she as a Hindu may find it impossible to sing a particular bhajan. This is no obstacle to openness. Rather faithfulness to the reality that is being celebrated then and there may demand from the partners of one group or other that they take an attitude of worshipful silence at this stage of dialogue.

236

Conclusion

As I have mentioned at the very beginning of this paper, the encounter of persons at the religious level stands always the risk of becoming discourses "on" religion. At the level of ordinary Christians--the same is often true of those of other faiths--the great block is the possessive, self-sufficient, language which they use to express their own particular self-understandings that prevents them from joining the dialogue-pilgrimage of hope. They would prefer to be tourists in the world of religions! Thus they can avoid all religious tensions! But for a Christian to be a Christian in our society today, the above attitude seems increasingly to be no longer an option. For, dialogue for him flows from his Christian faith in God's saving presence in the religious traditions of mankind and is the expression of the firm hope in the fulfillment of all things in Christ.[7]

NOTES

[1] Albert Nambiaparambil, "A Hindu Self-Understanding," Bulletin of the Vatican Secretariate For Non-Christian Religions. (Vatican, 1973).

[2] The Church In India Seminar of Bangalore (1969), The Theological Consultation of Nagpur in Evangelization, Dialogue and Development (1971), the All India Consultation of Patna (1974) which studied dialogue in relation to evangelization, in preparation for the Synod in Rome, the National Consultation of the Directors of Dialogue Groups and Movements in Rishikesh (1980) and the World Conference of Religions in Cochin (1981)-to which the C.B.C.I. Commission for Dialogue extended full cooperation are just a few mile-stones.

[3] The Guidelines for Inter-Religious Dialogue, the C.B.C.I. Dialogue Commission (Cochin: K.C.M. Press, 1977), p. 4.

[4] See "Final Declaration of the World Conference of Religions on Religion and Man," Cochin, Nov. 15-21, 1981. No. 5. For copies of the Declaration and proceedings, write to: The Secretariate, World Fellowship of Inter-Religious Councils, Chavara Cultural Center, Cochin 682011.

[5] Ibid. No. 14.

[6] Report of the Workshop No. 4 on the Political Dimension of our Religious Concern for Man.

[7] The Guidelines for Inter-Religious Dialogue, p. 4. See also C.B.C.I. Calcutta Session (1974)--Workshop Reports.

THE HINDU-CHRISTIAN DIALOGUE AND THE
INTERIOR DIALOGUE

James D. Redington

Interreligious dialogue necessitates not only a mutual revealing of beliefs, symbols, and values, but an interior dialogue within each dialogue partner as well. In this interior dialogue the truths which are being revealed are weighed, tested, and, it is hoped, reconciled into each person's faith and commitment. The present essay's suggestion amounts to this: though most Christians are not directly involved in the Hindu-Christian dialogue in India, or the dialogues with the other great religions, few can without loss exempt themselves from an interior dialogue of their personal faith with the world religions. For it is clear that a plurality of great religions exists and will continue to exist; and, if it is meaningful to think in terms of God's plans, or actions in history, these religions did not come about by chance, nor are they irrelevant to us. Through the interior dialogue, then, we are all connected with the interreligious dialogues taking place around the world; and they are connected with us.

Nevertheless, I want to say a good deal about the Hindu-Christian dialogue in India. For two reasons. First, the interior dialogue is best described in the context of the beliefs and values of (at least) two religious traditions in dialogue. Second, I am a participant of sorts in the Hindu-Christian dialogue, and I have some questions which were raised by the dialogue scene I observed in India in 1980 and again in 1983. Consequently I propose (1) to describe those central issues in the dialogue which raised substantive questions and (2) to present the idea of the interior dialogue, with the help of excellent writings by Raymond Panikkar and John A. T. Robinson.

THE HINDU-CHRISTIAN DIALOGUE
Dialogue's Starting Point

My first consideration stems from the fundamental theological question which impels the whole dialogue movement, especially from the Christian side: Since God wills to save all people, how is He doing so?[1] From this religious impulse--this curiosity to see where and how God is acting--to dialogue with the other religious traditions of the world is a short step. The Second Vatican Council shows clear signs of this reasoning in the declaration Nostra Aetate. After teaching that God alone is the final goal of all peoples as well as their origin, and stating that "His providence, His manifestations of goodness, and His saving designs extend to all," the declaration exhorts Christians as follows: "prudently and lovingly, through dialogue and collaboration with the followers of other religions...acknowledge, preserve, and promote the spiritual and moral goods found among them, as well as the values in their society and culture."[2]

One line of theological reasoning which has appeared frequently in the Christian tradition is excluded by the Council approach: the notion that God intends to save some, but not all, people. A second line, more difficult to evaluate, is the more widely held opinion that God's "plan" is to save all people through the Christian Church. A distinguished past participant in the Hindu-Christian dialogue, Robert Antoine, S.J., of Calcutta (d. 1982), has described well the picture that impresses itself upon the mind of a Christian in Asia. Christian evangelism is experiencing some degree of success there, and Christian faith is lively; but there is no question of the major Asian religions fading out before a "triumphant" Christianity. And so Antoine drew the theological conclusions: in light of the evident historical failure of the approach that would convert all to Christianity, dialogue with other faiths is the stance indicated. Put another way (still by Antoine): if God did not intend to save all people through historical Christianity, we must look at things seriously and anew, to try to see again what God's intent might be. The way in which it seems best to do this at present is through dialogue.[3]

It is also important to see this impulse to dialogue expressed subjectively, the way in which it is felt most vividly. In this context I experience my own faith in the God who works to save all as a motive force leading me directly, in a spirit of loving curiosity, to learn about the other religions of the world and to engage in dialogue with believers of those religions. George Gispert-Sauch, S.J., professor of systematic theology and Indology at Vidyajyoti Institute of Religious Studies in Delhi, sees dialogue as growing directly out of his Christian commitment as localized in India. The questions about God's grace and salvation vis-a-vis Hinduism (especially), he says, spring forth naturally for anyone who looks seriously.[4] And Ronald Prabhu, S.J., who has conducted many dialogue sessions at Ashirvad Retreat House in Bangalore, reports that Hindus would not, in general, be led to dialogue as something flowing naturally from their religious insight, although they are open to it when it is initiated. Rather, the need for dialogue flows straight out of his own Christian faith, in the form of a desire to see how God has manifested Himself in other religions.[5] This discovery of God in other religions, especially under the divine name "Truth," is one of the dialogue's most exciting facets. Finally, Raymond Panikkar sees dialogue as stemming from Christianity's most characteristic commandment: love of neighbor. He writes: "Dialogue is not bare methodology but an essential part of the religious act par excellence: loving God above all things and one's neighbor as oneself. If we believe that our neighbor lies entangled in falsehood and superstition we can hardly love him as ourselves . . . Love for our neighbor also makes intellectual demands."[6]

The Christian concern for the salvation of all, then, and the dialogue with the world's other religions which it has given rise to, are seen ultimately to stem from the foundational motives of the faith: love of God and love of neighbor.

A Soteriological Application

Against this background a question rises from my own Hindu-Christian dialogue experience. My experience has been with a learned Hindu guru, Shri Shyam M. Goswamy of Bombay, first as his student, but over many years now as a friend and informal dialogue partner as well. Shri Shyam was teaching me the doctrines of Vallabhacarya (hereafter Vallabha), the theologian/ saint who founded the Hindu system of which Shri Shyam is a guru. When we came to the question of Krishna's saving grace (for Krishna is the Supreme God in this system), Shri Shyam portrayed the tradition's teaching as follows:

Krishna's Grace is unlimited, and occurs anywhere and everywhere as Krishna wishes. Saving Grace not only occurs outside our system as well as within it, but we may even expect to be able to see traces of Krishna's Grace in other religions and cultures. What Vallabha has taught us is a Path of Grace which we are certain will lead us to salvation. In the trackless vastness of Krishna's Grace, therefore, Vallabha has demarcated this Path. It does not exhaust God's Grace, but it is our Path.[7]

In the years since, I have thought about this teaching of Vallabha's especially when my reading touches upon the traditional dictum[8] Extra ecclesiam nulla salus. After reading one such essay, the following line of questioning began to crystallize. Though the Christian faith can proclaim itself to be universal, and indeed potentially be so - i.e. it can save all, or, more accurately, God can save all through it - cannot another faith, say Hinduism or Buddhism, also proclaim that it can save all, and will try to? The point is this: Is the further conclusion which Christians usually make justified: that, since all can be saved through faith in Christ, is it God's plan that salvation actually come to all people by this one path? Might this not be jumping to an unwarranted conclusion and attempting to limit the scope of God's grace? It is natural for a way of salvation to rejoice in itself and to spread itself by preaching and conversion. In fact, Buddhism and Vallabha's as well as other traditions of Hinduism, along with Christianity and Islam, have done this systematically. But does the joyful experience that here is an assured way of salvation automatically mean that God intends all to be saved by it? Certainly, many further questions are raised by this one - for example, the nature as well as the implications, psychological, social, and religious, of felt, intimately experienced salvation. There is also the question of New Testament passages which appear to teach that salvation comes through Jesus Christ alone.[9] But what has occurred to me as useful is to highlight this question against a new background. This line of thinking reminds me of Hans Küng's suggestion that we turn into a positive statement the negative dictum "Outside the Church no salvation," making it read instead "Salvation inside the Church!"[10] That this rightly joyful assurance means also that all must be saved in this way is what is questionable.[11]

My second line of questioning relates more to the project of creating an Indian Christian theology than to the Hindu-Christian dialogue; but the two endeavors are far from separate. My consideration involves the application of a Hindu doctrine and practice, sannyāsa ("renunciation"), to Christianity in India. Two of the great Christian sannyāsis of our times, Swami Abhishiktananda (Dom Henri le Saux, O.S.B.) and Father Bede Griffiths, have participated prominently in the Hindu-Christian dialogue and have written eloquently about sannyāsa.[12] But for our purposes no more is needed than a statement of the essence of sannyāsa, so that I can then make a suggestion about its role in inculturating the Christian churches of India.

Sannyāsa, then, is the renunciation of all forms and formulations - social, cultural, religious - in order simply to "be" one with the Absolute. To this end the sannyāsi ritually (in his last ritual) interiorizes the sacrificial fires he had formerly fostered so carefully, dons the ochre robe, takes a new name (such as Abhishiktānanda - "he whose Joy is the Anointed One"), leaves the caste system (and consequently, for example, is buried rather than cremated at death), wanders forth from home and family, etc. It is precisely his (or her, in some modern, and certainly in Christian, practice) essence to be bound by no rule, subject to no convention of this minutely ordered but provisional world. He is the preeminently free one - free to embody the

Absolute, the Transcendent, the Beyond - free to be what we all are potentially and hope one day to be manifestly.

My line of questioning has to do with Christian sannyāsis: Are the sannyāsis the most important people in the Indian Christian churches? Badly expressed, but put thus for this reason: perhaps only the sannyāsis will renounce totally the Western-church basis of their Christianity. In the case of all other Indian Christians, the Westernized Christian churches are still very much present, as a padding to fall back upon, as it were, if the attempts at inculturation do not work (or becomes tedious, or truly frightening). But what seems essential is so to commit oneself to inculturation that there is no other church to "come back to." In this context the sannyāsis may be the most important people, at least in terms of sign value, and perhaps also in fact; for a Christian sannyāsi would take, in effect, two sannyāsas, one from Indian culture and convention (i.e., from his "world") and another from Western-church convention. This latter renunciation might be characterized (to modify slightly a famous phase from the Western tradition) as a life lived etsi Roma non daretur ("even though Rome" - by which I mean rhetorically to include all the Western churches - "be not assumed"). If some such thoroughness of commitment is not present in sannyāsis with or without the ochre robe, to speak of genuine Indianization of the Church seems unrealistic.

Christology Revisited

My third consideration takes us to what, for most of the Christian participants at least, is the heart of the dialogue: the person and nature of Jesus Christ and his relation to the non-Christian religions. I do not intend to review the substantial and still growing literature which just the Hindu-Christian dialogue,[13] not to mention the other dialogues, has generated on this subject; but I note here a few ways in which Indian Christian theologians are speaking about Jesus Christ, and then make a critical comment.

Veteran dialogue participant Ignatius Hirudayam, S.J., pursued an illuminating line of thought when I spoke with him at his beautiful dialogue center, Aikiya Alayam, in Madras.[14] He pointed out that we Christians would be presumptuous if we assumed we knew the face of the present and future Christ and could describe him completely. This is precisely what we cannot do, he continued, with the cosmic Christ, the Christ of faith (who, I reflected, is the only Christ). Christ is present and working, with his Spirit, in every faith. And, he concluded, all salvation is through this Christ.

Again, Gispert-Sauch[15] gives us valuable background on these questions. According to him, many Indian Christian theologians would not accept the statement "Jesus is really unique as Christ" without qualification.[16] When I asked whether, in a contemplated theological conference which would have the question of uniqueness of Christ as its focus, a uniqueness of Christ could not be taken for granted, while the modes of that uniqueness would be the conference's subject matter, Gispert-Sauch said no. A uniqueness would not be allowed to be presumed; the presumption or presupposition of uniqueness would definitely be questioned and made a subject.

Let me exemplify this tendency from an important Indian Christian theologian. Panikkar has found the distinction between "Jesus" and "Christ" fruitful for the dialogue and dialogue theology. The advantage of such a distinction can be seen in a passage where he asserts that the basis for the universalism of Christianity "lies in the Christian conception of Christ: he is not only the historical redeemer, but also the unique Son of God . . . the only ontological . . . link between God and the World."[17] But the disadvantage – which has sometimes led to Panikkar's being criticized for paying too little attention to the human, historical Jesus – may perhaps be seen in another recent passage of his. As the first among a number of theses for dialogue, Panikkar says: "Christ is the Lord, but the Lord is neither only Jesus nor does my understanding exhaust the meaning of the world."[18]

What occurs to me in this context is a criticism in the form of a caveat. I am in sympathy, indeed in solidarity, with the theological effort I have been describing. But, as occasionally a tendency shows itself to make Jesus the "Christ for Christians," as it were, while making "the Christ" the embodiment of the Absolute's self-revelation in all religions, the following question occurs to me. Is this the Christological counterpart of the ecclesiological move: outside the Church there is no salvation, therefore we define the Church as excluding one? Together with Kung,[19] I find untenable the notion that we must keep expanding the Church's walls so as to include all people, even those who quite consciously want no part of being, or being called, Christian. Likewise, on the Christological level we may be attempting to redefine Christ so that he belongs to every faith. The question and caveat, then: Are we expanding the meaning of Christ beyond all meaningfulness? It may be true that Christ is present in all religions; but let us not so drive a wedge between "Christ" and "Jesus of Nazareth" that our dialogue theology will ring true neither to Christians nor to non-Christians. Perhaps it is preferable to use some other theological categories, either traditional, such as the ecclesia ab Abel or the notion of a "cosmic religion,"[20] or new. More likely it will prove best to continue, delicately, with the distinction-in-unity between Jesus and ("the") Christ. To lose patience with the complexities would be a mistake; for, to phrase the caveat in one final way, can anyone truly believe a "Christology" that does not have Jesus as its central exemplification?

Good Effects on Ecumenism?

The final consideration in this first part stems from a question I asked Ignatius Hirudayam in Madras. I have noticed for some years that, on the Christian side of the dialogue, most of the Catholics at least seem to have a personal preference, among the Hindu systems, for the Advaita Vedânta of Shankara.[21] Yet I knew that Hirudayam, whose dialogue has involved him predominantly with the more theistic Shaiva Siddhanta tradition, would likely have a fruitful difference of opinion from the advaitic majority. So I asked him whether he thought that the preference of so many Christian participants for Shankara's Advaita constitutes a problem for the Christian side of the dialogue.

Hirudayam answered in the affirmative. He put the problem in classical Shaiva Siddhānta terms: you followers of advaita (say the Shaivas) have been dazzled by what you have seen (the identity between Atman, "the Self," and Brahman, "the Absolute"), but you are like a frog which has jumped only three fourths of the way across a well! Come further, to the final union with Shiva, which is nondual but nonetheless does not destroy the I.

I found this answer partially helpful, in that it agreed with my fear that a strong preference for advaita might, ironically, start a new history of Hindu sectarianism among the Christians who are in dialogue; and partially unhelpful, in that it substituted a preference for another Hindu system over the advaita system. And the claims of these two systems cancel each other out perfectly; for just as the Shaiva theism claims to include the advaita experience, so does advaita claim to include, and then pass beyond, theism. So it could happen that one intolerant inclusivism would be exchanged for another.

245

But what seems more important is the further consideration which this inquiry prompted in me. Although a Christian's entry into dialogue may involve penetrating deeply into a particular Hindu system, Christians in the dialogue should not choose their personal "type" of Hinduism and act as if it is the only valid one. This would be the Hindu sectarian mistake (and a Hindu in dialogue could make the corresponding mistake by holding out strongly for one Christian sect over all the others). Perhaps, instead, one of the unexpected fruits of the dialogue will be the other religion's teaching us how to live tolerantly with the differences of doctrine, church, sect, etc., within our own religion, and our teaching them how to tolerate theirs. If our partners in dialogue can enter profoundly into our religion and yet tolerate our differences, and we tolerate theirs, perhaps we can show each other how to heal the differences within our own folds. Thus "the wider ecumenism," as Eugene Hillman calls Christianity's dialogue with the other religions of the world, would help bring about ecumenism within one's own religion. This is rather unexpected, and at least a bit idealistic, but it does not seem impossible.

THE INTERIOR DIALOGUE
Definition

Now that we have experienced something of the atmosphere and central questions of the Hindu-Christian dialogue, it should be possible to define the interior dialogue more clearly and to consider some ways of going about it. "Interior dialogue" is a term I am suggesting as a substitute for the other two terms ("inner dialogue" and "intrareligious dialogue") by which I have seen this phenomenon designated.[22] Robinson provides some background and clarification for the first term: "What Murray Rogers calls 'the inner dialogue' which is a precondition of the outer for which the terms are the same. And it is from this inner dialogue, if not from the exposure required for the outer, that this book has been born and to which it forms an invitation."[23]

Inner dialogue, then refers to the entire process and impulse which lead one to desire outer or interreligious dialogue. In addition, inner dialogue refers to the effects of outer dialogue on one's own faith – effects which take place before, during, and after outer dialogue. Panikkar gives us a more complete explanation of the phenomenon, which he calls the "intrareligious dialogue": "Interreligious dialogue is today unavoidable; it is a religious imperative and a historical duty for which we must suitably prepare. But we often hear more talk about interreligious dialogue than actual dialogue. In order to sidestep this pitfall, I would like to begin by stressing the often-neglected notion of an intrareligious dialogue, i.e., an inner dialogue within myself, an encounter in the depth of my personal religiousness, having met another religious experience on that very intimate level. In other words, if interreligious dialogue is to be real dialogue, an intrareligious dialogue must accompany it."[24]

Inner dialogue must, then, accompany outer dialogue if the latter is to be substantial. What I propose is the expansion of the scope of this inner dialogue from those only who participate in interreligious dialogue to all searchers for the truth in this era of dialogue. This would be not an addition to but a logical consequence of my line of thinking, as Robinson has also shown when he announced his book as an "invitation" to all his readers to initiate an inner dialogue. Finally, since usage is still fluid and I think my term a bit better, I propose for this phenomenon the name "interior" dialogue. It is a word with more resonances in spiritual tradition than "inner," and simultaneously it is less complicated and unclear than "intrareligious." The interior dialogue, then, is the interaction, the testing, and, with the help of grace, the reconciliation within one's personal faith of the beliefs, symbols, and values of the different faith system which one is deeply considering.

On the Importance of Being Two-Eyed

Probably the best way to present the suggestions I make toward a theology of the interior dialogue is to divide them into two areas: how to see and how to believe. The first question is one of perception: how to view the interrelation between one's own religion and the other religion being considered. It would, of course, be dishonest to proceed in an a priori manner here, as if one could prepackage all one is going to see. Yet there is an incipient consensus among dialogue participants on how best to see. To know this way of perceiving is much more helpful than to be dropped anew, as it were, into this complicated panorama.

To be concrete: dialogue theologian Ignatius Puthiadam sees a "complementarity" between Hindu and Christian truths. It is not new to see, for example, Hinduism as stressing the eternal while Christianity stresses the historical. But it is new to perceive that this complementarity can be expected, and even described in a systematic way. Puthiadam sees such a complementarity both between the different moods he experiences while praying in a Hindu temple and a Christian church and between the major theological truths of the two religions. He perceives a "principle of complementarity" by which he discovers not only "the unknown

247

Christ and Christianity of Hinduism, Buddhism and Jainism, but the unknown Hinduism, Buddhism and Jainism of Christianity."[25] Similarly, Ignatius Hirudayam sees, in grand historical perspective, the various world religions as mutually corrective though systems and movements.

But the most vivid formulation of this way of seeing comes from a newcomer to the field of dialogue, John A. T. Robinson, whose Truth Is Two-Eyed has brought acknowledged illumination to such professionals as Antoine. Robinson's title refers to the way of seeing he proposes. But it is not actually truth that is two-eyed; rather, it is the observer who must hold two quite different, apparently opposed eyes in steady focus on truth.[26] These two eyes, present in every person's religious vision, might be named the prophetic and the mystical, or the relational (as in "I-Thou") and the nondual (as in "That art thou").[27] The great virtue of the "two-eyes" image is the simultaneity of different angles of vision it stresses. In this it surpasses complementarity, in which the two (or more) elements, though both essential, might be viewed one after the other. If the prophetic and mystical eyes view a religious truth simultaneously, then even the dominance of one eye over the other which often enough occurs will not distort one's religious vision.

For example, consider the uniqueness of Christ, a major sticking point of the Hindu-Christian dialogue and of other religions' dialogues with Christianity. The prophetic eye, often dominant in Christianity, stresses the historicity and uniqueness of Christ, that he is "once for all," while the mystical eye, so typical of Hinduism, provides the necessary scope for Christ's universality, that he is "once for all." If both were not present, emphasis on historical uniqueness would render universality less and less credible. Or, conversely, Christ would be so cosmic as to lose all concreteness. So, the two-eyed view of Christ is that he is unique and universal.[28] This example should shed light on the possible problem I outlined earlier, that of separating "Jesus" from "Christ." Overemphasis of the historical and unique would leave us with only Jesus, while similar insistence on universality yields a faceless, placeless Christ. Both "unique" and "universal" are true - true, in fact, in a way analogous, and not coincidentally, to "true God and true man." But to insist on one at the other's expense would distort the truth.

Two-eyedness, as also complementarity, does not mean that everything is correct and nothing wrong, or vice versa. It is a means of weighing a religious statement, experience, etc., from each of two fruitful but different perspectives, one of which may show a richness and validity to which the other was blind. It may not be excessive to say that the epistemology of religious knowing, especially in terms of the interior dialogue, has been broadened by this simple image, which encourages us to expect both the prophetic and the mystical, in mutually illuminating and mutually corrective ways. Far from inducing spiritual schizophrenia, this two-eyedness would make each of us attend to the full range of vision of the human spirit, and not our usual, more comfortable, partial range.

One final connection with respect to this way of seeing, a synthetic insight which Bede Griffiths has expressed in his Vedanta and Christian Faith.[29] If Robinson's two eyes can be called the relational and the nondual, then the Gospel of John shows a kind of two-eyedness we find nowhere else; for there Jesus speaks of his Father, himself, and his disciples as being related in a nondual way. Griffiths explains this phenomenon (using the word "identity" as I have been using the word "nonduality," though elsewhere the two do not always mean the same) as follows:

His [Christ's] was an experience of identity in relationship. He does not say, I am the Father-that he could never say-but "I and the Father are one" (John 10.30). It is a unity in duality, by which he can say, "I am in the Father and the Father in me" (John 14.10), which is yet based on an identity of being, by which he can say "He who sees me, sees the Father" (John 14.9). It is the experience of the Absolute in personal relationship, and that would seem to be the distinctive character of the Christian experience of God.

Thus, in John, the relational "I-Thou" and the nondual "that art thou" are not finally opposite or even separate, but mutually present in Jesus, the Father, and ideally, all human persons. It has long been sensed that the Gospel of John is the key New Testament writing for the Hindu-Christian dialogue.[30] We have here good evidence as to how its way of seeing illumines the interior dialogue as well.

Faith and Beliefs

Thus far with regard to seeing. Now what about believing? For this kind of seeing is not yet believing; at least, the process by which this seeing becomes believing remains to be traced. Tracing this process is what must concern us now.

First we should take notice of a phenomenon that occurs in interreligious dialogue and can therefore be expected in the interior dialogue as well. Deep understanding of a particular teaching of another religion involves, for many if not for all partners in dialogue, an experience of the truth of that teaching. One reaches a conviction, often strong, with regard to the teaching.

Our question is: What is the status of that conviction, that experience of truth, with respect to our religious faith? For example, what place in a Christian's faith can there be for a perception of profound truth on the central Hindu teaching that Atman is Brahman?

Panikkar, probably the leading contemporary explorer of dialogue, presents this problem best, though without being able as yet to solve it completely. I will introduce some of his insights, then comment and ask some questions. Panikkar speaks of understanding the dialogue partner's position or belief as involving assent to the truth of that position, and even as leading to conversion to that position. The following seems to constitute his fullest statement of his thesis:

The next step [in dialogue] is to understand the other's position, and at once a tremendous difficultly arises. I can never understand his position as he does--and this is the only real understanding between people--unless I share his view; in a word, unless I judge it to be somewhat true...When I say I understand a proposition and consider it untrue, in the first place I do not understand it because, by definition, truth alone is intelligible (if I understand a thing I always understand it sub ratione veritatis); in the second place I certainly do not understand it the way of someone who holds it to be true. Accordingly, to understand is to be converted to the truth one understands.[31]

Let us look at Panikkar's major assertion and, equally important, at its language. A person in dialogue must endeavor to understand the dialogue partner's religious position as the partner himself does. If this effort succeeds, the first person assents in some way to the truth of the partner's position--and this to such degree that it might even be said he is converted to the truth of the position. My response is that Panikkar is speaking of something profoundly true, but that the language of "conversion," though experientially correct, may be confusing theologically.

That one must, in dialogue (interior as well as interreligious), strive to understand the partner's religion as he understands it is the only position that makes sense upon reflection. Otherwise a person may simply read his own religious categories into a very different religion. And that, when the process of understanding succeeds, the person judges the partner's position to be in some way true, both I and many others who have been in dialogue can attest. The problem is with the use of the term "conversion," because this term has for so long connoted the abandoning of one position and the embracing of a new belief as "the truth." But I am quite certain that Panikkar means embracing a newly discovered truth without a presumptive necessity of abandoning a former belief which supposedly covered the same ground. Perhaps this is new ground that simply was not covered, or known of, before. Hence the joy of discovery and conversion to truth is real; but the idea of rejection and replacement that "conversion" often connotes is not present.

Panikkar, well aware after much feedback of the difficulty of communicating this important dialogue experience, is considering the possibilities of the idea of "conviction," perhaps especially of an archaic English noun, "convincement," for carrying his meaning.[32] And so the formulation of this, one of the most exciting and important experiences of dialogue, is not yet complete or satisfactory. But though the word may not yet be there, the thing is, and "conversion" is not so much a wrong term as a potentially confusing one. Lastly, for completeness' sake, it should be pointed out that Panikkar does not anticipate a hasty, unimpended attainment by dialogue partners of "understanding" and "conversion" with regard to every belief of their respective religions. Moreover, understanding should never be pretended where it does not exist. Instead, the beliefs not understood are the matter for continuing dialogue, whose end has scarcely been contemplated as yet.[33]

To apply this line of thinking to our example: I, for one, certainly have not had the definite experience that Atman is Brahman, the act of complete knowledge which, according to Hindu tradition, brings final release from the round of rebirths. But it would be accurate to say that I have had a passing but profound illumination of its truth, some perception of and some effects of which remain with me. This is the truth that I "assent to," or, if the language be properly qualified, am "converted to."

Now the ground is prepared for our final question: Can I also say that I "believe" such a truth? Both the interreligious dialogue and the interior dialogue will frequently pose this question; and, as with the question of understanding and/or being converted to another's position, it may be more important to begin speaking about such a central phenomenon than to wait for perfect formulation and solution before saying anything. In fact, some excellent, though perhaps not final, formulations have been made by Panikkar and by Bernard Lonergan. These I shall explain briefly, then comment upon and apply.

Both theologians tackle the question in terms of a distinction between faith and beliefs. For Panikkar,[34] faith is a constitutive human dimension – the dimension in which a person relates to his or her destiny – while beliefs are the person's formulations to himself and others of his faith. While beliefs composed of human language are integral to a person's expression of his faith to himself and others, and therefore integral to his faith, beliefs do not reach to and adequately express the term or object of faith, i.e., God, or the Transcendent, while faith does indeed reach and relate to its object. More briefly: faith really relates to the Infinite, while beliefs are the finite expressions of that relation, which by the very fact of being finite cannot capture the object of faith.[35] Beliefs are necessary for faith, but they are not identical with faith. In a homogeneous cultural world, in which dogmas are often taken to be faith itself rather than dogmas of faith, beliefs will be thought to be identical with faith. It is in a world of dialogue that the distinction between faith and beliefs, between the transcendence of faith and the relativity, though not relativism, of beliefs, becomes important.[36]

Similarly, Lonergan contends that "by distinguishing faith and belief we have secured a basis both for ecumenical encounter and for an encounter between all religions with a basis in religious experience."[37] For Lonergan, "Faith is the knowledge born of religious love,"[38] while belief is the expression – again, a human necessity partially constitutive of faith – of that knowledge. These beliefs can be different in different cultures and epochs, and yet stem from a deeper unity of faith and love.[39] Once again, then, a distinction between faith and beliefs is seen as essential for a world in dialogue. The immediate intention of Lonergan's beliefs stem from a faith and love whose source is the same. But the distinction seems applicable to our present problem too: the question of whether another religion's belief, now seen as stemming from that profound faith and love that grounds beliefs, can be affirmed as in some way true for all who see it.

To frame the question, this essay's final question, with the help of Panikkar's terms: What does the distinction between faith and beliefs have to do with the interior dialogue? Precisely this:

those truths which I have understood, assented to, even "been converted to" in dialogue of either kind, can now become beliefs which express my faith. These teachings, says Hindu or Buddhist, can prove to be such accurate and fruitful expressions of my pursuit of my human destiny, that I can say I believe in them, that they express my faith.[40]

I can anticipate an objection, and I cannot yet answer it entirely. Do I mean that everyone can believe everything that seems to them noncontradictory to their own religion? This possible extreme of individual interpretation must, it seems to me, be avoided. Yet I am starting from the other end: there must be some scope for believing some of the truths one discovers so genuinely in dialogue. Panikkar's and Lonergan's distinctions between faith and beliefs, and my presentation of this question for both the interreligious and the interior dialogue, may afford a beginning of discourse on this phenomenon.

What we dialogue theologians are endeavoring to do, then, is to lay a Christian theological foundation for a very important aspect of our experience: our perceived belief in teachings of religions other than our own Christianity.[41] I have used belief in the Ātman/Brahman identity as an example which applies to me, and which must have been true at a far deeper level for Abhishiktananda, among others. There is clearly much to be thought out on how the different beliefs we hold harmonize. Perhaps aesthetic thinking can help us more than discursive thinking here. Perhaps, for example, there are different moods and moments of faith experience for which different beliefs are more or less relevant, or "right." This beginning of a thought I hope to develop elsewhere. Meanwhile, the distinction between faith and beliefs makes room within Christian theological categories for an experience that is more and more frequent in dialogue: truth is being perceived, discovered, recognized; and there must be room for that truth in my Christian faith.

This must suffice for now. I hope that my suggestions concerning soteriology, the place of the sannyāsi, the crucial relation of "Jesus" and "the Christ," and the wider ecumenical possibilities of freedom from Christian dialogue. Further, I hope that those many inquirers engaged, all over the world, in what I have proposed to name the interior dialogue will find that these thoughts on how to see and how to believe, enriched by appropriation through their own experience, can combine to form an incipient theology of that same interior dialogue.[42]

NOTES

[1] I speak of the "Christian side" when my axiom that God wills to save all, and my dependence on the Vatican Council document Nostra aetate, might more exactly be considered Catholic. I hope I can be pardoned in this for being more heuristic than exact; yet I am also grateful to Monika Hellwig for the above observation.

[2] Nostra aetate 1 and 2 (The Documents of Vatican II, ed. Walter M. Abbott, S.J. [New York: America, c1966] 661 and 662-663).

[3] This "theological conclusion" and its paraphrase is a reconstruction of part of my conversation/interview with Antoine on July 24, 1980, in Calcutta. In this, as in all the interviews to which I shall refer, I did not use a tape recorder, and so I cannot cite the exact words. But I wrote down the conversations no more than a few hours after they had taken place, and so they are close to exact. For a published example of Antoine's opinions, cf. his essay "Like the Grain of Wheat," in God's Word among Men, ed. George Gispert-Sauch, S.J. (Delhi: Vidyajyoti Institute of Religious Studies, 1973) 139-47.

[4] From our conversation at Vidyajyoti on July 15, 1980.

[5] Our conversation took place on July 7, 1980, in Mangalore. Several other participants in dialogue would disagree with, or qualify substantially, what Prabhu has said about Hindus not initiating dialogue. But none, to my knowledge, would disagree with his positive assertion: for Christians, dialogue springs directly from their faith experience.

[6] The Intrareligious Dialogue (New York: Paulist, 1978) 10.

[7] In line with this teaching, Shri Shyam, when he was the editor of the system's monthly journal, prepared for each issue a section which he entitled "Fragrance of Grace" (Hindi "Pusti Saurabh"). Typically, the section featured a quotation which showed clear evidence of God's grace and love.

[8] Joseph Neuner, "Votum ecclesiae," God's Word among Men (n. 3 above) 147-66.

[9] Cf. J. A. T. Robinson's enlightening discussion of several such passages in his Truth Is Two-Eyed (Phila.: Westminster, 1979) 105-7; cf. also Paul Knitter, "World Religions and the

Finality of Christ: A Critique of Hans Kung's On Being a Christian," Horizons (1978) 153-56.

[10]The Church (New York: Doubleday, Image Books, 1976) 410.

[11]Some readers may find it helpful if I try to place this theological suggestion of mine among other contemporary Christian theological positions on the question of Extra ecclesiam nulla salus and the normativity of Jesus Christ for salvation (a topic of major concern in my next section). To do this, I will use the four positions explained by J. Peter Schineller in his "Christ and Church: A Spectrum of Views," TS 37 (1976) 545-66. I reject position 1, which holds that "Jesus Christ and the Church are the constitutive and exclusive way of salvation" (550). I find also inadequate position 2, the "anonymous Christian" position, in which Christ and the Church are not exclusively but constitutively necessary for salvation. I see the soteriological position I have just described as falling somewhere between Schineller's positions 3 and 4 (he sees his four positions as exclusive of one another, and I disagree with respect to positions 3 and 4). Position 3's emphasis that God's grace extends to all people, with Jesus Christ and the Church having a normative but not constitutive role in the salvation of all, is nearly congruent with my present suggestion. The only difference is that I cannot "in dialogue . . . point to the superiority or normativeness of the Christian witness" (564). I say that the salvation I know in Jesus Christ is normative in that it will illumine for me, in dialogue, other ways by which God has saved and is saving people. This takes me some distance toward Schineller's position 4, an apophatic stance, yet one in which God's grace extends to all, and Jesus Christ is one of many ways of radical epistemological scepticism which Schineller presents as an attribute of position 4.

[12]Cf. particularly Abhishiktānanda's "Sannyāsa" (pp. 1-56 in his The Further Shore [Delhi: Indian Society for the Propagation of Christian Knowledge, 1975]), which has been made required reading for even the Hindu candidates for sannyasa at one of the finest ashrams in Rishikesh (the ashram is the Shivananda Ashram, and Gispert-Sauch my source for this information). For examples of Bede Griffiths' writings on sannyasa, cf. his Christ in India (New York: Scribner's, 1966) 59-63, and his Return to the Centre (Springfield, Ill.: Templegate, 1977) 9-15.

[13]Cf., e.g., Raymond Panikkar, The Unknown Christ of Hinduism (2nd Ed.; Maryknoll, N.Y.: Orbis, 1981); M. M.

Thomas' deliberately countertitled The Acknowledged Christ of the
Indian Renaissance (2nd ed.; Madras: Christian Literature
Society, 1976); S. J. Samartha, The Hindu Response to the
Unbound Christ (Madras: Christian Literature Society, 1974);
Klaus Klostermaier, Kristvidya (Bangalore: Christian Institute for
the Study of Religion and Society, 1967).

[14]On August 4, 1980, under the same conditions as mentioned
for the previous conversations.

[15]In the conversation of July 15, 1980 (n. 4 above).

[16]My understanding here is that quite a number of Indian
theologians - Gispert-Sauch did not say whether he is among them
- would not admit absolute uniqueness of Jesus, although they
might well hold for a uniquenss and necessity of Christ in senses
which they would further define. By an "absolute uniqueness" of
Jesus I mean a claim that salvation comes only through Jesus of
Nazareth, who is the totality of Christ.

[17]The Unknown Christ of Hinduism, 83.

[18]The Intrareligious Dialogue 36 (the sentence is meant to
stand by itself, although I do not find all its referents clear).
Two theologians who have criticized the first edition of The
Unknown Christ on the above-mentioned ground are S. J.
Samartha (The Hindu Response to the Unbound Christ, 165) and
John B. Chethimattam (in "R. Panikkar's Approach to
Christology," Indian Journal of Theology 23 [1974] 219-22). I
agree with their criticism of Panikkar's first edition, but find the
second edition better on this question, though still occasionally
problematic (e.g., 29 and 56-57).

[19]Cf. esp. The Church 409-11.

[20]Robin Boyd, in his excellent Indian Christian Theology
(2nd ed.; Madras: Christian Literature Society, 1975) 294, sees
Abhishiktananda, "the Panikkar group," Bede Griffiths,
World Religions [London: Burns & Oates, 1967]) as theologians
who find the idea of a primal "cosmic religion" a useful one.

[21]This seems especially true for the monk/sannyasi
participants, though not for them alone. Robinson also notices
this (Truth Is Two-Eyed 13).

[22] I am not the first to use the term "interior dialogue." Lucien Richard uses it without elaboration, but in approximately the meaning I describe here, in his "Some Recent Developments on the Question of Christology and World Religions," Eglise et theologie 8 (1977) 209. Eric J. Sharpe also uses the term, but in a different sense (the contemplative/mystical aspect of interreligious dialogue), in his "Goals of Interreligious Dialogue," in John Hick, ed., Truth and Dialogue in World Religions (Phila.: Westminster, 1974) 87-89. But I think I am the first to suggest adoption of the term both as preferred usage and in the present meaning.

[23] Truth Is Two-Eyed 7. Robinson cites as his reference in dialogue theologian Murray Rogers' work the chapter "Hindu and Christian - A Moment Breaks," in H. Jai Singh, ed., Inter-Religious Dialogue (Bangalore: C.I.S.R.S., 1967) 104-17; unfortunately this very promising book is out of print.

[24] Cf. The Intrareligious Dialogue 40.

[25] Page 313 in Puthiadam's "Reflections on Hindu Religious Texts," in D. S. Amalorpavadass, ed., Research Seminar on Non-Biblical Scriptures (Bangalore: National Biblical, Catechetical, and Liturgical Centre, 1974) 300-313; cf. 309-13 on complementarity generally; 309 on P.'s experience of the different "moods."

[26] I am indebted for this astute clarification to my student Leanne Simon.

[27] Truth Is Two-Eyed 9-10.

[28] For this example cf. ibid. 97-103. Unique and Universal is also the title of an introduction to Indian theology (ed. John B. Chethimattam, Bangalore, 1972) which Robinson has cited favorably here and elsewhere.

[29] Los Angeles: Dawn Horse, 1973; I shall be quoting from p. 55.

[30] Cf. Abhishiktananda's chapter "The Johannine Upanishads," in his Hindu-Christian Meeting-Point (Bangalore: C.I.S.R.S., 1969) 85-102; and, more recently, the volume of essays, India's Search for Reality and the Relevance of the Gospel of John, ed. C. Duraisingh and C. Hargreaves (Delhi: I.S.P.C.K., 1975).

[31] The Intrareligious Dialogue 9.

[32] Learned in conversation with Panikkar, in Washington, D.C., May 3, 1981. One brief published example of the language of "conviction" combined with "conversion" and the intrareligious dialogue may be found in The Intrareligious Dialogue XXVI. The article in which Panikkar has thus far treated this question most thoroughly is in German: "Verstehen als Uberzeugtsein," in Neue Anthropologie 7 (ed. H. G. Gadamer and P. Vogler; Stuttgart: Thieme, 1975) 132-67; but he indicated that more is likely to be seen.

[33] It was in the conversation just mentioned that I asked Panikkar what happens when understanding is not reached.

[34] Cf. his Myth, Faith and Hermeneutics (New York: Paulist, 1979) 204-6, within the chapter titled "Faith as a Constitutive Human Dimension." Besides the above chapter, Panikkar has written a book on this subject: L'Homme qui devient Dieu: La foi dimension constitutive de l'homme (Paris: Aubier, 1969).

[35] Cf. esp. The Intrareligious Dialogue 12-13 and 18-22; and, e.g., the following (from Myth, Faith and Hermeneutics 198): "the act of faith grasps things in themselves. Its formulation is only a conceptualization of some 'thing' that transcends it."

[36] Cf. The Intrareligious Dialogue 18-21.

[37] Bernard J. F. Lonergan, S. J., Method in Theology (New York: Herder & Herder, 1972) 119.

[38] Ibid. 115.

[39] Ibid. 119.

[40] My expressing this conclusion in an individualistic way reflects merely the dominant present mode of dialogue experience, and in no way intends to exclude rich communitarian insight, language, and action in dialogue.

[41] Panikkar witnesses to this: "It is precisely because I take seriously Christ's affirmation that he is the way, the truth and the life that I cannot reduce his significance only to historical Christianity. It is because I also take seriously the saying of the Gita that all action done with a good intention reaches Krsna and the message of the Buddha that he points the way to liberation, that I look for an approach to the encounter with religions that will contain not only a deep respect for but an enlightened

confidence in these very traditions – and eventually belief in their messages" (The Intrareligious Dialogue 54).

[42]Reprinted with the permission of the author and the editor of Theological Studies; the article appeared in Theological Studies, 44 (1983):587-603.

BUDDHIST-CHRISTIAN DIALOGUE

Winston L. King

My first writing about the possibility of Buddhist-Christian dialogue, Buddhism and Christianity: Some Bridges of Understanding (London: 1963), was one result of my first-ever contact with a Buddhist culture, that of the Burmese. It was pleasant to write, for I had found the Burmese charmingly unpretentious, friendly, and nonaggressive in their explanations of Buddhism. Hence the writing was done in a fully ecumenical mood on my part; I tried in every way to find common ground between Christianity--that is, my own version of liberal Christianity--and the Theravada Buddhism.

It was only later in retrospect that I fully realized the depth of the polite but total disinterest in Christianity on the part of nearly all of my Burmese Buddhist friends, and the reason for it was their absolute confidence that Buddhism embodied the ultimate and perfect religious truth so that there was no need to be interested in or concerned about anything else in the way of religion. It was only later that I also realized the underlying and basic doctrinaire rigidity of the Theravada Buddhism that I found in Burma. The age-old Pali Canon was the embodiment of plenary inspiration, to use a Christian term, for the words of the Buddha contained in his discourses in the Three Baskets were infallibly and literally true as they stood.

In any case the aforesaid book was written hopefully and optimistically. Undoubtedly, as I now see it, I greatly underestimated the difficulties of genuine interreligious dialogue in any depth or existential reality and thought that I had accomplished more than I had. Perhaps this failure was due to some extent to the plane on which I sought rapprochement, for it was primarily on the level of doctrine that I attempted to come within speaking distance of Buddhism. This was because the disparity of doctrines had struck my attention most forcibly in my studies and experience, and seemed to be the greatest obstacle to any dialogue. There were no-God versus God, no-soul versus soul, karma versus grace, man as qualitatively different from all other life versus common nature and the interwoven destinies of all forms of sentient beings.

The result was an attempt to throw at least some gossamer filaments--optimistically called "bridges"--from the Christian side of the chasm of nonunderstanding across to the Buddhist side in the hope of finding anchorage there in some sort of Buddhist "likeness." Underlying my confidence of success was a history of religion's assumption that similar structures and functions could be found in both religions as religions, for example, that they both represented searches for some sort of salvation, that they both recognized some sort of ultimate reality of salvational consequence, that both found some actions leading to salvation and others not, and so on. The enterprise itself resulted in such "bridges" as the following: the Buddhist equivalent of God in the combination of dharma, karma, Nirvana, and the Buddha--a "god in four parts"; finding in the Buddha and Christ a similar compassion; seeing the mystic prayer of quiet as analogous to meditation; drawing out likenesses between Christian and Buddhist selflessness; and discovering implicit and structural grace in the Buddhist doctrinal system and in the power of the Buddha.

It could not be called an outstandingly successful bridge-building achievement in any sense of the word. One reviewer observed that he could not see much doctrinal, intellectual, or experiential traffic coming across my bridges-- even in the book itself. For some Christians too much had been conceded to "the opposition." And from the Buddhists there was not much more than a monk's indulgent semichuckle as he allowed that in the hymn lie "The angels adore Thee all veiling their sight," devas might somewhat meaningfully replace "angels" if we also took "Thee" out as a personal God reference. Later I was told that he did not approve of my books on Buddhism.

Aside from my own unskillfulness as a bridge builder with the materials at hand, what was wrong with my effort? Was my version of Christianity too superficial, too one-sided to make any real connection with Buddhism possible? Did I choose the wrong approach points? Did I remain "too Christian," that is, too dogmatically committed, to make meaningful contact? Or more basically and generally, are all attempts at doctrinal rapprochement between Christianity and Buddhism fated to fail? Some would answer "yes" to this last question, and say that only by experience-related efforts can there be successful contact between the two traditions. In part I agree, though the matter of interfaith dialogue is not solved by a simple appeal to pure experience. I shall return to this a little later.

However, even in Burma I did not confine myself solely to the intellectual investigation of Buddhism. In our second year there my wife and I took a 10-day meditation course at the International Meditation Center in Rangoon under the late U Ba Khin, a lay meditation master. (This I have written about in an appendix to my A Thousand Lives Away, 1964.) Ever since then I have been concerned with the meditational, that is, experiential, approach to Buddhism.

But I have asked myself since: Was even my short dip into actual meditation under Buddhist auspices a truly "Christian-Buddhist encounter"? I think now that my answer must be no. Why? Because it was not a genuine existential encounter on my part, but a kind of psychosomatric experiment. (The Center was willing to receive even such meditators from the highways and hedges, requiring no declaration of any intention to become a Buddhist.) So I shifted my internal gears into neutral and went through the ten days with an "open" mind to see what would happen. Interesting things did happen in a superficial way, but did not markedly influence my religious stance at the time simply because I never really expected or intended them to.

Perhaps there was a greater influence than this suggests, for some years later I shifted my church membership from the Protestant denomination that I had belonged to for nearly thirty years to the Friends, largely because I found their silent worship more congenial than the sermonic and structured type of service. Since then other meditation experiences in Japan have confirmed me in this preference.

Be this as it may, two or three questions are raised in my mind at present about Christian-Buddhist encounters. The first is the question alluded to earlier: Is shared experience the only and sufficient route to genuine interreligious encounter or dialogue in the deepest sense? This has been persuasively argued by many. Some would argue it on a mystical level: all mysticisms, in their thrust beyond words and in the experience of an ultimate Oneness, are essentially at one with each other—if they could forget their differing doctrinal statements, mere word structures at best. Many others, who would not call themselves mystics, believe that basic human experiences, particularly the religious ones, have a common quality which enables men to share existentially despite linguistic differences, if only those can be put aside.

Thus, after participating in a set of Christian-Buddhist retreats with Japanese Buddhist monks and scholars living, meditating, and discussing with European Catholic monks in their monasteries, Professor Jikai Fujiyoshi noted that the group which had no interpreters but simply meditated together in silence for two or three weeks felt close to each other at the end of the visit and embraced each other with tears at their parting. But in his own group where "we were engaged almost solely in . . . discussion. . . . The more we argued, the more we realized the differences. There was no point for a meeting at the level of theology." In the end he concluded that "Christians in Europe know the concept of sunyata or Emptiness philosophically and they may be able to understand it intellectually, but their claim that God is identifiable with Nothingness or Emptiness is not really correct." Hence this theological encounter only separated Christians and Buddhists further.

The reasons for the success of experience over discussion are obvious. Experience is essentially direct, emotional, nonverbal, but beliefs are verbalized. With words come differences, as language systems and intellectual discussions amply testify. In the religious context, deep emotion gathers around key terms; they become the banners and rallying points of faith. But nonverbal emotion and awareness can be shared even between sworn (intellectual) enemies. A glance, a facial expression, a touch of the hand, a bodily posture give their clear message irrespective of the language barriers. Face to face with basic human situations, men are able to communicate important messages and fellow feeling wordlessly. And Buddhism, with its deep conviction of the possibility of pure, true experience, untainted by intellection, feels especially akin to all types of wordless communication of the truth.

Despite my sympathy for this approach to religious "dialogue," however, I cannot quite convince myself that "experience only" is the best or only avenue for existential religious encounter. That is to say, divisive as doctrinal discussion is, doctrinal questions must sooner or later be squarely faced if there is to be any genuine, fully existential encounter between any two religious traditions. To be sure, "experience only" encounters are valuable in that they can provide a sense of fellowship and human solidarity in facing the ultimate concerns of humanity, even though from differing stances. But they can do little more than that, and it is foolishly romantic to think otherwise. For there is no such thing, some Zen talk to the contrary, as "pure" experience completely undefiled by any ideation, covert or overt. Nor does the statement quite ring true from a contemporary Theravada-Vipassana meditation teacher that "Dhamma . . . should be taken not as a religion but as an ideal way of life," since he then goes on to expound at length the Buddha's path to liberation. It is clearly a public relations ploy; vipāssana remains firmly ensconced in the Buddhist doctrinal tradition.

To repeat: All experiences, except the purely physical sensory experiences--and these many times too--have some ideational context. Especially is this true of the experiences had within religious traditions, no matter how elastically portrayed. For example, take prayer and meditation. There are Buddhist prayers and there is Christian meditation of course. But though Buddhist prayers on the popular level may be functionally almost indistinguishable from Christian prayers in that both appeal to the Highest Powers for some sort of benefit otherwise unobtainable, prayers are never really in the central Buddhist tradition at its higher levels. There, prayers are essentially meditational exercises designed to affect the meditator's own attitudes. Classically, Christian meditation has been thought of, even in mystical circles, as a preparation for prayer. And prayer, even though it be the unitive prayer of quiet that has passed beyond the pale of outright petition, is never less than or different from a waiting before an Other in surrender and openness.

What then happens when a Christian, as so often occurs today, decides to meditate in the Zen manner? Is what ensues "Buddhist" meditation? Or is it Christian-Buddhist, or Buddhist-Christian meditation? Most Catholics who thus meditate see it as a means or method for enhancing their own personal spiritual discipline with no doctrinal implications involved. The late Thomas Merton has written that Zen has no message, but is only a way of seeing, of becoming aware of, one's existential selfhood. (Whether Zen meditators would agree, I am not certain.) I would say, in consonance with what William Johnston once wrote, that when a Christian sits on a pillow to meditate Zen fashion, he is sitting on a Christian pillow, and that the Zen Buddhist meditator in doing the "same" meditation, even side by side with the Christian, is sitting on a Zen pillow, even though he would "kill" the Buddha if he met him.

Does this then shut the door completely to genuine existential religious dialogue or the intermingling of religious experiences? There seems to me to be at least four possible ways here. One is that of conversion, which begins with a genuinely existential encounter, that is, the willingness to let one's contacts with another faith fundamentally modify his own faith and belief. But then, of course, dialogue is over for that person, and my own observation is that converts as a rule are not much interested in remaining in dialogue with the faith that they have left behind them, except to make other converts.

There is the second theoretical possibility of trying to make contact with another faith from somewhere between the lines, either by someone who is semi-ex-faith A (his inherited one) and interested/attracted to faith B, but not yet willing to be committed to it; or the nonreligious version of working for self-development from a psychological-existential base with no serious concern for belief systems or commitment to them. No doubt some in our day of rejected or loosely held religious beliefs thus work out viable patterns of life conduct. But neither of these is a method that engages religious traditions as such in dialogue, and they may end up, both religiously and psychologically, nowhere in particular, with the engine of existential significance and action still in neutral.

There is, thirdly, the use of the other faith's spiritual techniques, say meditation, with no intention of modifying one's own faith or belief system in any fundamental way, but simply improving it. At its shallowest this seems to me to be the essence of some (or much?) of the present Catholic, and some Protestant, practice of Zen meditation. This is quite legitimate, though I have heard some Buddhist converts maintain that such "Christian-Buddhist" meditation is bogus Buddhism, even bogus spirituality. That is, a faith commitment to the doctrinal context of a spiritual discipline—in this case Buddhism—is necessary to make that discipline genuinely fruitful. But whether bogus or not, such practices have seemed to numbers of Christians to have genuinely deepened their own Christian lives.

Some, of course, are fearful of doing even this much. When I spoke on Buddhist meditation to a group of missionaries in Burma, I was immediately classified as hostile to Christianity, and a Christian friend in Burma said that he did not feel free to do Buddhist meditation, much as he was interested, because it would seem to his Christian friends that such meditation would be a confession of the superiority of Buddhism to Christianity.

There is among Buddhists in Burma and Japan, it seems to me, a reverse-similar attitude that likewise inhibits any faith interaction on their part. It takes the form of a polite but almost total disinterest in Christianity, except sometimes a scholarly-argumentative one. The implication seems to be, as suggested previously, that Nirvana and Emptiness are so much superior to Heaven and God, that there is little use in troubling oneself about the latter. Very practically speaking, it is much more difficult for a Buddhist to genuinely share in Christian devotional forms of prayer and adoration to God, than for a

sunrise or near evening makes a great difference. Therefore it is meaningless to say simply "an hour": "an hour" is an abstraction. Time is heterogeneous; each hour has its own color, its own message, its distinct entity. One is free to interpret all this with an astrological bent, but astronomy would support my point just as well. To perceive no difference among days and hours is to ignore the fact that time--which physics discusses as though it were merely a conception--is an actuality. It is to miss the message and radiance of time and to see only its alternating velocities.

It is obvious that this conception of time could have unsettling consequences. Industry might find more than one difficulty in the view that time cannot be hurried, cannot be altered by what is accomplished in it. But, this is off my subject. I will contain myself in the mind of India, where it is known that time is rhythm and therefore heterogeneous. To take a non-Indian example, consider Ravel's Bolero. From this example we may begin to see what rhythm means. If it is merely heard it is maddening; it can be endured only if it is not listened to, but danced, only if one enters and moves with its rhythm. All the music of India is like that.

I have learned in the West to be as clear as possible, to proceed from one to two to three. So, to summarize, I have said what time is not for India, and what it is: a rhythm that purely is.

Life, which we all agree exists within time, is not an illusion nor a finality, not a straight line, but rather a circle. Or, according to the Purana - and more than one Purana - time is still more like a spiral than a circle, but no straight line in any case. Life is not a dream, but neither is it anything solid and uniform. It has no end or culmination and thus no meaning, no finality of itself. It is simply a game, diverting for those who play it well and boring for those who do not, for those who would change the rules, for those who have traded childlike innocence for the tedious reflectiveness of adulthood (who, since they have not understood the game abandon it for the theoretical ennui they call "philosophy" or perhaps "civilization"). When life is not sufficiently diverting we fabricate diversions or seek to escape life altogether. India, however, finds the game itself sufficient and hence has no need to invent distractions. Life is a game which, so long as it is played according to the rules, does not need transcendental attachments. India did not turn to metaphysics for what was already its own: simple, living physicality.

Being play, life is not only diverting, but beautiful as well. It embodies no final tragedy; if we lose, we begin again and, thanks to the bit of experience we acquired, play the game a little better. It is not that life can be played with, but that life itself is the game. We have no need of teleological thought to pierce the crust of things and open the core to us. Life itself is core and secret.

Life is thus simply a gift, something bestowed on us like air and water, and the country we were born to and the language we speak and the culture which first nurtured us. All these are gifts. All these are part of the game that is the gift. For traditional India life is a gift to be received with both hands, not to exploit or manipulate, but to enjoy. It is gratuitous, and--if you'll allow me ,to play the philologist--gratifying.

In discussing the third characteristic of time I will pay tribute to Hellenic culture--and avoid the less widely comprehensible Sanskrit--by coining a little Greek word: mesocosm. Man is neither cosmos nor microcosm; he is mesocosm. He is neither creator nor the whole creation, not spectacle nor spectator (as the entire Western tradition from Plato onward would have us believe). Rather, he is an intermediary, something provisional and constitutionally itinerant. This is the definition of his place in the universe. Indian philosophers express this concept well with the phrase sad asad anirvacanīyam: not being, nor not-being, nor the denial of the two nor the synthesis of the two, but their constant passage through experience - in Hebrew, pasca - the everlasting transit, the silence between two crescendos in one symphony. The Brahmasūtra seeks to guide its students to the recognition of nothingness between temporal points, the intemporal reality between two points which we apprehend as real.

This is in essence the meaning of the meditation of Yoga: not to achieve a concentration which then explodes and provokes more trauma and psychosis, but to strip away the discrimination that separates one thing from another, to unite things indiscriminately, to attain awareness of that moment of silence and transition. For a moment the Yogi may fly between one moment of existence and another, and in that flight discover that reality is no still point of the earth but the passage among them. The symbol of Hindu experience could be a NO PARKING sign. The only permanence is the lack of permanence. You cannot park even thought, for by nature you yourself are intermediary, a mesocosm, a moving thing.

This discourse should not be equated with Heraclitean becoming or Parmenedian non-being, which are both linked to the concept of time. In Indian thought there is no becoming and nothing which becomes; there is only transition, mesocosm.

I mentioned before that, India's conception of time as rhythm and as transition is subject to criticism by the West. What is it good for? Can civilization be built upon it? Can it set railroads into motion or institute systems of taxation? Though now they fade away, it is well to note that these conceptions served India for many centuries.

The second great symbol of Indian civilization, which in varying forms is a universal conception, is space. For India, space is neither to pass through nor to remain in, neither is it something that can be conquered or mastered--as we say we reach the moon by "conquering" space. Since it is neither a place we pass through nor the place we pause at, space is not an external barrier which man must surmount or break or even acknowledge. Space is Dasein or Existenz, to seek a rough equivalent, even while recognizing that translation is treacherous.

Space is not "outside"--not that which separates us from the moon or some other place. Nor is it "inside," an internal and immanent location. In a sense, I am space. Where I am, space is. Without a cue from Gabriel Marcel, India can say, "as I am body and I am soul." If I am soul, then surely I am body. I do not have body or soul, but am body and soul. If I say that I have hands but that I am soul, I divide soul from body and body from soul. India has never made this separation, nor accepted it when made by others. I am soul and body and not disparate components.

To divide body from soul is reflection. Reflection for India is a loss of innocence, a second-rate, second-hand understanding. To assume that reflection, a method of returning to knowledge in Western conception, is equivalent to departing from knowledge, seems contrary to the law that declares returns are not departures. But India has never believed that the soul need contemplate its solitary self. For India, space is that of which we are constituted, the Dasein, the being there-ness which is not outside, not inside, a concept which I understand by transcending. It is true that we may speak reflectively of it, but our words will never get to the root of it.

It is not quite fair to accuse the West of deifying logos, but we may see the difference between its conceptions of the primacy of the Word and India's by refering to the Satapathabrahmana:

275

One day the Word and the Spirit went to Prajápati
because they were arguing over which was greater and more
powerful. The Word began, "I am by far greater because
you, Spirit, you, Mind, are powerless to manifest yourself.
You are poor and powerless and impotent unless I reveal you,
unless I, Logos, I Vác, express what you are thinking inside
yourself. Without manifestation there is no force, no
concreteness, no epiphany, nothing tangible at all.
Therefore I am mightier than you."

Spirit answered, "No, it is actually you who are the
tool. If I do not breathe into you and tell you what to say
you babble meaninglessly. From within I fill you with
speech."

It is one of the Orient's crucial moments when Prajápati,
Father of Gods, decides in favour of Spirit. All the greatness of
the West aligned itself in favour of the Word, Logos. The
pre-eminence of Spirit over Word is perhaps the cornerstone of
traditional India. When Prajápati decided in favour of Spirit,
then Vac, the Word, was angered. Consequently, though India
has had great intuition, the Word deserted her and she has not
always been able to express herself adequately. India has had
keen joy of spirit, but her people died at thirty-three. The fable
continues:

Väc, with an angry countenance, said, "Since you give me
second place, I will no longer be your instrument at all,
Prajápati." Thus, when the supplicant makes an offering to
Prajápati he does not speak aloud, but in a whisper.

Logos refused to serve Prajápati because he was subordinated
to Spirit.

The theology of logos has been the subject of many books in
many a library. But the very concept "theo-logy," the Word of
the Spirit, is a contradiction in terms. It is impossible to study
or analyze Spirit by means of the Word, for Spirit is clearly the
obverse of Logos, its complement and not its subject.

We have already seen that space is equivalent to existence,
the Dasein, the ākāśá, that which I am: neither within, nor
without, but am. Space is all-pervading, and that which is, is
space. Literature and philosophical texts will say that we are
enfolded and covered by space, that it is what clothes, limits, and
manifests us. Without space we would not be what we are, but
isolated, absolutely excommunicated. When the man of India came

out of the cave where he had first taken refuge, he did not wrap reason about him as another cave, another integument to separate him from the animals that he might dominate them, from angels that he might scoff at them, from God that he might rationalize Him. Because of his basic conception of space, the Indian lives in communion with angels and demons, earth and elements, animal and herb, God and gods, in community with all.

There is no tradition in yesterday's India that the individual is a self-sufficing or autonomous unit that occasionally interacts with other such isolated units. The smallest unit it would recognize is the extended family, and beyond that, the unit of caste. The law of karma is precisely this cosmic solidarity among all existing things. Man is no exception. He is never alone. There are ever the angels, or if modern man prefers, the virus. But virus or angel, they are always with us. Man need never feel isolated, for there are angels and beasts, wife, children, family, community. Privacy and exclusive intimacy are egoistical aberrations seen in those who believe they must isolate themselves in a sort of spiritual air-conditioner for the sake of self-realization. Instead, it is karma upon which achievement is based, for it is all-pervading, necessary, real, and as material as it is spiritual.

Space is not place, not an exterior reality through which one passes. It is existence. It is the verticality of existence, referring not to the distance between one thing and another, but to the manner in which these things are manifest. Whereas horizontal space may be measured in 1-2-3 uniform kilometres, vertical space is unique and non-repeatable. When a mother embraces her child or a lover his lover, the act is precious in part because it cannot be acted again. Truly human activities are those which are unique and non-replicable. They cannot be interchanged nor compared either absolutely or in relation to anything else. They are self-justifying, and we are delighted to have undertaken them even when their consequences are hard and immediate. One says, "It is worthwhile to have lived five, ten, twenty years to attain this moment, this encounter, this glance, this experience." Authentic human life is always unique, and so involved with the essence of the man who lives it as to be temporal, incomparable, unrecordable.

If ordinary temporality can be abstracted from an experience, then that experience cannot be called long or short, past, or potential. Non-authentic life is datable and, belonging to the horizontal of experience, replicable, temporal, and historic.

277

What can be seen constantly in the reactions of the Indian people, even today, is that there is not existential anguish about discovering the meaning of life. Already somewhat affected by the perturbations of the West, I ask myself whether life has meaning and what that meaning might be. But for the Indian, if life has meaning, it has meaning; if not, not. My awareness of that meaning is purely extraneous. If I base my reception of life on my understanding of life, then I may discover many bizarre and various things, but the true heart of existence will elude me because it has nothing to do with my understanding of it. If meaning is there, then it is there. If it is not there, it is not there. Hence my effort to disclose the secrets of existence is at best a pastime which is either very beautiful or very perilous. But it cannot find the profundities I seek. It will not enlighten me that repose relies on coming to understand a thing which is, in the ordinary sense, unlearnable.

Obviously this leads to a non-economic, even anti-economic organization of society, for it is not repeating, improving, magnifying which count, but the doing of a thing that cannot be planned or replicated. If you go to Delhi you will see that most of the difficulties faced by the Planning Commission exist because it calculates in paradigms and patterns which do not correspond to the sensibilities of traditional India.

Third concern: Man. What is the identity of man? What is the experience of being human? It is puruṣa, sacrifice. A Greek equivalent for this word would be theandrism: more than man, less than God. When India uses the word "man" it is thinking of something greater than men, and when it uses "God," of something not so great as God. Man is this middle ground; man is the encounter of the empirical experience of his own being with the idea of God.

Man is God precisely because one must add immediately that God is man. This is neither tautology nor pantheism. It is puruṣa. Puruṣa is sacrifice, and by sacrificing what he thought he was, man becomes more than he thought he could be.

Let me explain. A prime contributor to India's ruin--an elegant ruin, at least; there are many ways to die--is the fundamental conception of classical Brahman civilization, "simplicity as perfection." The word "perfection" is treacherous for our understanding. "Perfect" is per-factum--something is perfect when it is full, when it is rich, when it holds all it can hold. For twenty-five centuries the sphere of Parmenides has been the symbol of perfection in the Western world. Per-factum.

Roundness. Fullness. More. As Saint Paul speaks of clothing
oneself with Christ, the function of the symbology of liturgy is
to clothe the intermediary one in ever more glorifying vestments.
A bishop wears two crowns; the Pope, three. The more crowns
the more authority, power and richness. This kind of symbolism
dictates our Western conception of perfection.

But the concept India would call perfection comes closer to
our concept of "simplicity." It is not the Parmenedian sphere, but
the dimensionless point. In fact, the ideal Brahmanic education
would peel from a man as from an onion all that is accidental--
neti, neti: not this, not that--and leave him in a state of
absolute freedom. Not sphere, but point.

This leads us to the consideration of Indian asceticism.
Western asceticism seems to say, with Aesop's fox, "This fruit is
good and desirable, but I am an ascetic and may not have it:
therefore I renounce it. There is positive value in this, yet I
renounce it." India sees immediately that this is "sour grapes"
and says, "You are not convinced that the fruit is bitter. You
try, but don't reach, so you say it is green."

To India asceticism is leaving the fruit only when truly
convinced of its bitterness. Asceticism is the renunciation of
that which has no value, that which causes no hardship to lose.
It is a discipline whereby one is not enslaved by that which is no
longer useful. It is not costly, and he who renounces does not
envy those who have. I renounce the bitter fruit in the hope of
higher things.

Renunciation of the less for the great leads us again to
theandrism, because mankind's great sickness is his desire to
preserve his own distinct existence, which, if he is truly more
than he seems to be, should be a delight to forfeit rather than a
calamity. To sacrifice what he seems to be, should be for man a
sweet dissolution into what he truly is. Religion has a particular
meaning for India. Though the etymology of the word points to
religare, in India it signifies not the binding, but the unbinding
by which one offers oneself, ceases to be, escaping one's own
individuality. This is sacrifice. Living life means losing what
it appears to be. He who would save the little core he calls self
has little faith in God, or whatever you conceive to move the
universe.

When a drop falls in the ocean, we think it disappears--as
though its whole existence were the surface tension that made it a
separate thing. If personality consists of the barriers that
separate me from you, then obviously all is lost when the drop is

279

in the Ocean. But if the essence of the drop is the water itself and not the film of surface tension, then the drop is not lost but transformed into the whole ocean. India has never confused the film with the water, and considers that human condition best which ends soonest. Man is puruṣa, the sacrifice, and is in as much as he loses himself, in as much as he abandons the desire to be what he thinks he is. Man is to the degree that he unmakes himself-- reversing Prajapati's sacrifice, Prajapati who dismembered himself in the act of creation. The enlightened man sacrifices himself so as to restore that broken divine body.

Life, like a fire, is lived by burning and consuming. Sacrifice is the fundamental law, the primary experience of a man as a theandric being, whose perfection is simplicity even unto dissolution. Here I must speak of sacred eschatology; that this, the ends of man are his own ending. It is then that rejuvenation occurs, then that one gains new life, or if you will, rebirth, salvation, liberation. This eschatology is not a thing dependent on time. It is not merely the end of a sequence of events. Only if it were, only if it were a sort of cosmic climax would the discussion of modern theologians as to the futility of Christ's sacrifice be understandable. This end, this eschatology cannot be anticipated. It does not come, it does not arrive; it has been a thousand years and it has not come. Liberation will not come from that direction. We shall not be saved by an historical event. To wait is not to hope.

Within the realm of eschatology, as I have called it, of salvation, liberation, of culmination, it has been my experience that death is not in front of me, but behind me. The West, on the other hand, from Plato to Heidegger, has conceived philosophy as a preparation for death: in Heidegger's phrase, "being-unto-death." This is a conceptual dead end to the great speculation on death. Considering this inclination of Western thought, it seems common sense to see death before us, to view our lives as a preparation for a good death. We are so used to thinking our lives a Sein zum Tod that we have become comfortable with the fear of it.

The experience of the large mass of Hindu (and later the Buddhist) world is quite otherwise. Let us say parenthetically that much might have been different in Vietnam if America had understood that the Buddhist attitude toward death is not that of an American soldier. One cannot count on a Buddhist's fear of death. Philosophy at times can take to itself great magical potency.

280

The Indian sense of death is this: I am in as much as I begin at death and gather more life unto myself. I do not move toward death, I move away from it; and the further away death recedes, the more authentic life becomes. The more present and immediate life becomes, the further it moves from death, which is a phenomenon of the past. I live not toward my end, but successively away from it.

I have tried to relate a tradition that an Indian philosopher would have explained in the simplicity of experience, speaking of the law of karma, of the nature of samsāra. I have spoken of immanence, the immanence of time, space, of man himself in the non-time we would call eternity, in the non-being which we would call nothingness, in the non-human we would call God. I speak as a true Indian without melancholy for the passing of what has endured for centuries, out of which men have built a civilization and a life. For all things are destined--not condemned, but destined--to pass, and perhaps both East and West know that only by death can life be imparted anew.[1]

NOTE

[1]Reprinted from *Religion and Society*, 27 (1980), 64-74, with the permission of the author.

RELIGIOUS EXPERIENCE IN THE
SECOND AXIAL PERIOD

Ewert Cousins

The twentieth century has witnessed an increasing interest in religious experience. William James gave impetus to this interest with his Gifford Lectures in 1901-1902, published under the title: The Varieties of Religious Experience.[1] In the 1960's interest in religious experience reached a high pitch in the United States chiefly among the younger generation, but also among academicians and scientific researchers. The discovery of psychedelic drugs led to extensive scientific research in religious states of consciousness. Abraham Maslow launched the Humanistic Psychology movement, focusing on the creative aspect of religious experience in his book Religions, Values, and Peak Experiences.[2] In depth psychology, C.G. Jung had early acknowledged the significance of religious experience in psychic growth and had extended his horizons beyond Western culture through his concept of the archetypes of the collective unconscious. In the 1960's this cross-cultural dimension became concrete through the gurus and spiritual teachers from the East who invaded the West, teaching Oriental meditation and bringing religious experience into a global context. This interest in global religious experience was supported by many decades of research in the history of religions which had amassed a vast store of data on primitive cultures and the established religions of the East and West. Among the religious traditions themselves, there had grown an increasing ecumenical climate of openness to other traditions, mutual respect, interest and enrichment. In fact, the encounter of world religions has become the major religious event of our times. This encounter has drawn the interest in religious experience to a level of mature crystallization, for it focuses on experience rather than institutions, on spirituality rather than creeds; and it reveals the depth and variety of religious experience in a global context, while at the same time searching for dimensions of unity.

It is fitting that a volume entitled Religious Experience: East and West Meet should be dedicated to Father John Chethimattam. For in his research, publishing and teaching, the theme of religious experience in the meeting of East and West has been his central concern. Through the years I have been personally enriched by his work. As a colleague of mine at Fordham University since 1967, he has had many discussions with me on this theme; I have been enlightened by his books and articles and by the journal Dharma, of which he is an associate editor. In 1979 he invited me to give a paper at the International Seminar on Religious Experience: Its Unity and Diversity, sponsored by his congregation's Centre for Indian and Inter-Religious Studies in Rome. There I came into firsthand contact with the excellent work the Carmelites of Mary Immaculate are doing in the area of cross-cultural research into religious experience. Again through Father Chethimattam, in 1981 I was invited by Father Albert Nambiaparampil to give a paper at the World Conference of Religions on Religion and Man in Cochin, where once again I observed, this time in India, the work that the Carmelites of Mary Immaculate are doing in the field of interreligious dialogue.

Inspired and enlightened by Father Chethimattam's work, I would like to explore in the present paper religious experience in the Second Axial Period. I am drawing the concept of the Axial Period from Karl Jaspers in his book The Origin and Goal of History, where he describes the transformation of consciousness that occurred in the first millenium B.C. -- a transformation that radically affected religious experience and the subsequent history of the world religions. I claim that at the present time we are going through a Second Axial Period, which will have a comparable effect on religions and religious experience. First, I will explain my notion of the Second Axial Period, indicating the forces that are shaping it and highlighting the two major factors influencing religious experience: the encounter of world religions and the secularization of culture. Secondly, I will explore the significance of the encounter of religions for religious experience in the Second Axial Period, focusing on the problem of religious identity in the midst of diverse religious experience. Thirdly, I will examine the effects of secularization on religious experience in the Second Axial Period, indicating how the world's religious traditions must transform themselves and their religious experience in order to come to grips with the problems raised by secularization.

The Second Axial Period

Observing the phenomena of the first millenium B.C., Karl Jaspers notes that a striking transformation of consciousness occurred in three geographical regions: China, India and Persia, and the Eastern Mediterranean including Israel and Greece. This transformation took place apparently without significant influence of one area upon the other. Jaspers calls this era the Axial Period because it "gave birth to everything which, since then, man has been able to be." He continues: "It would seem that this axis of history is to be found in the period around 500 B.C., in the spiritual process that occurred between 800 and 200 B.C. It is there that we meet with the most deepcut dividing line in history. Man, as we know him today, came into being. For short, we may style this 'Axial Period.'[4]

In the Axial Period the transformation of consciousness was mediated by great spiritual teachers who emerged in the three pivotal regions. In China Confucius and Lao-Tzu taught; In India the Upanishads, Mahavira and the Buddha appeared; in Persia, Zoroaster; in Israel, the prophets: Elijah, Isaiah and Jeremiah; in Greece, the philosophers: Socrates, Plato and Aristotle. These teachers mediated a transformation from the mythic, cosmic, ritualistic, collective consciousness of primitive peoples to the rational, analytic, critical, individualistic consciousness that has characterized the mainstream of human history since the Axial Period.

We can grasp the significance of this transformation by comparing the qualities of Axial consciousness with those of primitive consciousness. The nature of primitive consciousness can be examined through archeological research, through a study of the surviving forms of primitive culture -- for example, the American Indians -- and through the residue of this form of consciousness within the consciousness of the Axial Period. First, it is important to note that the transformation was not abrupt, but was prepared for by an intermediate period of the great empires of Egypt, Assyria, Persia, and China. Granted this intermediate period, the radical nature of the transformation can best be seen by contrasting Axial consciousness with its primitive antecedents.

The most distinctive quality of primitive consciousness is a lack of the foundational element of Axial consciousness: distinct individual identity which allows one to separate himself or herself from the tribe and the cosmos. Primitive peoples experienced themselves as part of the totality. They felt that they were linked in an organic fashion to the cosmos and the cosmic cycles, whether they were food-gatherers, hunters, herders or farmers. They grounded their religious life in the change of the seasons and the fertility cycles; they were sensitive to nature symbolism in a much deeper way than the Axial peoples, often naming themselves from animals or objects in nature. They related to life through myth and ritual, drawing from nature powerful symbols which gave expression to their deepest spiritual longings. A similar sense of fusion existed also with the tribe. They experienced corporate not individual identity, for their psychic and spiritual energy flowed through the collectivity of the tribe. Ostracism from the tribe was

285

the worst of fates; for it cut them off from their vital roots, leaving them to psychological and even physical death.

The Axial Period altered this structure of consciousness, producing a new form of relatedness to the world and the community. In the Axial Period there emerged a sense of independent individual identity. No longer was the human person fused with the cosmos and the tribe; rather he could separate himself out from the cycles of the seasons and the fertility of nature and embark on his own individual spiritual journey. No longer was he embedded in the matrix of the tribe; rather he could radically criticize the structure of society, as Socrates and the Hebrew prophets did. No longer was he related to the universe and events through myth and ritual; rather he could use his newly acquired analytic reason to determine the scientific structure of the natural world and record the events of history. In fact, he could turn his analytic,reflective consciousness on himself, arriving at a new awareness of himself, his capacities and his place in nature and history.

It was during this period that the world religions as we know them came into existence. Although they have roots in the Pre-Axial Period, their present form embodies the distinctive consciousness of the Axial Period. In fact, their message can be seen as a charting of the spiritual path within the horizon of Axial consciousness. This is true of the religions that crystallized in this period: Hinduism, Buddhism, Jainism, Zoroastrianism, Taoism, Confucianism and Judaism. It is true also of the religions that appeared later but with roots in this period: Christianity, Islam and Sikhism. In the great religions of the Axial Period, the individual spiritual path became a possibility. Because of the emergence of individual identity, the person could now come to a self-reflexive grasp of his psyche in relation to the Good, according to the Greeks, or of his ātman in relation to Brahman, according to the Indians. He could then pursue his journey toward his goal through the inner way, disengaged from cosmic rhythms and rituals, and from the collectivity of the tribe.

Monasticism as a way of life came into being in the Axial Period; for equipped with the new individual identity, one could take the stance of a marginal person in society, become a beggar, free himself from the tasks of the tribe and from the cycle of sexual reproduction. Having made a radical break from nature and the community, he could pursue his spiritual path as a hermit or a member of a community of monks with a similar structure of consciousness. Although mythic, ritualistic, cosmic and collective forms of consciousness survived in the Axial religions, they were subordinated to the new Axial consciousness, often remaining subliminal or unconscious. It is safe to say with Jaspers that, "in this age were born the fundamental categories within which we still think today, and the beginnings of the world religions, by which human beings still live, were created."[5]

Although the Axial Period opened many spiritual possibilities, it had some negative effects. At the same time that it generated individual consciousness, it tended to alienate the person from nature and the community. In opening up to the individual spiritual journey, it produced an other-worldly attitude, directing attention away from matter and the rootedness of the human community in the earth. If we look at the maps of the spiritual journey charted in the Axial Period, we will find that they are directed to the individual and present a path which proceeds in an ascent from matter to spirit to the divine. There is, of course, a spectrum of attitudes, with Taoism at one end upholding an organic relation of the human with nature. Nevertheless, the approach of the great religions presupposes Axial consciousness, strongly emphasizing its distinctive characteristics in contrast with the mode of consciousness of the Pre-Axial Period.

Second Axial Period

I believe that we are passing through a Second Axial Period. For centuries forces have been building up which are now reaching a climax. I call this the Second Axial Period because I believe that it is producing a transformation of consciousness as significant as that of the First Axial Period and that this transformation is affecting the great religions of the world in a profound fashion. According to Teilhard de Chardin, the forces of evolution are in a process of moving toward "planetization": an organic global consciousness brought about by the spherical shape of the earth, the development of science, technology and communication and the increase of population. According to Teilhard, the forces of divergence, which for millenia have caused the human community to separate, have shifted to those of convergence. Like the meridians on a globe that separate at the equator and converge at the pole, the human community after its long history of divergence is moving toward convergence in global consciousness.[6] In a similar way, the eminent historian of spirituality, Jean Leclercq discerns that we are presently in a period of mutation that is global in scope and global in content since it is producing global consciousness.[7]

What are the characteristics of the consciousness of the Second Axial Period? It is global in two senses: (1) In a horizontal sense, it is global in being comprehensive, encompassing the entire world and the human community as a whole. (2) In a vertical sense, the Second Axial Period is pressuring the human community to extend its consciousness back into the earth, into matter and the biological substratum that supports life on our planet. The pollution of the environment, the exhaustion of natural resources, the threat of nuclear holocaust are forcing the human community to reexamine its roots in the earth, to relate itself harmoniously to its ecological base if life is to survive at all on our planet. To state it briefly, in the Second Axial Period the human community is rediscovering on a global level the characteristics of the consciousness of the Pre-Axial Period without losing the distinctive values of Axial consciousness. We must rediscover the cosmic and collective consciousness of primitive peoples but integrated into the individual consciousness, with its analytic, critical modes of self-reflection. Thus the consciousness of the Second Axial Period would be more integral and multi-dimensional than the consciousness of either the Pre-Axial or the Axial Periods.

The impact on religion of Second Axial consciousness will be enormous, comparable in its own way to the transformation of consciousness in the Axial Period that produced the world religions as we know them. Already this influence is being manifested in the two major religious phenomena of our time: The meeting of world religions and the secularization of culture. In each case religious experience is being both deepened and transformed as it moves into the context of the horizons of the Second Axial Period.

The Encounter of Religions

In an unprecedented way the religions of the world are meeting each other in an atmosphere of mutual interest, respect and enrichment. Often in the past, the meeting of religion has been hostile -- in war and persecution. At times, on the contrary, it has been not only tolerant but even mutually creative. All of these meetings, however, have been regional; the present encounter is global. Areas of misunderstanding -- even of hostility -- still exist, but the most striking religious phenomenon of our time is the mood of openness that surrounds the present encounter of religions on a global scale.

What effect is this encounter having on religious experience? First, it is deepening and supporting the classical forms of religious experience in each major tradition. When believers meet and share their belief, they sustain each other in their belief. They give support to the basic religious experience that underlies their belief. Particularly in the West, believers have been preoccupied for several centuries with maintaining their belief in the face of secularization. They feel alienated from their religious experience, embattled by trends in secular culture. They have expended enormous intellectual energy to relate their belief to science, atheism and agnosticism: to maintain their belief in the face of unbelief, to nourish their religious experience in an indifferent and even alien cultural environment. When a Western Christian, for example, meets a Hindu in interreligious dialogue, he discovers another world: the world of Hindu belief, of Hindu religious experience. The Christian and Hindu recognize that each is rooted in religious experience, that religious experience is cherished by each as the highest value. They have no need to hide their religious experience, to dress it in secular clothes, to translate it into secular language, to make it negotiable in the secular marketplace. They can relax in the fact that they both stand on a rockbottom of religious belief, where their mutual acknowledgement assists each to grasp the firmness of their positions.

Having been supported by a basic mutual affirmation, they can open to a second phase of the encounter: mutual enrichment in specific areas. At first one discovers similarities; for example, the Christian can discern common elements in his understanding of the soul as image of God and in the Hindu affirmation of the ātman, or in his belief in the Trinity and in the attribution of Brahman of sat, chit, and ānanda. He must not jump to hasty conclusions, but be aware of differences ranging from elements in the experience itself to the deeper metaphysical and theological presuppositions. A second phase of enrichment comes from the discovery of complementary experiences: those which have not been cultivated within one's own tradition, but which harmonize with one's own and fulfill it by way of complementarity. For example, Raimundo Panikkar has pointed out the significance of silence in Buddhism[8] in relation to the silence of the Father in the Christian Trinity. Since Christianity is primarily a religion of the Word, silence has not been cultivated as a spiritual path so centrally as in Buddhism. By the encounter with Buddhism, the Christian can discover the significance of silence for the spiritual journey and in relation to this central mystery of the Trinity by discerning the silence of the Father as that depth of the mystery out of which the eternal Word is spoken. The very complementarity of the Trinitarian relations becomes the model of the complementarity of Buddhism and Christianity.

Partners in the interreligious dialogue will find that praying together is a very effective way to deepen and enrich their religious experience. Prayer and meditation will bring them together on an experiential level. It will give them mutual support and enrichment in their religious experience, revealing similarities and complementarities in their traditional methods of prayer. In the recent past Christians have been greatly enriched by exploring and appropriating to themselves the spiritual wisdom contained in the Orient's practice of meditation.

In their encounter with other religions, Christians will find not only similarities and complementaries but also differences. Of course, these are merely superficial differences due to cultural variations and diversity of symbolic forms; but after these are passed and one penetrates through the areas of similarity and complementarity, he will very likely encounter significant differences on the level of experience which imply metaphysical and theological differences. At the present stage of interreligious encounter, it is difficult to discern how deep these differences go. For example, the non-dualism one meets in the radical advaitan position seems at variance with essential elements in the Christian experience and belief. On one level, it is possible to see advaita as a negation of radical dualism and a move toward a Trinitarian relation. But it can also be a move to the point of monism, denying all differentiated relationship. These areas of primordial difference enter into the absolute-exclusive claims of each tradition, through which each affirms for itself a uniqueness among world religions.

Once they discover their common ground as believers and are enriched by the similarity and diversity of their religious experience, a problem arises: What of their religious identity? How can they remain Christian, or Buddhist, or Hindu in the midst of such diversity? Granted, they share a common ground in the face of secularization, yet what of their distinct identity in the face of religious pluralism? In the global consciousness of the Second Axial Period, pluralism is the dominant motif. Having been supported and enriched by meeting other believers, they are now threatened by the very belief they have encountered. What will be the form of religious identity in the Second Axial Period? It is too early to answer that question. But this much is clear: the approach cannot be through a foolhardy abandonment of one's religious identity -- with its accompanying religious experience and historical continuity -- or by a naive leap into an abstract common denominator that lacks religious depth and historical rootedness. It is only by plunging more deeply into one's own identity that one can achieve creative encounter with the other traditions.

What, then, are the characteristics of religious experience in the Second Axial Period? It is primarily multi-dimensional. The religious experience of the Second Axial Period will have expanded horizons, opening to by way of mutual relationship and assimilating where possible the vast range of human religious experience as this has taken shape through history. Even religious identity will be multi-dimensional; for, instead of emphasizing the differences of religions, it will be searching for interrelations. It will strive to relate to other traditions from its own absolute claims while supporting the absolute claims of the other.

Religious Experience and Secularization

The process of secularization in Western culture has threatened religious experience. It has turned attention away from the spiritual to the material, focusing on science, technology, and political, social and economic dimensions of life. At times it has been hostile to religious experience; at other times it has merely ignored religion; but even in ignoring religion it has not been passive for it has cultivated a "secular" form of consciousness that presents an obstacle to the cultivation of religious experience. Granted these problems, secularization has prepared the way for a new type of religious experience which is emerging in the Second Axial Period, since it has brought into focus precisely the area that had receded in the transformation of consciousness in the First Axial Period: the natural world and all that this implies for human life. Unlike the primitive, Pre-Axial consciousness, secular consciousness experiences this realm in a non-religious way. The challenge, then, facing the religions in the Second Axial Period is to rediscover the religious significance of the natural world, the spiritual significance of the secular. The religions must accomplish this not by abandoning the spiritual achievements of the First Axial Period, but by recapitulating the positive dimensions of Pre-Axial consciousness and integrating these with Axial consciousness within the global context of the Second Axial Period. Each of the world religions must tap the spiritual resources of its own tradition in creative response to contemporary secular problems and in ecumenical collaboration with the other religions.

Already the religions have accepted the challenge. For example, liberation theology has tapped the resources of Christianity towards alleviating social, political and economic oppression in Latin America, in the Third World as a whole and in the case of minorities in the First World. In a similar way the Neo-Hindu movements of Ramakrishna and Gandhi have attempted to meet the challenges of our time by drawing upon the spiritual resources of Hinduism, yet transforming these to meet contemporary problems. An excellent example of religious concern for the secular in an ecumenical context can be found in the World Conference of Religions on Religion and Man, organized by the Chavara Cultural Centre at Cochin, under the leadership of Father Albert Nambiaparampil, November 15-20, 1981. The focus of the conference was on the social, economic, political and humanistic dimensions of the human situation. On successive days orientation papers were given by a Hindu on "Social and Economic Dimensions of Our Religious Concern for Men"; by a Muslim on the "Political Dimension"; by a Buddhist on "Humanistic, Scientific Aspects" and by a Christian on the "Spiritual Dimension." In the workshops that followed, the three hundred delegates from these and other traditions discussed the issues in an ecumenical climate and produced a joint declaration touching each of the above areas. In this way the secular dimensions of experience were integrated into religious consciousness in an ecumenical setting.

What are the characteristics of this new secular religious experience? It is both secular and religious -- not secular alone or religious alone, but an integration of the two. It does not look upon the secular as merely a stepping stone to the spiritual and the divine. Rather, it takes the secular seriously on its own terms, but out of a deeply religious motivation. It is not static, but dynamic, seeking to achieve solutions to human problems and a transformation of the religions themselves in relation to these problems. It is not anti-traditional, but traditional in the sense that it roots itself in an historical religious tradition from which it draws spiritual resources. However, it is not frozen into a previous phase of that historical tradition, but can move creatively into the future. Finally, it is global in that it perceives secular problems within a global horizon and in that it relates to the other traditions ecumenically not only on the religious level but in a common confrontation of the global problems facing the human race.

This, then, is a profile of religious experience in the Second Axial Period. According to my analysis, as we move further into the future, religious experience will go through a deepening and a transformation that will produce a much more complex, sophisticated form of religious consciousness than that of previous eras. For it will include the cosmic and collective dimensions of the Pre-Axial Period with the individual, critical, analytic dimensions of the First Axial Period. It will be both religious and secular, other-worldly and this-worldly, eternal and historical, mythic and scientific, wholistic and analytic, ritualistic and meditative, ecumenical and rooted in its distinct identity, involved in a personal and a collective spiritual journey. This multi-dimensional religious experience will find its place within a global horizon which encompasses the earth and the human community as a whole.

NOTES

[1] William James, The Varieties of Religious Experience (New York: Longmans, Green and Company, 1902).

[2] Abraham Maslow, Religions, Values, and Peak Experiences (Columbus, OH: Ohio State University Press, 1964).

[3] Karl Jaspers, Vom Ursprung und der Geschichte (Zurich: Artemis, 1949); English translation by Michael Bullock, The Origin and Goal of History (New Haven: Yale University Press, 1953).

[4] Jaspers, The Origin and Goal of History, p. 1.

[5] Ibid., p. 2.

[6] Pierre Teilhard de Chardin, Le Phénoméne humain (Paris: Editions du Seuil, 1955), pp. 268-269.

[7] Cf. the summary of Leclercq's position in my article "Raimundo Panikkar and the Christian Systematic Theology of the Future," Cross Currents, 29 (1979), pp. 142-143.

[8] Raimundo Panikkar, The Trinity and the Religious Experience of Man (New York: Orbis Press, 1973), pp. 44-50.

EPILOGUE

TOWARDS A WORLD THEOLOGY:
AN INTERRELIGIOUS APPROACH TO
THEOLOGICAL ISSUES

John B. Chethimattam

The New Interreligious Mood

Today World Religions have entered a new era of common understanding and cooperation in their search for the salvation of humanity. They are no longer viewed upon as competing ideologies demanding the total allegiance of the same people. Taking their origin and developing in different historical contexts and socio-cultural and political situations, they are considered distinct systems and traditions that represent varying ways of faith and provide solutions to the basic problems of humanity such as the origin, nature and meaning of human existence and of human society, reasons and roots of suffering, source of evil in the world, and the question of one's survival after the tragedy of death. In the euphoria of human freedom claimed after the end of World War II, there emerged a new attitude of sharing and cooperation in the relationship among religions in contrast to the exclusivism and antagonism that characterised their outlook towards each other in the earlier period.

This new willingness to enter into dialogue with each other even from the part of religions that claimed direct revelations from God is owing to a number of religious factors that have come to the full awareness of humanity only in recent times. First of all, all have come to recognize that, though religion deals with the divine reality, it is very much a human phenomenon: the way human beings understand God and express that understanding in words, gestures, rituals, and traditions. Even though God is said to communicate himself directly in Revelation through words and deeds, still that communication is expressed and transmitted in human words, narratives, and events that need to be interpreted so that one may come to the rational realization that God is actually and directly present in those words, stories, and events. Although the disciples of Christ encountered the Son of God in bodily form, they needed to use their reason and interpret their experience in order to arrive at the conclusion that it was not an ordinary Jewish Rabbi, but really the Son of God that they encountered in Jesus of Nazareth. Even if we had today a tape-recording of the sermons of Jesus or a videotape of his working of a miracle, that by itself need not convince us that Jesus is really the Son of God; the evidence has to be analyzed and interpreted.

A second discovery that radically altered the traditional attitudes among religions is the place and role of the individual knowing subject in the perception even of the most clear and obvious objective truths of religion. The principle on which various religions based their programmes of persecution against members of other religions--hardly there is any religion on the face of the earth which did not practise persecution of other religionists at one time or other -- was that error has no right. Beliefs and traditions contrary to what one in all sincerity of faith accepted as true had to be false. Hence one could in no way tolerate them without compromising one's own faith. This is the reason why religious authorities with the best of intentions justified and authorised the burning of heretics and witches.

But belief systems and traditions have no value unless accepted by conscious beings; and rational beings cannot accept ideas and systems except under the aspects of truth and good. No one can accept evil or falsehood for its own sake. Any error lives in the minds of those who accept it on account of the element of truth trapped in it. Hence the effective way of fighting error is not burning people who in good faith follow it, but rather recognizing and thus liberating the truth factor hidden in the particular erroneous system, at the same time rejecting the falsehood, and thereby liberating the human beings caught in the limitations of the particular truth. Even the most perfect religion is not absolute truth, but is characterised by various limitations, social, cultural, political and the like; and, therefore, needs liberation in interaction with other truth systems. Interreligious dialogue, therefore, even for the most perfect of religions is not a luxury, but a need lest it should remain a prisoner to its own limitations.

But the most important reason for interreligious cooperation is the universality of religious problems and of religious truths. If there is a God, there is a God also for the atheist; and, if that God is really triune, the divine reality is a Trinity also for the Unitarians. One's particular preferences and prejudices and immediate concerns cannot affect the objective state of affairs. All claims of superiority and position of privilege made by one religion over the other often stem from national pride and attempts at economic, political, and cultural domination of one group over others. One of the first discoveries Christianity had to make before it could launch its mission to evangelize the world is expressed in the words of St.Peter at Caesarea addressing the Gentile Cornelius and his companions: "I begin to see how true it is that God shows no partiality. Rather, the man of any nation who fears God and acts uprightly is acceptable to him."

(Acts, 10:34-35). One comes to the idea of God in searching for the meaning of one's own life, the source of existence, ultimate support in all one's needs, and the final hope of one's survival after death. That God, who is evidently a conscious being that brought man into existence cannot be imagined to be silent. He can be expected to disclose to man in various ways details concerning His own divine reality, the nature and source of man's problems like sin and suffering, the way to resolve them, and what man has to do in order to realize his own goal in life and attain the final happiness destined for him.

The fact that the Creator does not remain simply outside his creation but is immanent in it and enters into intimate communion with his own creatures is a matter of special interest to all religions. All religions, even those which do not deal with a personal God, in one way or another discuss the question of the ultimate meaning of reality, the existence and nature of the divine, divine revelation and incarnation, the questions of human sin and suffering, and salvation and the reconstitution of the authentic human family. Today no religious tradition can formulate its faith and scheme of practice in isolation from other systems and traditions. In the past, too, this interaction existed, but with the difference that different religious traditions developed and modified themselves in reaction and opposition to other religions. Today they have to learn from each other. No religion can deal with other systems in an attitude of confrontation, treating them as if they were pure error, creations of the devil, or at best simply inadequate human attempts to arrive at the incomprehensible reality of the Transcendent. Even the condescending statement often found in official documents of the Church that other religions and their religious texts contained "seeds of the Word" is a contradiction in terms. The Word of God, if it is truly divine, cannot be taken piecemeal. If truly "seeds of the Word" are recognized, there the Word of God himself is there. Religions should be considered like any other field of human endeavor, say science, technology, art, and philosophy, as parallel efforts of the human race, assisted by Divine Providence to find adequate solutions for the deepest problems of man.

I. Divine Revelation

The starting point of all theology is the divine self-disclosure to man. With any amount of efforts from the side of man God remains incomprehensible. Even though through reasoning from the nature of created things one can arrive at the existence of a Creator and deduce certain divine characteristics like infinity and intellectuality, these remain human projections,

In this way we know more what God is not than what He actually is. God has no aspects or parts and hence cannot be known piecemeal.

So some religions like Buddhism and Jainism would deny the usefulness of all inquiry into God. According to them religion should place the emphasis on liberating man from his present sickness of ignorance, passion, attachment to material things, and the like. Revelation, therefore, for them is essentially the faithful handing down of religious wisdom tracing its origin to the illumination received by eminent leaders like Siddartha Guatama Buddha or Vardhamana Mahavira. Here the relevant question, as far as man is concerned is what purpose the "revealed doctrine" serves in liberating humanity from its present bondage.

But most religions would deny that the divine reality is the Great Unknown. For human beings who constantly experience their sinfulness, limitation, and the need for help, God is paradoxically the best known ground of existence and at the same time the most profound and incomprehensible mystery. In and through every finite thing, even a blade of grass or a drop of dew, one is encountering the one Author of all things, the beginningless Beginning the independent First Cause of all activity, the subsistent Existence, pure and infinite Good, the governing and directing Intelligence, and the Source of all beauty and order in the universe. We get another glimpse of the same divine reality through the reports of theophanics and miraculous happenings in which people could discern an intervention from outside the ordinary course of nature since certain basic laws of nature got suspended for a moment, or certain things achieved results far beyond their normal competence. More marked is the experiences of the divine presence in the providential course of the history of peoples and nations that seem to indicate an overarching plan and design, a higher purpose and superior goal than that of the natural and normal course of human events. This is said to be the salvific meaning of history that is worked out in, through and some times even against the profane meaning of history.

Perhaps the most radical difference in the perception of religious experience between the Judeo-Christian tradition and the other religions is history. In these traditions the divine is intuited by the individual as the transcendental meaning of one's existence as if in flash in a moment which seems to transcend time. The religious community arises as the fellowship of those who have such time-arresting experience of the Transcendent. On the other hand, for the Judeo-Christian tradition the community is first

298

created by a special call from God gathering up and constituting a hardnecked and unsuspecting group into a "Chosen People," the "People of God" with a special mission towards the rest of humanity. Experience of God occurs for them in the context of that community and in the providential course of its history. For Israel the legend of its miraculous liberation from the slavery of Egypt and the story of its freedom from the long captivity of Babylon become a symbol not only of the origin of the universe as a creative liberation from the primeval chaos but also of the continuing presence of Yahweh in the midst of "His" people guiding its destinies and leading it to the liberation of all humanity. For Christianity all history before Christ leads up to the "Christ event," the sacrificial death and resurrection of Christ, and the history after Christ is a preparation of the world for his second coming at the end of the world. In the miraculous event of the raising of Christ from the dead is contained as if in miniature the overarching plan of God for the salvation of all humanity and also the ever-continuing presence of God in the world as the Lord of history.

For Hinduism, on the other hand, any true Revelation of God can be received only through an intuitive experience. Every other means of right knowledge like inference, analogy, and even Scripture presents the divine in forms and idioms of man's daily experience. No other form can really present God who transcends all forms and images. Hence they can only dispose and prepare a mind and lead it up to the intuitive experience which is intimately personal. In the same way, one who has attained that intuitive experience cannot communicate it to others directly but can only help them through indirect means to dispose themselves to receive the same experience. Hence the scope and goal of all religion is the attainment of the direct and intuitive self-disclosure of the divine reality, which by its very nature implies a certain identity between the knower and the known. The Mundaka Upanishad neatly states the fact: the knower of Brahman becomes even Brahman. All divine revelation implies an effective divinization of the recipient.

The Christian concept of revelation brings in another dimension: The scope of divine revelation is not merely to provide us with some information on the divinity, to construct an ontology of God, but rather to reveal man to man himself with God as the horizon of the full meaning of his life. In this way Jesus Christ, fully man and fully God at the same time in the unity of a single divine personality is the fullness of divine revelation since he reveals man to man himself. He shows how the human consciousness is fully open to the divine and at the same time also totally committed to the salvation of all humanity in the sacrifice of the Cross. Further, what fully reveals God to humanity in Jesus Christ is the divine personality of Christ, the Son of God. What the disciples experienced in Jesus especially the Risen Lord, was not a mere humanity, nor mere divine power and activity, but the one who is Son of God and son of man at the same time, the Messiah, the one mediator between God and humanity. In Christ the human race met with the Godhead in bodily form. Christ's personality is in a way transparent since the Son as Son cannot be understood without encountering the Father, and that too only under the guidance of the Spirit given by Christ.

II. The Problem of God

The experience of the self-disclosure of God in whatever form naturally leads one to the problem of the divine reality. God, the ultimate meaning of human existence, Creator and final goal of all things, should naturally be the one unifying principle of all religions and peoples. But unfortunately this was not always the case. This history of humanity bears witness to the numerous religious wars that split the human race into opposing camps and brought nation against nation and religion against religion. One of the basic reasons for these religious wars was that the specific approaches to God followed by particular traditions were very much dictated by the socio-political concerns of those peoples. To counteract the bad effects generated by such conflicts and divergent concerns, one has to emphasize the complementarity of the different approaches to God, the ultimate meaning of human life.

For the Greeks caught up in the constant conflicts among city states and wars with the Persians and other world powers, the search for the ultimate meaning of existence focussed on what was the really real in a world of appearance, the source of stability in a universe of flux. The main philosophical principle was stated by Parmenides when he said, "What is and can be thought of is Being, and non-being is not." Plato defined this ultimate Being, the form of all forms as the Good, the sun of the intellectual world, since from it everything derived its goodness and intelligibility. For Aristotle this absolute reality was the Immovable Mover, Thought thinking itself, which moved all things not by physical force but as the object of their knowledge and love. Plotinus identified this supreme Good and the Immovable Mover with the One which produced all things through the Nous, the storehouse of all ideas; and the Medieval Scholastics discovered in this Greek idea of the Absolute the best metaphysical definition of God, the Creator of all things, who was also by that very reason their final end. For, He is the infinite Good and supreme intelligible to which all beings tend through their proper activities, especially human beings through their knowledge and will. St. Augustine's statement: "O Lord you created us for you and our heart is restless until it rests in you" indicates the place of God as the final goal of human life. Similarly, Aquinas formulates its intellectualist version: "Our intellect in knowing anything tends to the infinite. A sign of this is that given any finite quantity our intellect can think of something greater. This inclination of the intellect to the infinite would be in vain unless there is some infinite thing. So there is something infinite which we call God."

The search for God in the East, on the other hand, was prompted by the inner needs of man, his experience of suffering and the desire to find its roots and ultimate solution. Naturally the root of suffering was located in the radical ignorance of one's true self and the confusion between the immutable spiritual self and the material principle of evolution and individuality. The time-space bound and evolving material aspect of life naturally postulates not only an immediate principle of matter but also a transcendent spiritual self: Anything structured and composed of several parts, argues the Samkhyakārikā, is for the sake of the unstructured and simple spiritual self, which is the true ground, goal and directive principle. So the changing material existence of man points to the individual spiritual self as its authentic and responsible subject. But the existence of many individual selves is an indication of the limited character of their existence and consciousness, and so demands an ultimate Self of all, pure, infinite and immutable consciousness, subsisting by itself. This is the Hindu view of the Absolute Reality, Ātman-Brahman, which identifies in itself the radically distinct dimensions of being, consciousness and bliss.

The nomadic and semi-nomadic tribes of the Middle East moving up and down what is known as the fertile crescent, constituted by the Nile and Euphrates and Tigris valleys connected by the Palestinian coast, looked on God as some one, a powerful leader who could protect his people from the dangers of desert life. Each clan and tribe had its own special God. Israel addressed its God as Yahweh, who described himself to Moses as "I am Who Am," the one who really is, or more literally the one who is faithful to himself, namely to the promise he has made to his people. This powerful Lord who owes allegiance and fidelity